ACCA

F3/FFA FINANCIAL ACCOUNTING

REVISION QUESTION BANK

For Examinations from September 2017 to August 2018

This training material has been published and prepared by Becker Professional Development International Limited: www.becker.com/acca

Acknowledgement

Past ACCA examination questions are the copyright of the Association of Chartered Certified Accountants and have been reproduced by kind permission.

The examination will consist of 35 two mark multiple choice questions (MCQs) and two 15 mark questions in Section B (see Specimen Exam included). Section B will test consolidations and accounts preparation. The consolidation question could include a small amount of interpretation and the accounts preparation question could be set in the context of a sole trader or a limited company.

This Revision Question Bank includes non-MCQ questions on topics that will **not** be examined in Section B but are provided for comprehensive revision. These are indicated *

CONTENTS

Question		*Page*	*Answer*	*Marks*	*Date worked*
MULTIPLE CHOICE QUESTIONS – BOOKKEEPING					
1	Accruals and prepayments	1	1001	26	
2	Depreciation and disposals	4	1002	32	
3	Receivables and payables	9	1004	36	
4	Inventory	14	1008	8	
5	Books of prime entry and control accounts	16	1009	30	
6	Journal entries	21	1011	14	
DOUBLE-ENTRY AND RECORDING TRANSACTIONS					
*7	Rook *(ACCA J00)*	23	1012	16	
*8	Addax *(ACCA J02)*	24	1013	9	
*9	Riffon *(ACCA D03)*	24	1014	12	
CONTROL ACCOUNT RECONCILIATIONS					
*10	United *(ACCA J95)*	25	1015	9	
*11	Scimitar *(ACCA D97)*	26	1016	12	
*12	Otter *(ACCA D99)*	27	1016	15	
*13	Atanga *(ACCA J07)*	28	1017	7	
BANK RECONCILIATIONS					
14	MCQs Bank reconciliations	28	1017	18	
*15	George *(ACCA J99)*	31	1018	17	
SUSPENSE ACCOUNTS					
16	MCQs Suspense accounts	32	1019	22	
*17	Andromeda *(ACCA J01)*	36	1021	15	
*18	Arbados *(ACCA J04)*	37	1022	9	
*19	Lorca *(ACCA D06)*	37	1022	11	
ADJUSTMENT TO PROFIT STATEMENTS					
*20	Pride *(ACCA Pilot Paper 2001)*	38	1023	14	
*21	Choctaw *(ACCA J05)*	39	1024	8	
*22	Rampion *(ACCA J06)*	39	1025	11	

All ACCA past exam question and answers have been updated, where necessary, to take account of changes in syllabus and developments in IFRS.

Question		*Page*	*Answer*	*Marks*	*Date worked*
INCOMPLETE RECORDS					
23	MCQs Incomplete records	40	1026	36	
*24	Lamorgan *(ACCA D01)*	46	1028	10	
*25	Altese, Senji & Aluki *(ACCA J03)*	47	1029	9	
*26	Hasta *(ACCA J07)*	48	1030	11	
REGULATORY FRAMEWORK					
27	MCQs Regulatory Framework	48	1031	16	
*28	IASB *(ACCA J98)*	50	1031	8	
CONCEPTUAL FRAMEWORK					
29	MCQs Qualitative characteristics	50	1032	38	
*30	Four concepts (ACCA D98)	54	1033	12	
*31	Materiality *(ACCA J01)*	54	1034	11	
*32	Comparability *(ACCA J04)*	55	1035	5	
IAS 1 *PRESENTATION OF FINANCIAL STATEMENTS*					
33	MCQs IAS 1	55	1036	32	
34	Arbalest *(ACCA D97)*	60	1037	15	
35	Perseus *(ACCA J01)*	61	1038	15	
36	Cronos *(ACCA D02)*	62	1040	15	
37	Abrador *(ACCA D03)*	63	1041	15	
38	Minica *(ACCA J04)*	65	1042	15	
39	Shuswap *(ACCA J05)*	66	1043	15	
CAPITAL STRUCTURE AND FINANCE COSTS					
40	MCQs Capital structure and finance costs	67	1044	36	
*41	Reserves and issues *(ACCA J03)*	72	1046	6	
*42	Armani	72	1047	8	
IAS 2 *INVENTORIES*					
43	MCQs IAS 2	73	1047	20	
*44	Sampi *(ACCA J98)*	76	1049	5	
*45	P, Q & R *(ACCA D94)*	76	1049	8	
IFRS 15 *REVENUE FROM CONTRACTS WITH CUSTOMERS*					
46	MCQs Revenue	77	1051	10	
IAS 16 *PROPERTY PLANT AND EQUIPMENT*					
47	MCQs IAS 16	79	1051	26	
*48	Non-current assets *(ACCA J92)*	82	1053	17	

Question		*Page*	*Answer*	*Marks*	*Date worked*
IAS 38 *INTANGIBLE ASSETS*					
49	MCQs IAS 38	83	1054	16	
*50	Lion *(ACCA D04)*	85	1055	12	
*51	Aircraft *(ACCA J07)*	86	1056	10	
IAS 37 *PROVISIONS, CONTINGENT LIABILITIES AND CONTINGENT ASSETS*					
52	MCQs IAS 37	86	1056	16	
*53	Reserves *(ACCA D94)*	89	1057	12	
IAS 10 *EVENTS AFTER THE REPORTING PERIOD*					
54	MCQs IAS 10	89	1058	18	
*55	Aluki (IASs 2, 10 & 37) *(ACCA D03)*	92	1059	9	
*56	Quapaw (IASs 2, 10 & 37) *(ACCA J05)*	92	1059	6	
*57	Umbria (IAS 10, 16 & 37) *(ACCA D05)*	93	1060	10	
IAS 7 *STATEMENT OF CASH FLOWS*					
58	MCQs IAS 7	93	1061	24	
59	Crash *(ACCA Pilot Paper 2001)*	97	1062	15	
*60	Marmot *(ACCA J02)*	98	1063	10	
61	Renada *(ACCA J04)*	99	1064	15	
62	Sioux *(ACCA J05)*	100	1065	15	
63	Joyce *(ACCA D06)*	101	1067	15	
CONSOLIDATED FINANCIAL STATEMENTS					
*64	MCQs Consolidated financial statements	102	1068	44	
65	Haydn & Strauss	108	1072	15	
66	Dublin & Belfast	110	1073	15	
67	Helios & Luna *(ACCA D02)*	111	1075	15	
68	Bradshaw & Martin *(ACCA D09)*	112	1076	15	
INTERPRETATION OF FINANCIAL STATEMENTS					
69	MCQs Interpretation of financial statements	113	1076	26	
*70	Beta *(ACCA D98)*	116	1078	15	
*71	Weden *(ACCA J02)*	118	1079	10	
*72	Apillon *(ACCA J03)*	119	1080	9	
ACCA SPECIMEN EXAM (2 hours)					
Section A					
	35 MCQs	121	1081	70	
Section B					
1	Keswick Co	131	1085	15	
2	Malright Co	132	1085	15	

Question 1 MCQs ACCRUALS AND PREPAYMENTS

1.1 A company has sublet part of its offices and in the year ended 30 November 20X6 the rent receivable was:

Until 30 June 20X6	$8,400 per year
From 1 July 20X6	$12,000 per year

Rent was paid quarterly in advance on 1 January, April, July, and October each year.

What amounts should appear in the company's financial statements for the year ended 30 November 20X6?

	Statement of profit or loss	*Statement of financial position*	
A	$9,900	$2,000 in sundry payables	
B	$9,900	$1,000 in sundry payables	
C	$10,200	$1,000 in sundry payables	
D	$9,900	$2,000 in sundry receivables	(2 marks)

1.2 A business compiling its financial statements for the year to 31 July each year pays rent quarterly in advance on 1 January, 1 April, 1 July and 1 October each year. The annual rent was increased from $60,000 per year to $72,000 per year as from 1 October 20X6.

What figure should appear for rent expense in the business's profit or loss for the year ended 31 July 20X7?

A $62,000
B $63,000
C $69,000
D $70,000 (2 marks)

1.3 Beek receives rent for subletting part of its office premises to a number of tenants. In the year ended 31 December 20X6 Beek received cash of $318,600 from its tenants.

Details of rent in advance and in arrears at the beginning and end of 20X6 are as follows:

	31 December 20X6	*31 December 20X5*
	$	$
Rent received in advance	28,400	24,600
Rent owing by tenants	18,300	16,900

All rent owing was subsequently received.

What figure for rental income should be included in Beek's profit or loss for 20X6?

A $341,000
B $336,400
C $316,200
D $300,800 (2 marks)

1.4 At 1 July 20X6 a company had prepaid insurance of $8,200. On 1 January 20X7 the company paid $38,000 for insurance for the year to 30 September 20X7.

What figures should appear for insurance in the company's financial statements for the year ended 30 June 20X7?

	Profit or loss	*Statement of financial position*
A	$27,200	Prepayment $19,000
B	$39,300	Prepayment $9,500
C	$36,700	Prepayment $9,500
D	$55,700	Prepayment $9,500

(2 marks)

1.5 A company sublets part of its office accommodation. In the year ended 30 June 20X7 cash received from tenants was $83,700. Details of rent in arrears and in advance at the beginning and end of the year were:

	In arrears	*In advance*
	$	$
30 June 20X6	3,800	2,400
30 June 20X7	4,700	3,000

All arrears of rent were subsequently received.

What figure for rental income should be included in the company's profit or loss for the year ended 30 June 20X7?

A $80,600
B $83,400
C $84,000
D $85,800

(2 marks)

1.6 A business sublets part of its office accommodation. The rent is received quarterly in advance on 1 January, 1 April, 1 July and 1 October. The annual rent has been $24,000 for some years, but it was increased to $30,000 from 1 July 20X6.

What amounts for this rent should appear in the company's financial statements for the year ended 31 January 20X7?

	Profit or loss	*Statement of financial position*
A	$27,500	$5,000 in sundry receivables
B	$27,000	$2,500 in sundry receivables
C	$27,000	$2,500 in sundry payables
D	$27,500	$5,000 in sundry payables

(2 marks)

1.7 During 20X6, Benz paid a total of $60,000 for rent, covering the period from 1 October 20X5 to 31 March 20X7.

What figures should appear in the company's financial statements for the year ended 31 December 20X6?

	Profit or loss	*Statement of financial position*
A	$40,000	Prepayment $10,000
B	$40,000	Prepayment $15,000
C	$50,000	Accrual $10,000
D	$50,000	Accrual $15,000

(2 marks)

1.8 Jam is preparing its financial statements for the year ended 30 June 20X7. Its draft trial balance includes:

(1) A balance for office expenses (including rent) paid in the financial year of $89,100
(2) A balance for prepayment of rent at 1 July 20X6 of $9,500

On 31 May 20X7 Jared paid three months' rent in advance of $15,300.

Which of the following will be the figure for office expenses in Jam's statement of profit or loss for the year ended 30 June 20X7?

A $60,400
B $88,400
C $89,100
D $93,500 (2 marks)

1.9 Brindal acquired five apartments on 1 June 20X6 and immediately rented them out to different tenants. Brindal has a credit balance on its rent receivable account in the trial balance extracted as at 31 May 20X7 of $22,850. The bookkeeper has calculated that rents in arrears as at 31 May 20X7 amounted to $4,490 and rents in advance at the same date amounted to $7,720.

What was Brindal's rental income for the year ended 31 May 20X7?

A $19,620
B $22,850
C $26,080
D $37,340 (2 marks)

1.10 Holly began trading on 1 July 20X6. The business is now preparing its financial statements for the year ended 30 June 20X7. Rent is charged for the year from 1 April to 31 March, and was $1,800 for the year ended 31 March 20X7 and $2,000 for the year ended 31 March 20X8. Rent is payable quarterly in advance on 1 March, 1 June, 1 September and 1 December.

What is the charge to Holly's statement of profit or loss for rent for the year ended 30 June 20X7?

A $1,650
B $1,700
C $1,850
D $1,900 (2 marks)

1.11 On 1 June 20X6, Heather paid an insurance invoice of $2,400 for the year to 31 May 20X7.

How will this be accounted for in Heather's financial statement for the year ended 31 December 20X6?

	Statement of profit of loss	*Statement of financial position*
A	$1,000	$1,400 prepayment
B	$1,400	$1,000 accrual
C	$1,400	$1,000 prepayment
D	$1,200	$1,200 prepayment

(2 marks)

1.12 On 1 January, a business had prepaid insurance of $10,000. On 1 August it paid, in full, an insurance invoice of $36,000 for the year to 31 July 20X7.

What amounts will be included in the financial statements for the year ended 31 December 20X6?

	Statement of profit or loss	*Statement of financial position*
A	$15,000	$21,000
B	$22,000	$23,000
C	$25,000	$21,000
D	$25,000	$15,000

(2 marks)

1.13 During the year ended 30 September 20X6, Priceless Co recorded the following cash transactions:

(1) Payment of an annual insurance premium of $12,000 for the period to 31 December 20X6

(2) Receipt of $6,000 in respect of rent from a tenant covering the three month period to 30 November 20X6

What is the impact on the profit and net assets of making the year-end adjustments for prepaid income and expenditure at 30 September 20X6?

	Profit	*Net assets*
A	Decrease $1,000	Increase $1,000
B	Decrease $7,000	Increase $7,000
C	Decrease $1,000	Decrease $1,000
D	Increase $7,000	Increase $7,000

(2 marks)

(26 marks)

Question 2 MCQs DEPRECIATION AND DISPOSALS

2.1 A business purchased a motor car on 1 July 20X6 for $20,000. It is to be depreciated at 20%per year on the straight line basis, assuming a residual value at the end of five years of $4,000, with a proportionate depreciation charge in the year of purchase.

The $20,000 cost was correctly entered in the cash book but posted to the debit of the motor vehicles repairs account.

How will the business profit for the year ending 31 December 20X6 be affected by the error?

A Understated by $18,400
B Understated by $16,800
C Understated by $18,000
D Overstated by $18,400

(2 marks)

2.2 A company's policy as regards depreciation of its plant and machinery is to charge depreciation at 20% per year on cost, with proportional depreciation for items purchased or sold during a year.

The company's plant and machinery at cost account for the year ended 30 September 20X6 is shown below:

Plant and machinery – cost

		$			$
20X5					
1 Oct	Balance (all plant purchased after 20X2)	200,000			
			20X6		
20X6			30 Jun	Transfer disposal account	40,000
1 Apr	Cash-purchase of plant	50,000	30 Sept	Balance	210,000
		250,000			250,000

What should be the depreciation charge for plant and machinery (excluding any profit or loss on the disposal) for the year ended 30 September 20X6?

A $42,000
B $43,000
C $45,000
D $51,000 (2 marks)

2.3 The plant and machinery at cost account of a business for the year ended 30 June 20X7 was as follows:

Plant and machinery – cost

20X6		$	*20X6*		$
1 July	Balance	240,000	30 Sept.	Transfer disposal account	60,000
20X7			*20X7*		
1 Jan	Cash-purchase of plant	160,000	30 Jun	Balance	340,000
		400,000			400,000

The company's policy is to charge depreciation at 20% per year on the straight line basis, with proportionate depreciation in the years of purchase and disposal.

What should be the depreciation charge for the year ended 30 June 20X7?

A $68,000
B $64,000
C $61,000
D $55,000 (2 marks)

2.4 A business's statement of profit or loss for the year ended 31 December showed a profit of $83,600. It was later found that $18,000 paid for the purchase of a motor van had been debited to motor expenses account. It is the company's policy to depreciate motor vans at 25% per year, with a full year's charge in the year of acquisition.

What would the profit be after adjusting for this error?

A $70,100
B $97,100
C $101,600
D $106,100 (2 marks)

2.5 The plant and machinery cost account of a company is shown below. The company's policy is to charge depreciation at 20% on the straight line basis, with proportionate depreciation in years of acquisition and disposal.

Plant and machinery – cost

20X6	$	*20X6*	$
1 Jan Balance	280,000	30 June Transfer disposal	14,000
1 Apr Cash	48,000		
1 Sept Cash	36,000	31 Dec Balance	350,000
	364,000		364,000

What should be the depreciation charge for the year ended 31 December 20X6?

A $64,200
B $67,000
C $68,600
D $70,000 (2 marks)

2.6 Sam's statement of profit or loss for the year ended 31 December 20X6 showed a profit of $83,600. It was later found that $18,000 paid for the purchase of a motor vehicle on 1 January 20X6 had been debited to motor expenses account. It is the company's policy to depreciate motor vehicles at 25% per year.

What is Sam's profit for the year after adjusting for this error?

A $70,100
B $97,100
C $101,600
D $106,100 (2 marks)

2.7 On 1 January 20X4 Joffa purchased a new machine at a cost of $96,720. Delivery costs were $3,660 and internal administration costs of $9,450 were incurred. At that time Joffa planned to replace the machine in five years, when it would have no value, and to depreciate the machine on a straight line basis.

Joffa decides on 1 January 20X6 that the machine only has one remaining year of useful life. There is no expected change to the residual value at the end of its life.

What is the depreciation expense in respect of this machine for the year ended 31 December 20X6?

A $33,460
B $58,032
C $60,228
D $65,898 (2 marks)

2.8 On 1 April 20X5 Herepath bought a Foxy car for $23,500. The company's depreciation policy for cars is 30% per annum using the reducing balance method. On 1 April 20X7 the Foxy was part-exchanged for a Vizgo car, which had a purchase price of $28,200. Herepath paid the seller $19,350, in final settlement.

What was Herepath's profit or loss on the disposal of the Foxy?

A $7,835 profit
B $2,665 loss
C $5,150 loss
D $6,250 loss (2 marks)

2.9 Redruth commenced trading on 1 April 20X4. The carrying amount of plant and equipment in Redruth's financial statements as at 31 March 20X6 was $399,960. The cost of these assets was $614,500. On 31 March 20X7 an asset costing $11,500 was acquired. Depreciation is charged on plant and equipment monthly at an annual rate of 25% straight line. There are no residual values.

What is the carrying amount of Redruth's plant and equipment in its statement of financial position at 31 March 20X7?

A $254,960
B $257,835
C $299,970
D $308,595 (2 marks)

2.10 A car was purchased for $12,000 on 1 April 20X3 and has been depreciated at 20% each year on a straight line basis assuming no residual value. The company's financial year end is 31 December and its policy is to charge a full year's depreciation in the year of purchase and no depreciation in the year of sale. The car was traded-in for a replacement vehicle on 1 August in 20X6 for an agreed figure of $5,000.

What was the profit or loss on the disposal of the vehicle in the year ended 31 December 20X6?

A Loss $1,144
B Profit $200
C Profit $1,000
D Profit $2,600 (2 marks)

2.11 A company bought a machine on 1 October 20X2 for $52,000. The machine had an expected life of eight years and an estimated residual value of $4,000. On 31 March 20X7 the machine was sold for $35,000. The company's year end is 31 December. The company's policy is to depreciate assets on a straight-line basis with a full year's depreciation in the year of purchase and none in the year of sale.

What is the gain or loss on disposal of the machine?

A Loss $13,000
B Gain $7,000
C Gain $10,000
D Gain $13,000 (2 marks)

2.12 SSG bought a machine for $40,000 in January 20X3. The machine had an expected useful life of six years and an expected residual value of $10,000. The machine was depreciated on the straight-line basis where a full year's charge in made in the year of purchase and none in the year of sale. In December 20X6, the machine was sold for $15,000. The company includes any profit or loss on disposal of assets with depreciation expense in its financial statements. Its year end is 31 December.

What is the total amount charged to the statement of profit or loss over the life of the machine?

A $15,000
B $20,000
C $25,000
D $30,000 (2 marks)

2.13 A company purchased equipment for $80,000 on 1 July 20X3. The company's accounting year end is 31 December and it has a policy to charge a full year's depreciation in the year of purchase. Equipment is depreciated on the reducing balance basis at 25% per annum.

What is the carrying amount of the equipment at 31 December 20X6?

A $18,984
B $25,312
C $29,531
D $33,750 (2 marks)

2.14 Stroma's reporting date is 30 September. Stroma purchased a machine on 1 April 20X3 for $200,000. The machine was estimated to have a useful life of eight years and depreciated at 25% per annum using the reducing balance method. On 31 January 20X6 the machine was sold for $90,000. Stroma charges a full year's depreciation in the years of purchase and disposal.

What is the profit or loss arising on the disposal of the machine to be included in the statement of profit and loss for the year ended 30 September 20X6?

A Loss $22,500
B Loss $10,000
C Profit $5,625
D Profit $26,719 (2 marks)

2.15 On 1 September 20X4 Cyanne purchased a non-current asset for $88,000 which had a useful life of four years and no residual value. The company's policy is to depreciate non-current assets at 25% per annum on the reducing balance basis.

When preparing the financial statements for the year to 31 October 20X6, the accountant calculated the depreciation charge on the straight line basis.

What will be the effect of correcting the depreciation charge on profit for the year to 31 October 20X6?

A Reduced by $5,500
B Increased by $5,500
C Reduced by $16,500
D Increased by $16,500 (2 marks)

2.16 Strad depreciates non-current assets on the reducing balance basis at a rate of 25% per annum. At 1 May 20X6, the company's non-current assets had cost $680,500 and accumulated depreciation was $285,900. In the year to 30 April 20X7, Strad bought new assets which cost $32,800. All assets are depreciated for a full year, irrespective of the date of acquisition.

What is the depreciation charge for the year to 30 April 20X7?

A $98,650
B $106,850
C $178,325
D $249,800 (2 marks)

(32 marks)

Question 3 MCQs RECEIVABLES AND PAYABLES

3.1 At 30 September 20X5 a company's loss allowance for trade receivables amounted to $38,000, which was 5% of the receivables at that date.

At 30 September 20X6 receivables totalled $868,500. It was decided to write off $28,500 of debts as irrecoverable and to keep the loss allowance at 5%.

What should be the total expense in profit or loss for the year ended 30 September 20X6 for irrecoverable debts?

A $32,500
B $33,925
C $42,000
D $70,500 (2 marks)

3.2 At 1 July 20X6 a company had a loss allowance for receivables of $83,000. During the year ended 30 June 20X7 debts totalling $146,000 were written off. At 30 June 20X7 it was decided that $218,000 was required as a loss allowance for receivables.

What is the total amount that should appear in profit or loss for the year ended 30 June 20X7 for irrecoverable debts?

A $11,000
B $155,000
C $281,000
D $364,000 (2 marks)

3.3 At 31 December 20X6 a company's trade receivables totalled $864,000 and the loss allowance for receivables was $48,000. It was decided that debts totalling $13,000 were to be written off, and the loss allowance for receivables adjusted to 5% of the receivables.

What figures should appear in the financial statements in respect of receivables (after accounting for the loss allowance)?

	Profit or loss	*Statement of financial position*
	$	$
A	8,200	807,800
B	7,550	808,450
C	18,450	808,450
D	55,550	808,450

(2 marks)

3.4 The receivables ledger control account below contains several incorrect entries:

Receivables ledger control account

	$		$
Opening balance	138,400	Credit sales	80,660
		Contras against credit balances in payables ledger	1,000
Cash received from credit customers	78,420	Discounts allowed	1,950
		Irrecoverable debts written off	3,000
		Dishonoured cheques	850
		Closing balance	129,360
	216,820		216,820

At the point of sale, customers are not expected to take advantage of settlement discounts.

What should the closing balance be when all the errors are corrected?

A $133,840
B $135,540
C $137,740
D $139,840 (2 marks)

3.5 Alpha buys goods from Beta. At 30 June Beta's account in Alpha's records showed $5,700 owing to Beta. Beta submitted a statement to Alpha as at the same date showing a balance due of $5,200.

Which of the following could account fully for the difference?

A Alpha has sent a cheque to Beta for $500 which has not yet been received by Beta
B The credit side of Beta's account in Alpha's records has been undercast by $500
C An invoice for $250 from Beta has been treated in Alpha's records as if it had been a credit note
D Beta has issued a credit note for $500 to Alpha which Alpha has not yet received

(2 marks)

3.6 At 30 June 20X7 a company's loss allowance for receivables was $39,000. At 30 June 20X7 trade receivables totalled $517,000. It was decided to write off debts totalling $37,000 and to adjust the loss allowance for receivables to the equivalent of 5% of the trade receivables based on past events.

What figure should appear in profit or loss for these items?

A $22,000
B $23,850
C $24,000
D $61,000 (2 marks)

3.7 Ordan received a statement from one of its suppliers, Alta, showing a balance due of $3,980. The amount due according to the payables ledger account of Alta in Ordan's records was only $3,110. Comparison of the statement and the ledger account revealed the following differences:

(1) A payment sent by Ordan for $270 has not been allowed for in Alta's statement
(2) Alta has not allowed for goods returned by Ordan $180
(3) Ordan made a contra entry, reducing the amount due to Alta by $320, for a balance due from Alta in Ordan's receivables ledger. No such entry has been made in Alta's records

What difference remains between the two companies' records after adjusting for these items?

A $100
B $460
C $640
D $740 (2 marks)

3.8 At 1 January 20X6 a company had a loss allowance for receivables of $18,000. At 31 December 20X6 the company's trade receivables were $458,000. It was decided:

(1) To write off debts totalling $28,000 as irrecoverable
(2) To adjust the loss allowance for receivables to the equivalent of 5% of the remaining receivables

What figure should appear in the company's profit or loss for the total of debts written off as irrecoverable and the movement in the loss allowance for receivables for the year ended 31 December 20X6?

A $31,500
B $32,900
C $49,500
D $50,900 (2 marks)

3.9 A company purchases all goods on credit. The following payables ledger control account contains some errors:

Payables ledger control account

	$		$
Purchases	963,200	Opening balance	384,600
		Cash paid to suppliers	988,400
Discounts received	12,600	Purchases returns	17,400
Contras with amounts receivable in receivables ledger	4,200		
Closing balance	410,400		
	1,390,400		1,390,400

What should the closing balance be when the errors have been corrected?

A $325,200
B $350,400
C $358,800
D $376,800 (2 marks)

3.10 An extract of Moon's draft trial balance as at 31 October 20X6 includes the following:

	Debit	*Credit*
Loss allowance for receivables as at 1 November 20X5		$6,546
Trade receivables	$251,760	

As at 31 October 20X6 Grundle's balance to Moon of $1,860 is irrecoverable. Blenheim owes $12,650, but Moon believes a loss allowance of 40% of this amount is necessary.

What is the total debit required to Moon's irrecoverable debts expense account?

A $374
B $1,860
C $3,346
D $6,920 (2 marks)

3.11 At its year end of 31 July 20X7 Hussar has trade receivables of $578,645, a loss allowance in respect of Cusack as at 1 August 20X6 of $1,200 and a charge for irrecoverable debts expense of $3,290. The following have still to be accounted for:

(1) Cusack's account was settled in full in the year
(2) A loss allowance of $250 is required against the account of Dancer
(3) $89 was received at 31 July 20X7 in respect of an amount written off two years ago, but only the cash book has been updated for this

What amounts should be shown in the financial statements as at 31 July 20X7?

	Statement of profit or loss	*Statement of financial position*
A	$2,251	$578,395
B	$2,340	$577,606
C	$2,340	$578,395
D	$3,451	$578,395

(2 marks)

3.12 Quince's trial balance extracted as at 31 May 20X7 includes the $456,875 for inventory as at 1 June 20X6. Inventory was physically counted on 31 May 20X7 and its cost has been established at $572,904. Of this, inventory costing $27,485 is damaged and is estimated to have a net realisable value of only $15,000.

What amount of closing inventory should appear in Quince's financial statements as at 31 May 20X7?

A $456,875
B $545,419
C $560,419
D $572,904

(2 marks)

3.13 Samantha, a sole trader, does not keep a receivables control account or a sales day book and is not registered for sales tax. The bookkeeper has discovered the following errors and omissions in Samantha's accounting records:

(1) A cheque for $180 from a customer has been returned unpaid by the bank. No entries have been made in the accounting records for the return of the cheque

(2) A credit note for $12 was sent to a customer but was mistaken for an invoice by Samantha's accounts clerk when recording it

Which of the following journals will be entered in Samantha's general ledger accounts in order to correct these items?

A Dr Receivables $156, Dr Sales $24, Cr Cash $180
B Dr Cash $180, Cr Receivables $156, Cr Sales $24
C Dr Receivables $168, Dr Sales $12, Cr Cash $180
D Dr Irrecoverable debt expense $180, Dr Receivables $24, Cr Cash $180, Cr Sales $24

(2 marks)

3.14 On 1 May, East owed a supplier $1,200. During the month of May, East:

(1) Purchased goods for $1,700 and the supplier offered a 5% discount for payment within the month

(2) Returned goods valued at $100 which had been purchased in April

(3) Paid $1,615 for the goods delivered in May

What is the balance on the supplier's account at the end of May?

A $1,015
B $1,100
C $1,185
D $1,300 (2 marks)

3.15 The revenue of a company was $4 million and its receivables were 7.5% of revenue. The company wishes to have a loss allowance of 3% of receivables, which would result in an increase of 25% of the current allowance.

What is the charge to profit or loss for irrecoverable debts?

A $1,800
B $2,250
C $9,000
D $12,000 (2 marks)

3.16 On 31 March 20X7, the balance on the receivables control account of Peak Co is $425,700. The bookkeeper has identified that the following adjustments for receivables are required:

Irrecoverable debt recovered	$2,000
Specific allowance	$2,400

It was decided that a further allowance for receivables of 2% should be made for expected credit losses. The allowance for receivables on 1 April 20X7 was $1,900.

What was the receivables expense for the year ended 31 March 20X7?

A $6,966
B $8,866
C $8,966
D $10,866 (2 marks)

3.17 The total of a list of balances in Retro Co's receivables ledger was $633,700 on 30 September 20X6. This did not agree with the balance on Retro Co's receivables ledger control account. The following errors were discovered:

(1) A credit balance on an individual customer's account of $200 was incorrectly extracted as a debit balance

(2) An invoice for $3,223 was posted to the customer account as £3,232

(3) The total of the sales returns day book was overcast by $500

What amount should be shown in R Co's statement of financial position for accounts receivable at 30 September 20X6?

A $633,291
B $633,409
C $633,491
D $633,791 (2 marks)

3.18 Viki Co's balance on the payables control account at 30 September 20X6 of $147,000 does not agree to the total of the list of payables ledger balances. The following errors have been found:

(1) A credit note from a supplier for $250 has been omitted from the purchase day book

(2) An invoice for $75 has been posted twice to the supplier's account on the payables ledger

(3) Cash paid to suppliers of $32,000 has been posted to the payables control account as $23,000

What is the total on the payables control account after all errors have been corrected?

A $146,925
B $137,750
C $137,675
D $137,825 (2 marks)

(36 marks)

Question 4 MCQs INVENTORY

4.1 At 30 September 20X6 the closing inventory of a company amounted to $386,400. The following items were included in this total at cost:

(1) 1,000 items which had cost $18 each. These items were all sold in October 20X6 for $15 each, with selling expenses of $800

(2) Five items which had been in inventory since 2001, when they were purchased for $100 each, sold in October 20X6 for $1,000 each, net of selling expenses

What figure should appear in the company's statement of financial position at 30 September 20X6 for inventory?

A $382,600
B $384,200
C $387,100
D $400,600 (2 marks)

4.2 The inventory value for the financial statements of Q for the year ended 31 December 20X6 was based on an inventory count on 4 January 20X7, which gave a total inventory value of $836,200. Between 31 December and 4 January 20X7, the following transactions took place:

	$
Purchases of goods	8,600
Sales of goods (profit margin 30% on sales)	14,000
Goods returned by Q to supplier	700

What adjusted figure should be included in the financial statements for inventories at 31 December 20X6?

A $834,300
B $838,100
C $842,300
D $853,900 (2 marks)

4.3 A business had an opening inventory of $180,000 and a closing inventory of $220,000 in its financial statements for the year ended 31 December.

Which of the following entries for these opening and closing inventory figures are made when completing the financial records of the business?

		Debit $	*Credit* $
A	Inventory account	180,000	
	Profit or loss		180,000
	Profit or loss	220,000	
	Inventory account		220,000
B	Profit or loss	180,000	
	Inventory account		180,000
	Inventory account	220,000	
	Profit or loss		220,000
C	Inventory account	40,000	
	Purchases account		40,000
D	Purchases account	40,000	
	Inventory account		40,000

(2 marks)

4.4 Franz is a manufacturer. Inventory is valued using the continuous weighted average method. At 1 August 20X6 it held inventory of 2,400 units of product Z, valued at $10 each. During the year the following transactions in product Z took place:

14 November 20X6	Sell	900 units
28 January 20X7	Purchase	1,200 units for $20,100
7 May 20X7	Sell	1,800 units

What was the value of Franz's inventory of Zobdo at 31 July 20X7?

A $9,000
B $11,700
C $15,075
D $35,100

(2 marks)

(8 marks)

Question 5 MCQs BOOKS OF PRIME ENTRY AND CONTROL ACCOUNTS

5.1 The following control account has been prepared by a trainee accountant:

Receivables ledger control account

	$		$
Opening balance	308,600	Cash received from credit customers	147,200
Credit sales	154,200	Discounts allowed to credit customers	1,400
Cash sales	88,100	Interest charged on overdue accounts	2,400
Contras against credit balances in payables ledger	4,600	Irrecoverable debts written off	4,900
		Loss allowance	2,800
		Closing balance	396,800
	555,500		555,500

At the point of sale, customers are not expected to take advantage of settlement discounts.

What should the closing balance be when all the errors made in preparing the receivables ledger control account have been corrected?

A $395,200
B $304,300
C $307,100
D $309,500

(2 marks)

5.2 **Which of the following correctly describes the imprest system of operating petty cash?**

A The petty cash float is replenished by regular periodic transfers of equal amount

B The petty cash float is replenished by periodic transfers of the actual expenditure in the period

C All expenses must be supported by a properly authorised voucher

D Petty cash is operated outside the business double entry accounting system

(2 marks)

5.3 The following receivables ledger control account for December prepared by a trainee accountant contains a number of errors:

Receivables ledger control account

	$		$
1 Dec Balance	614,000	30 Dec Credit sales	301,000
31 Dec Cash from credit customers	311,000	Discounts allowed	3,400
		Irrecoverable debts written off	32,000
Contras against amounts due to suppliers in payables ledger	8,650	Interest charged on overdue accounts	1,600
		Balance	595,650
	933,650		933,650

At the point of sale, customers are not expected to take advantage of settlement discounts.

What should the closing balance on the control account be after the errors in it have been corrected?

A $561,550
B $568,350
C $578,850
D $581,550 (2 marks)

5.4 The following receivables ledger control account for December has been prepared by a trainee accountant:

Receivables ledger control account

		$			$
1 Dec	Balance	318,650	31 Dec	Cash from credit customers	181,140
	Credit sales	161,770		Interest charged on overdue accounts	280
				Irrecoverable debts w/off	1,390
	Cash sales	84,260		Sales returns from credit customers	3,990
	Discounts allowed to credit customers	1,240		Balance	379,120
		565,920			565,920

At the point of sale, customers are not expected to take advantage of settlement discounts.

What should the closing balance at 31 December be after correcting the errors in the account?

A $292,380
B $292,940
C $295,420
D $377,200 (2 marks)

5.5 **Which of the following statements about a cash imprest system is/are correct?**

(1) At any point in time physical cash plus petty cash vouchers will be equal to the imprest balance

(2) There is no incentive to ensure all money disbursed is documented and supported by vouchers

(3) It is difficult to reconcile an imprest system because it is not known exactly how much should be in the float

(4) A fixed amount of cash is issued each month

A 1 only
B 4 only
C 1 and 3
D 2 and 4 (2 marks)

5.6 A trainee accountant has prepared the following receivables ledger total account to calculate the credit sales of a business which does not keep proper accounting records (all sales are on credit):

Receivables ledger total account

	$		$
Opening receivables	148,200	Credit sales	870,800
Cash received from customers	819,300		
Discounts allowed to credit customers	16,200		
Irrecoverable debts written off	1,500		
Returns from customers	38,700	Closing receivables	153,100
	1,023,900		1,023,900

At the point of sale, customers are not expected to take advantage of settlement discounts.

What is the sales figure when all the errors have been corrected?

A $835,400
B $848,200
C $877,600
D $880,600 (2 marks)

5.7 Johan enters into the following transactions with Marius, a supplier who is also a customer. Marius buys goods from Johan on credit terms. Johan agrees to make contra entries in Marius' individual ledger accounts.

Which of Johan's accounting records are affected by these transactions?

A Sales day book, payables ledger and sales ledger
B Purchase day book, payables ledger and sales ledger
C Sales day book and sales ledger
D Purchases day book and purchases ledger (2 marks)

5.8 At the end of December Rock's payables control account and its list of payables ledger balances fail to agree.

It is discovered that the total of the purchase day book for December has been recorded as $11,750. The correct figure is $17,150.

Which one of the following is the correct adjustment in the payables control account reconciliation?

A The control account balance should be reduced by $5,400
B The list of balances should be increased by $5,400
C The control account balance should be increased by $5,400
D The list of balances should be reduced by $5,400 (2 marks)

5.9 At 31 October 20X6 Osba had a receivables control account with a balance of $381,255. This balance was $782 more than the total on the list of receivables balances at the same date.

Which one of the following errors would account for this difference?

A A receipt from Ellie for $391 had been recorded on the debit side of Ellie's account. Correct entries were made in the general ledger

B The total column in the sales day book had been overcast by $782

C A customer returned some goods to Osba on 30 November 20X6. These had originally been invoiced at $782. Osba recorded a credit note in the sales day book which was debited to the customer's account

D An invoice to Plion plc for $391 had been recorded in the sales day book as a credit note (2 marks)

5.10 A company operates an imprest system for petty cash. At 1 July there was a float of $150, but it was decided to increase this to $200 from 1 August onwards. During July, the petty cashier received $25 from staff for personal use of the photocopier and a personal cheque for $90 was cashed for an employee. During July the company took $500 from its bank account to make up the imprest balance for petty cash.

What was the total expense paid from petty cash in July?

A $385
B $435
C $515
D $615 (2 marks)

5.11 Patrick starts a new business. During the first year the entries in the sales ledger control account are:

	$
Sales	250,000
Bank receipts	225,000
Sales returns	2,500
Irrecoverable debts written off	3,000
Dishonoured cheques	3,500
Contra with purchase ledger control account	4,000

What is the balance on the sales ledger control account at the end of the year?

A $12,000
B $19,000
C $25,000
D $27,000 (2 marks)

5.12 Norris operates an imprest system for petty cash. On 1 February, the float was $300. He decided that this should be increased to $375 at the end of February.

During February, the cashier paid $20 for window cleaning, $100 for stationery and $145 for coffee and biscuits. The cashier received $20 from staff for private use of the photocopier and $60 for a sundry cash sale.

What amount was drawn from the bank account for petty cash at the end of February?

A $185
B $260
C $315
D $375 (2 marks)

5.13 A sales tax registered company commenced trading on 1 December. In December, the company sold goods that attracted sales tax at 15% with a net value of $200,000, goods exempt from sales tax with a value of $50,000 and goods at 0% sales tax with a net value of $25,000.

All purchases in December, which were all subject to 15% sales tax, were $161,000, including sales tax.

What is the balance on the sales tax account at the end of December?

A Dr $9,000
B Dr $5,850
C Cr $5,850
D Cr $9,000 (2 marks)

5.14 Damien Co's transactions for the month of September 20X6 were as follows:

	$
Sales (including sales tax)	600,000
Purchases (excluding sales tax)	450,000

Damien Co is registered for sales tax at 20%. On 1 September 20X6 the sales tax account showed sales tax recoverable by Damien Co of $2,000.

What was the balance on the sales tax account on 30 September 20X6?

A $8,000 Dr
B $8,000 Cr
C $12,000 Dr
D $12,000 Cr (2 marks)

5.15 Paula Co is reconciling its receivables control account and has discovered the following items:

(1) An invoice for $110 had been recorded in the receivables ledger as $1,100

(2) A cash sale of $100 to a customer had been posted to the receivables ledger

Where should each of the corrections be recorded?

	Item 1	*Item 2*
A	Control account	Receivables ledger
B	Receivables ledger	Control account
C	Control account	Control account
D	Receivables ledger	Receivables ledger

(2 marks)

(30 marks)

Question 6 MCQs JOURNAL ENTRIES

6.1 Which of the following journal entries is correct according to its narratives?

		Dr $	Cr $
A	Wages account	38,000	
	Purchases account	49,000	
	Buildings account		87,000
	Labour and materials used in construction of extension to factory		
B	Directors' personal accounts:		
	K	30,000	
	L	40,000	
	Directors' remuneration		70,000
	Directors' bonuses transferred to their accounts		
C	Suspense account	10,000	
	Sales account		10,000
	Correction of error in addition – total of credit side of sales account $10,000 understated		
D	Discount received	7,000	
	Trade payables	61,000	
	Bank		68,000
	Payment to creditors after allowing for prompt payment discount		

(2 marks)

6.2 Which of the following journal entries is correct according to their narratives?

		Dr $	Cr $
A	Receivables ledger account	450	
	Irrecoverable debts account		450
	Irrecoverable balance written off		
B	Share premium	40,000	
	Share capital		40,000
	Bonus issue of 80,000 shares of $0.50 each		
C	Suspense account	1,000	
	Motor vehicles account		1,000
	Correction of error – debit side of Motor vehicles account undercast by $1,000		
D	Wages	2,500	
	Buildings		2,500
	Capitalisation of labour costs on self-constructed building		

(2 marks)

6.3 Which of the following journal entries are correct, according to their narratives?

		Dr $	*Cr* $
A	Suspense account	18,000	
	Rent received account		18,000
	Correction of error: $24,000 cash received for rent was posted to the rent received account as $42,000		
B	X receivables account	22,000	
	Y receivables account		22,000
	Correction of error: cash received from Y wrongly entered to X's account		
C	Share premium account	400,000	
	Share capital account		400,000
	1 for 3 bonus issue on share capital of 1,200,000 $0.50 shares		
D	ZX customer account	4,000	
	ZX supplier account		4,000
	Set off (contra) of amount due to supplier ZX against amount due from customer ZX		

(2 marks)

6.4 What journal entry is required to record goods taken from inventory by the owner of a business?

A Debit Drawings and Credit Purchases
B Debit Sales and Credit Drawings
C Debit Drawings and Credit Inventory
D Debit Purchases and Credit Drawings (2 marks)

6.5 Ewan, a sole trader, has taken goods during the year for his own use valued at $1,350. This has not been recorded.

What will be the effects of accounting for these drawings?

	Profit	*Assets and liabilities*
A	Increase profit	Decrease asset
B	Decrease profit	Increase liability
C	Increase profit	No effect
D	No effect	Decrease asset

(2 marks)

6.6 Leonard, a sole trader, extracts a trial balance as at 30 April 20X7. He subsequently discovers that drawings amounting to $38,100 have been debited to other expenses account in error.

What correcting entries must be made?

A Dr Capital account and Cr Other expenses account
B Dr Other expenses account and Cr Capital account
C Dr Drawings account and Cr Suspense account
D Dr Suspense account and Cr Other expenses account (2 marks)

6.7 North, which is registered for sales tax, received an invoice from an advertising agency for $4,000 plus sales tax. The rate of sales tax is 20%.

What are the correct ledger entries for this transaction?

	Debit $	*Credit* $	
A	Advertising 4,000	Payables 4,000	
B	Advertising 4,800	Payables 4,800	
C	Advertising 4,800	Payables 4,000 and Sales tax 800	
D	Advertising 4,000 and Sales tax 800	Payables 4,800	(2 marks)

(14 marks)

Question 7 ROOK

The following transactions of Rook took place in the year ended 31 March 20X7:

(a) The clearance of a difference in the list of account balances for which a suspense account had been opened. The difference was found to be caused by a $2,000 understatement of the debit side of the salaries account in the general ledger; (2 marks)

(b) The acceptance of a car worth $6,000 in settlement of a trade account receivable of $7,500 due from Wren. No other money will be received from Wren. The car is to be used by one of the sales representatives of Rook; (2 marks)

(c) The construction of an extension to Rook's factory using materials from inventory and the company's own labour force. The costs were:

Materials taken from inventory	$27,600
Labour	$18,500

(3 marks)

(d) Rook purchased a number of assets from Crow. It was agreed that the total purchase price was not to be paid immediately but was to remain as a loan to be repaid by Rook over several years. The assets purchased were:

	$
Motor vehicles	18,000
Plant and equipment	33,000
Goods for resale in the normal course of Rook's business	20,000
	71,000

(3 marks)

(e) The purchase of a car from Car Dealer on 18 March 20X7 for $20,000. On that date, Rook gave in part exchange a vehicle which had cost $18,000 and which had a written down value of $12,000. The agreed part exchange value of this vehicle was its written down value of $12,000. The balance of $8,000 is to be paid on 30 April 20X7. (6 marks)

Required:

Show journal entries, with narrations, to record these transactions. Note that entries to ledger control accounts are not required for item (b).

(16 marks)

Question 8 ADDAX

The following balances appeared in the statement of financial position of Addax at 31 March 20X6.

	$
Plant and equipment – cost	840,000
Accumulated depreciation	370,000

In the year ended 31 March 20X7 the following transactions took place:

(1) Plant which had cost $100,000 with a written down value of $40,000 was sold for $45,000 on 10 December

(2) New plant was purchased for $180,000 on 1 October 20X6

It is the policy of the company to charge depreciation at 10% per year on the straight line basis with a proportionate charge in the year of acquisition and no charge in the year of sale. None of the plant was over ten years old at 31 March 20X6.

Required:

(a) Prepare ledger accounts recording the above transactions. A cash account is NOT required. (5 marks)

(b) List the items which should appear in Addax's statement of cash flows for the year ended 31 March 20X7 based on these transactions and using the indirect method. Your answer should include the headings under which they should appear in accordance with IAS 7 *Statement of Cash Flows*. (4 marks)

(9 marks)

Question 9 RIFFON

The accounting records of Riffon included the following balances at 30 June 20X6:

		$
Office buildings	– cost	1,600,000
	– accumulated depreciation (10 years at 2% per year)	320,000
Plant and equipment	– cost (all purchased in 20X4 or later)	840,000
	– accumulated depreciation (straight line basis at 25% per year)	306,000

During the year ended 30 June 20X7 the following events occurred:

20X6

1 July — It was decided to revalue the office building to $2,000,000, with no change to the estimate of its remaining useful life.

1 October — New plant costing $200,000 was purchased.

20X7

1 April — Plant which had cost $240,000 and with accumulated depreciation at 30 June 20X6 of $180,000 was sold for $70,000.

It is the company's policy to charge a full year's depreciation on plant in the year of acquisition and none in the year of sale.

Required:

Prepare the following ledger accounts to record the above balances and events:

(a)	**Office building:**	**cost/valuation; accumulated depreciation; revaluation surplus.**	(6 marks)
(b)	**Plant and equipment:**	**cost; accumulated depreciation; disposal.**	(6 marks)
			(12 marks)

Question 10 UNITED

A company maintains a receivables ledger control account in the general ledger, and includes the balance on this account in its list of balances. It also maintains a memorandum individual receivables ledger.

The following errors relating to receivables have been discovered.

(1) A credit note for $90 had been entered as if it were an invoice.

(2) Sales of $400 had been entered on the wrong side of a customer's account in the individual receivables ledger.

(3) A settlement discount of $70 taken up by a customer who was not expected to accept the offer of a discount had been completely omitted from the records.

(4) An invoice of $123 had been entered in the sales day book as $321.

(5) No entry had been made to record an agreement to contra an amount owed to P of $600 against an amount owed by P of $700.

(6) Irrecoverable debts written off amounting to $160 had not been posted to the individual receivables accounts, though otherwise correctly treated.

Required:

Prepare journal entries to correct each of the errors described in (1) to (6) above. Accounts should be fully named, but narrative descriptions are not required.

(9 marks)

Question 11 SCIMITAR

Scimitar proves the accuracy of its ledgers by preparing monthly control accounts. At 1 September the following balances existed in the company's accounting records, and the control accounts agreed:

	Debit	*Credit*
	$	$
Accounts receivable ledger totals	188,360	2,140
Accounts payable ledger totals	120	89,410

The following are the totals of transactions which took place during September, as extracted from the company's records:

	$
Credit sales	101,260
Credit purchases	68,420
Sales returns	9,160
Purchases returns	4,280
Cash received from customers	92,700
Cash paid to suppliers	71,840
Cash discounts received	880
Irrecoverable debts written off	460
Refunds to customers	300
Contra settlements	480

At 30 September the balances in the ledgers, as extracted, totalled:

	Debit	*Credit*
	$	$
Accounts receivable ledger balances	To be ascertained	2,680
Accounts payable ledger balances	90	To be ascertained

An initial attempt to balance the two ledgers showed that neither of them agreed with their control accounts. The differences were found to be due to the following:

(1) A credit balance of $680 had been omitted when listing the accounts receivable ledger balances;

(2) A contra settlement of $500 had not been included in the totals of transactions prepared for the control accounts;

(3) A new employee had mistakenly entered five sales invoices into the purchases day book as if they had been purchase invoices and entered the amounts to new accounts payable ledger accounts. The total of these invoices was $1,360;

(4) A $20 cash refund to a customer was made that has not been included in the summary of transactions given above. The $20 was entered to the accounts receivable ledger as if it had been a cash receipt from the customer. This resulted in a $40 credit balance on the account, which was still outstanding at 30 September.

When these errors had been corrected both control accounts agreed with the personal ledgers.

Required:

Prepare the accounts receivable ledger and accounts payable ledger control (total) accounts for the month of September AFTER these errors had been corrected, and hence ascertain the missing totals of the ledger balances as indicated above (debit balances in accounts receivable ledger and credit balances in accounts payable ledger).

(12 marks)

Question 12 OTTER

Otter operates a computerised accounting system for its accounts receivable and accounts payable ledgers. The control accounts for the month of September are in balance and incorporate the following totals:

		$
Accounts receivable ledger:		
Balances at 1 September:	Debit	386,430
	Credit	190
Sales revenue		163,194
Cash received		158,288
Sales returns inwards		590
Credit balances at 30 September		370
Accounts payable ledger:		
Balances at 1 September:	Credit	184,740
	Debit	520
Purchases		98,192
Cash payments		103,040
Discounts received		990
Purchases returns outwards		1,370
Debit balances at 30 September		520

Although the control accounts agree with the underlying ledgers, a number of errors have been found, and there are also several adjustments to be made. These errors and adjustments are detailed below:

(1) Four sales invoices totalling $1,386 have been omitted from the records;

(2) A cash refund of $350 was paid to a customer, A Smith, whose account balance was a credit. This refund was mistakenly treated as a payment to a supplier with the same name;

(3) A contra settlement offsetting a balance of $870 due to a supplier against the accounts receivable ledger account for the same company is to be made;

(4) Irrecoverable debts totalling $1,360 are to be written off;

(5) During the month, settlement was reached with a supplier over a disputed account. As a result, the supplier issued a credit note for $2,000 on 26 September. No entry has yet been made for this;

(6) A purchases invoice for $1,395 was keyed in as $1,359;

(7) A payment of $2,130 to a supplier, B Jones, was mistakenly entered to the account of R Jones;

(8) A debit balance of $420 existed in the accounts payable ledger at the end of August. The supplier concerned cannot now be traced and it has been decided to write off this balance.

Required:

Prepare the accounts receivable and accounts payable ledger control accounts as they should appear after allowing, where necessary, for the errors and adjustments listed.

(15 marks)

Question 13 ATANGA

The receivables ledger control account of Atanga at 31 December shows a debit balance of $487,600. The list of receivables ledger balances at the same date totalled $455,800 debit. There were no credit balances.

On investigation the following errors and revisions were found:

(1) The sales day book had been overcast by $2,000;

(2) A debt of $8,550 is to be written off;

(3) A credit note for $1,200 was entered on the debit side of the customer's account;

(4) Contras against amounts owing to Atanga in the payables ledger totalling $16,100 were entered on the debit side of the receivables ledger control account;

(5) A credit note for $5,600 sent to a customer and recorded at that figure should have been for $4,500.

Required:

(a) Prepare a statement showing the necessary adjustments to the receivables ledger control account balance. (4 marks)

(b) Prepare a statement showing the necessary adjustments to the total of the list of receivables ledger balances. (3 marks)

(7 marks)

Question 14 MCQs BANK RECONCILIATIONS

14.1 Listed below are five potential causes of difference between a company's cash book balance and its bank statement balance as at 30 November:

(1) Cheques recorded and sent to suppliers before 30 November but not yet presented for payment.

(2) An error by the bank in crediting to another customer's account a lodgement made by the company.

(3) Bank charges.

(4) Cheques paid in before 30 November but not credited by the bank until 3 December.

(5) A cheque recorded and paid in before 30 November but dishonoured by the bank.

Which of the following alternatives correctly analyses these items into those requiring an entry in the cash book and those that would feature in the bank reconciliation?

	Cash book entry	*Bank reconciliation*
A	1, 2, 4	3, 5
B	2, 3, 5	1, 4
C	3, 4	1, 2, 5
D	3, 5	1, 2, 4

(2 marks)

14.2 Which TWO of the following statements about bank reconciliations are correct?

(1) If a cheque received from a customer is dishonoured, a credit entry in the cash book is required

(2) A difference between the cash book and the bank statement must be corrected by means of a journal entry

(3) Bank charges not yet entered in the cash book should be dealt with by an adjustment in the bank reconciliation

(4) In preparing a bank reconciliation, lodgements recorded before date in the cash book but credited by the bank after date should reduce an overdrawn balance in the bank statement

A 1 and 3
B 2 and 3
C 1 and 4
D 2 and 4

(2 marks)

14.3 The following bank reconciliation statement has been prepared for a company:

	$
Overdraft per bank statement	39,800
Add: Deposits credited after date	64,100
	103,900
Less: Outstanding cheques presented after date	44,200
Overdraft per cash book	59,700

Assuming the amount of the overdraft per the bank statement of $39,800 is correct, what should be the balance in the cash book?

A $19,900 overdrawn
B $68,500 overdrawn
C $59,700 overdrawn as stated
D $158,100 overdrawn

(2 marks)

14.4 Sigma's bank statement shows an overdrawn balance of $38,600 at 30 June. A check against the company's cash book revealed the following differences:

(1) Bank charges of $200 have not been entered in the cash book

(2) Lodgements recorded on 30 June but credited by the bank on 2 July $14,700

(3) Cheque payments entered in cash book but not presented for payment at 30 June $27,800

(4) A cheque payment to a supplier of $4,200 charged to the account in June recorded in the cash book as a receipt

Based on this information, what was the cash book balance BEFORE any adjustments?

A $16,900 overdrawn
B $34,100 overdrawn
C $43,100 overdrawn
D $60,300 overdrawn

(2 marks)

14.5 The following bank reconciliation statement has been prepared by an inexperienced bookkeeper at 31 December:

	$
Balance per bank statement (overdrawn)	38,640
Add: Lodgements not credited	19,270
	57,910
Less: Unpresented cheques	14,260
Balance per cash book	43,650

What should the final cash book balance be when all the above items have been properly dealt with?

A $5,110 overdrawn
B $33,630 overdrawn
C $43,650 overdrawn
D $72,170 overdrawn (2 marks)

14.6 The debit balance in Omar's cash book at the year end is $42,510. The following items appear in the bank reconciliation at the year end:

	$
Unpresented cheques	2,990
Outstanding lodgements	10,270

A customer's cheque for $2,470 was returned unpaid by the bank before the year end, but this return has not been recorded in the cash book.

What was the balance shown by the bank statement?

A $47,320
B $37,700
C $35,230
D $32,760 (2 marks)

14.7 Z's bank statement shows a balance of $825 overdrawn. The bank statement includes bank charges of $50, which have not been entered in the cash book. There are unpresented cheques totalling $475 and deposits not yet credited of $600. The bank statement incorrectly shows a direct debit payment of $160, which relates to another customer of the bank.

What bank balance should be shown in Z's statement of financial position?

A $590 overdrawn
B $540 overdrawn
C $790 overdrawn
D $840 overdrawn (2 marks)

14.8 In preparing a company's bank reconciliation statement at 31 March, the following items are causing the difference between the cash book balance and the bank statement balance:

(1) Unrecorded bank charges $380
(2) Error by bank $1,000 (cheque incorrectly debited to the account)
(3) Lodgements not credited $4,580
(4) Outstanding cheques $1,475
(5) Unrecorded direct debit $350
(6) Cheque paid in by the company that was subsequently dishonoured $400

Which of these items will require an entry in the cash book?

A 2, 4 and 6
B 3, 4 and 5
C 1, 2 and 3
D 1, 5 and 6 (2 marks)

14.9 A company has prepared its bank reconciliation at 31 March 20X7 taking the following information into account:

	$
Outstanding lodgements	5,000
Unpresented cheques	2,800
Bank charges shown in the bank statement but not recorded in the cash book	125

The adjusted cash book balance per the bank reconciliation was a debit balance of $1,060.

What was the balance as shown on the bank statement at 31 March 20X7?

A $1,140 debit
B $1,140 credit
C $1,265 debit
D $1,265 credit (2 marks)

(18 marks)

Question 15 GEORGE

George had completed his financial statements for the year ended 31 March, which showed a profit of $81,208, when he realised that no bank reconciliation statement had been prepared at that date.

When checking the cash book against the bank statement and carrying out other checks, he found the following:

(1) A cheque for $1,000 had been entered in the cash book but had not yet been presented.

(2) Cheques from customers totalling $2,890 entered in the cash book on 31 March were credited by the bank on 1 April.

(3) Bank charges of $320 appear in the bank statement on 30 March but have not been recorded by George.

(4) A cheque for $12,900 drawn by George to pay for a new item of plant had been mistakenly entered in the cash book and the plant account as $2,900. Depreciation of $290 had been charged to profit or loss for this plant.

(5) A cheque for $980 from a credit customer paid in on 26 March was dishonoured after 31 March and George decided that the debt would have to be written off, as the customer was now untraceable.

(6) A cheque for $2,400 in payment for some motor repairs had mistakenly been entered in the cash book as a debit and posted to the credit of motor vehicles account. Depreciation at 25% per annum (straight line) is charged on motor vehicles, with a full year's charge calculated on the balance at the end of each year.

(7) The total of the payments side of the cash book had been understated by $1,000. On further investigation it was found that the debit side of the purchases account had also been understated by $1,000.

(8) George had instructed his bank to credit the interest of $160 on the deposit account maintained for surplus business funds to the current account. This the bank had done on 28 March. George had made an entry on the payments side of the cash book for this $160 and had posted it to the debit of interest expense account.

(9) George had mistakenly paid $870 for repairs to his house with a cheque drawn on the business account. The entry in the cash book had been debited to repairs to premises account.

(10) George had also mistakenly paid $540 due to Paul, a trade supplier, to clear his account in the accounts payable ledger, using a cheque drawn on George's personal bank account. No entries have yet been made for this transaction.

The cash book showed a debit balance of $4,890 before any correcting entries had been made. The balance in the bank statement is to be derived in your answer.

Required:

(a) Prepare an adjusted cash book showing the revised balance which should appear in George's statement of financial position at 31 March. (6 marks)

(b) Prepare a bank reconciliation statement as at 31 March. (3 marks)

(c) Draw up a statement for George showing the effect on his profit of the adjustments necessary to correct the errors found. (8 marks)

(17 marks)

Question 16 MCQs SUSPENSE ACCOUNTS

16.1 A company's trial balance failed to agree, the totals being:

Debit	$815,602
Credit	$808,420

Which one of the following errors could fully account for the difference?

A The omission from the trial balance of the balance on the insurance expense account $7,182 debit

B Discount allowed $3,591 debited in error to the discount received account

C No entries made in the records for cash sales totalling $7,182

D The returns outwards total of $3,591 was included in the trial balance as a debit balance (2 marks)

16.2 A trial balance extracted from a sole trader's records failed to agree, and a suspense account was opened for the difference.

Which of the following errors would require an entry in the suspense account to correct them?

(1) Discount allowed was mistakenly debited to discount received account

(2) Cash received from the sale of a non-current asset was correctly entered in the cash book but was debited to the disposal account

(3) The balance on the rent account was omitted from the trial balance

(4) Goods taken from inventory by the proprietor had been recorded by crediting Drawings account and debiting Purchases account

A 1 and 2
B 2 and 3
C 3 and 4
D 1 and 3 (2 marks)

16.3 A company's trial balance does not balance. The totals are:

Debit	$384,030
Credit	$398,580

A suspense account is opened for the difference.

Which of the following pairs of errors could clear the balance on the suspense account when corrected?

A Debit side of cash book undercast by $10,000; $6,160 paid for rent correctly entered in the cash book but entered in the rent account as $1,610

B Debit side of cash book overcast by $10,000; $1,610 paid for rent correctly entered in the cash book but entered in the rent account as $6,160

C Debit side of cash book undercast by $10,000; $1,610 paid for rent correctly entered in the cash book but entered in the rent account as $6,160

D Debit side of cash book overcast by $10,000; $6,160 paid for rent correctly entered in the cash book but entered in the rent account as $1,610 (2 marks)

The following information is relevant for questions 16.4 and 16.5:

A company's draft financial statements for the year to 31 December showed a profit of $630,000. However, the trial balance did not agree, and a suspense account appeared in the company's draft statement of financial position.

Subsequent checking revealed the following errors:

(1) The cost of an item of plant $48,000 had been entered in the cash book and in the plant account as $4,800. Depreciation at the rate of 10% per year ($480) had been charged

(2) Bank charges of $440 appeared in the bank statement in December but had not been entered in the company's records

(3) A director paid $800 due to a supplier in the payables ledger by a personal cheque. The bookkeeper recorded a debit in the supplier's ledger account but did not complete the double entry for the transaction. (The company does not maintain a payables ledger control account)

(4) The payments side of the cash book had been understated by $10,000

16.4 Which TWO of the above items would require an entry to the suspense account to correct them?

- **A** 1 and 2
- **B** 1 and 4
- **C** 2 and 3
- **D** 3 and 4

(2 marks)

16.5 What would the company's profit become after the correction of the above errors?

- **A** $624,440
- **B** $624,760
- **C** $625,240
- **D** $634,760

(2 marks)

16.6 The following errors have occurred during Bombardier's recent accounting period:

(1) A discount received from Bernard had been debited to purchases but was correctly treated in the payables control account

(2) Goods returned by Cranberry had been debited to Cranberry's account in the receivables ledger and to the receivables control account but had been correctly treated in the sales account

Which of these errors would give rise to an entry in a suspense account?

- **A** 1 only
- **B** 2 only
- **C** Both 1 and 2
- **D** Neither 1 nor 2

(2 marks)

16.7 Hywel's trial balance includes a total amount for the sum of the individual receivables ledger accounts as listed out at the year end. The trial balance fails to agree and a suspense account is opened. The difference is found to be due to the following errors in Hywel's ledger accounts:

(1) The balance on Markham's receivables ledger account is $9,890. This is incorrectly included in the list of balances as $9,980

(2) A discount unexpectedly taken by Umberto of $33 was debited to his receivables ledger account

(3) The sales revenue account is overcast by $110

Three journals are drafted to correct these errors.

What is the overall effect of these journals on the suspense account?

- **A** $110 Cr
- **B** $46 Cr
- **C** $46 Dr
- **D** $86 Dr

(2 marks)

16.8 Llama maintains its petty cash records using an imprest system. The total petty cash float is topped up monthly to $300. Last month the following expenses were paid from petty cash:

	$
Stationery	36
Tea and coffee	60
Postage stamps	120

In error, the purchase of postage stamps was recorded as $12 and as a result $108 cash was added to the petty cash float.

Which one of the following will result from the error?

A An imbalance in the trial balance of $108 and a petty cash balance that is $108 less than it should be

B An understatement of expenses of $108 and a petty cash balance that is $192 less than it should be

C An understatement of expenses of $108 and a petty cash balance that is $108 less than it should be

D An imbalance in the trial balance of $192 and a petty cash balance that is $192 less than it should be (2 marks)

16.9 As at 31 December Isambard's trial balance failed to balance and a suspense account was opened. When the following errors were discovered and then rectified, the suspense account balance was eliminated.

(1) The debit side of the trial balance was undercast by $692

(2) A payment of $905 had been credited in the cash book but no other entry in respect of it had been made

What was the original balance on the suspense account?

A $1,597 Dr
B $213 Dr
C $213 Cr
D $1,597 Cr (2 marks)

16.10 Teebee maintains a purchases ledger control account in its general ledger. The bookkeeper is extracting a trial balance from a general ledger.

Which of the following errors in postings to the purchases ledger control account could cause the trial balance totals to be unequal?

(1) A transposition error
(2) An error of omission
(3) An error of principle

A 1 only
B 2 only
C 1 and 2 only
D 1, 2 and 3 (2 marks)

16.11 A company has a suspense account balance in its trial balance of $560 credit.

It was discovered that discounts allowed of $700 have been debited to, instead of credited to, the receivables control account.

What is the remaining balance on the suspense account after this error has been adjusted for?

A $140 debit
B $840 debit
C $1,260 credit
D $1,960 credit (2 marks)

(22 marks)

Question 17 ANDROMEDA

The list of account balances of Andromeda at 31 December 20X6 did not balance. On investigation the following errors and omissions were found. When all were corrected, the list of account balances agreed.

(1) A loan of $20,000 from Jason, one of the directors of the company, had been correctly entered in the cash book but posted to the wrong side of the loan account.

(2) The purchase of a motor vehicle on credit for $28,600 had been recorded by debiting the supplier's account and crediting motor expenses account.

(3) A cheque for $800 received from A Smith, a customer to whom goods are regularly supplied on credit, was correctly entered into the cash book but was posted to the credit of irrecoverable debts recovered account in the mistaken belief that it was a receipt from B Smith, a customer whose debt had been written off some time earlier.

(4) In reconciling the company's cash book with the bank statement it was found that bank charges of $380 had not been entered in the company's records.

(5) The total of the discounts received column in the cash book for December amounting to $2,130 had not been posted to the discount received account.

(6) The company had purchased some plant on 1 January 20X6 for $16,000. The payment was correctly entered in the cash book but was debited to plant repairs account. The depreciation rate for such plant is 20% per year on the straight-line basis.

Control accounts are not maintained.

Required:

Prepare journal entries with narratives to correct the errors, write up the suspense account and hence derive the opening balance on the suspense account representing the original difference.

(15 marks)

Question 18 ARBADOS

The draft financial statements of Arbados at 30 September have been prepared, but there remains a difference of $100, which has been temporarily inserted as a credit in a suspense account in the company's statement of financial position. On investigation the following errors were found:

(1) $8,700 paid for repairs to premises and correctly recorded in the cash book was debited to the premises asset account as $7,800.

(2) $1,000 received for the wreckage of a car destroyed in an accident while uninsured had been correctly entered in the cash book but not posted anywhere. The car had cost $30,000 and depreciation of $6,000 had already been charged on the car for the year to 30 September, making accumulated depreciation on the car at that date $12,000. No entries have yet been made to eliminate the cost and accumulated depreciation of the car.

It is the company's policy to charge no depreciation on an asset in the year of its disposal.

Required:

Prepare journal entries, including narratives, to correct the errors, record the loss of the car and clear the suspense account.

(9 marks)

Question 19 LORCA

Lorca's draft statement of profit or loss showed a profit of $830,000. However, the trial balance did not balance and a suspense account with a credit balance of $20,000 has been included in the statement of financial position for the difference.

The following errors were found on investigation:

(1) The proceeds of issue of 100,000 $0.50 shares at $0.70 per share were correctly entered in the cash book but had been credited to sales account.

(2) During the year $8,000 interest received on a holding of loan notes had been correctly entered in the cash book but debited to interest payable account.

(3) In arriving at the net sales and purchases totals for the year, the $48,000 balance on the returns outwards account had been transferred to the debit of sales account and the $64,000 balance on the returns inwards account had been transferred to the credit of purchases account.

(4) A payment of $4,000 for rent had been correctly recorded in the cash book but debited to the rent account as $40,000.

Required:

(a) Prepare journal entries to correct the errors. Narratives are NOT required. (7 marks)

(b) Calculate the revised profit after adjusting for the errors. (4 marks)

(11 marks)

Question 20 PRIDE

The following extracts have been taken from the trial balance of Pride at 31 March 20X7:

	$000	$000
Equity shares ($0.50 each)		250
Share premium account 1 April 20X6		180
Retained earnings 31 March 20X7		91
Land at cost	210	
Buildings – cost 1 April 20X6	200	
– accumulated depreciation at 1 April 20X6		120
Plant and equipment – cost	318	
– accumulated depreciation at 1 April 20X6		88
Receivables	146	
Cash at bank	50	
Payables		94
10% Loan notes (redeemable 20Y1)		100
Loss allowance for trade receivables		10
Suspense account		171

Notes:

(1) The retained earnings balance shown above includes $80,000 draft profit for the year before corrections for the following items:

(2) The balance on the suspense account is made up as follows:

	$000
Receipt of cash on 8 January 20X7 on the issue of 200,000 equity shares of $0.50 each at a premium of $0.30 per share	160
Proceeds of sale of plant *	11
	171

* Plant originally cost $18,000 and had been written down to $6,000 at 31 March 20X6.

The company's policy is to provide depreciation for a full year in the year of acquisition of assets and none in the year of sale.

(3) Depreciation is to be provided for on the straight line basis at the following annual rates:

Land	Nil
Buildings	2%
Plant and equipment	20%

(4) The loss allowance for trade receivables is to be increased to $12,000.

(5) Prepayments and accruals as at 31 March 20X7 are to be accounted for:

Prepayments	$8,000
Accrued expenses	$4,000

(6) The value of closing inventory used in arriving at draft profit for the year was $180,000.

Required:

(a) **Prepare an adjustment to profit statement.** (4 marks)

(b) **Prepare the statement of financial position of Pride as at 31 March 20X7 for publication complying as far as possible with the provisions of IAS 1 *Presentation of Financial Statements*.** (10 marks)

(14 marks)

Question 21 CHOCTAW

The draft financial statements of Choctaw for the year ended 31 December 20X6 showed a profit of $86,400. The trial balance did not balance, and a suspense account with a credit balance of $3,310 was included in the statement of financial position.

In subsequent checking the following errors were found:

(1) Depreciation of motor vehicles at 25% was calculated for the year ended 31 December 20X6 on the reducing balance basis, and should have been calculated on the straight-line basis at 25%.

Relevant figures: Cost of motor vehicles, $120,000. Carrying amount at 1 January 20X6, $88,000.

(2) Rent received from subletting part of the office accommodation $1,200 had been put into the petty cash box. No receivable balance had been recognised when the rent fell due and no entries had been made in the petty cash book or elsewhere for it. The petty cash float in the trial balance is the amount according to the records, which is $1,200 less than the actual balance in the box.

(3) Irrecoverable debts totalling $8,400 are to be written off.

(4) The opening accrual on the motor repairs account of $3,310, representing repair bills due but not paid at 31 December 20X5, had not been brought down at 1 January 20X6.

After the necessary entries, the suspense account balanced.

Required:

Prepare journal entries, with narratives, to correct the errors found, and prepare a statement showing the necessary adjustments to the profit.

(8 marks)

Question 22 RAMPION

The draft financial statements of Rampion for the year ended 31 December 20X6 included the following:

	$
Profit	684,000
Closing inventory	116,800
Trade receivables	248,000
Loss allowance for receivables	10,000

No adjustments have yet been made for the following matters:

(1) The company's inventory count was carried out on 3 January 20X7 leading to the figure shown above. Sales between the close of business on 31 December 20X6 and the inventory count totalled $36,000. There were no deliveries from suppliers in that period. The company fixes selling prices to produce a 40% gross profit on sales. The $36,000 sales were included in the sales records in January 20X7.

(2) In December 20X6 a customer ordered $10,000 of goods. These goods cost $6,000. Due to a clerical error the order was duplicated and goods were delivered and accounted for twice in December. On 10 January 20X7 the customer returned the goods in the second delivery in good condition.

(3) Goods included in inventory at cost $18,000 were sold in January 20X7 for $13,500. Selling expenses were $500.

(4) $8,000 of trade receivables are to be written off as irrecoverable.

(5) The loss allowance for receivables is to be adjusted to the equivalent of 5% of the trade receivables after allowing for the above matters.

Required:

(a) Prepare a statement showing the effect of the adjustments on the company's profit for the year ended 31 December 20X6. (5 marks)

(b) Show how the adjustments affect:

(i) Closing inventory;
(ii) Receivables, showing separately the deduction of the loss allowance.

(6 marks)

(11 marks)

Question 23 MCQs INCOMPLETE RECORDS

The following information is relevant for questions 23.1 and 23.2:

A is a sole trader who does not keep full accounting records. The following details relate to her transactions with credit customers and suppliers for the year ended 30 November 20X6:

	$
Trade receivables, 1 December 20X5	130,000
Trade payables, 1 December 20X5	60,000
Cash received from customers	687,800
Cash paid to suppliers	302,800
Discounts received	2,960
Irrecoverable debts	4,160
Amount due from a customer who is also a supplier offset against an amount due for goods supplied by him	2,000
Trade receivables, 30 November 20X6	181,000
Trade payables, 30 November 20X6	84,000

23.1 **Based on the above information, what figure should appear in A's statement of profit or loss for the year ended 30 November 20X6 for sales revenue?**

A $748,960
B $740,800
C $744,960
D $823,960 (2 marks)

23.2 **Based on the above information, what figure should appear in A's statement of profit or loss for the year ended 30 November 20X6 for purchases?**

A $283,760
B $325,840
C $329,760
D $331,760 (2 marks)

23.3 A sole trader fixes her prices by adding 50% to the cost of all goods purchased. On 31 October 20X6 a fire destroyed a considerable part of the inventory and all inventory records.

Her statement of profit or loss for the year ended 31 October 20X6 included the following figures:

	$	$
Sales		281,250
Opening inventory at cost	183,600	
Purchases	249,200	
	432,800	
Closing inventory at cost	204,600	228,200
Gross profit		53,050

Using this information, what inventory loss has occurred?

A $40,700
B $61,050
C $87,575
D $110,850 (2 marks)

23.4 The following information is available for the year ended 31 December for a trader who does not keep proper accounting records:

	$
Opening inventories at 1 January	38,000
Closing inventories at 31 December	45,000
Purchases	637,000
Gross profit percentage on sales	30%

Based on this information, what was the trader's sales figure for the year?

A $819,000
B $900,000
C $920,000
D $837,200 (2 marks)

23.5 Wanda keeps no accounting records. The following information is available about her position and transactions for the year ended 31 December:

	$
Opening net assets at 1 January	210,000
Drawings during the year	48,000
Capital introduced during the year	100,000
Closing net assets at 31 December	400,000

Based on this information, what was Wanda's profit for the year?

A $42,000
B $138,000
C $242,000
D $338,000 (2 marks)

23.6 A trader who fixes her prices by adding 50% to cost actually achieved a mark-up of 45%.

Which of the following factors could account for the shortfall?

A Sales were lower than expected
B Opening inventories had been overstated
C Closing inventories were higher than opening inventories
D Goods taken from inventories by the proprietor were recorded by debiting drawings and crediting purchases with the cost of the goods. (2 marks)

23.7 The following information is available for a sole trader who keeps no accounting records:

	$
Net business assets at 1 July 20X6	186,000
Net business assets at 30 June 20X7	274,000
During the year ended 30 June 20X7:	
Cash drawings by proprietor	68,000
Additional capital introduced by proprietor	50,000
Business cash used to buy a car for the proprietor's wife, who takes no part in the business	20,000

Using this information, what is the trader's profit for the year ended 30 June 20X7?

A $50,000
B $86,000
C $90,000
D $126,000 (2 marks)

23.8 **Which of the following factors could cause a company's gross profit percentage on sales to fall below the expected level?**

A Overstatement of closing inventories

B The incorrect inclusion in purchases of invoices relating to goods supplied in the following period

C The inclusion in sales of the proceeds of sale of non-current assets

D Reduction of overheads incurred in the production process (2 marks)

23.9 The following information is available for Orset, a sole trader who does not keep full accounting records:

		$
Inventory	1 July 20X6	138,600
	30 June 20X7	149,100
Sales for year ended 30 June 20X7		1,008,000

Orset makes a standard gross profit margin of 30%.

Based on these figures, what is Orset's purchases figure for the year ended 30 June 20X7?

A $695,100
B $705,600
C $716,100
D $785,885 (2 marks)

23.10 The following information is available about the transactions of Razil, a sole trader who does not keep proper accounting records:

	$
Opening inventory	77,000
Purchases	763,000
Sales	945,000
Mark up on cost	25%

Based on this information, what should be the cost of Razil's closing inventory?

A $70,000
B $84,000
C $85,750
D $131,250 (2 marks)

23.11 Plym is a retailer which is registered for sales tax which is at the rate of 20%. For the year to 30 June 20X7 Plym paid $69,600 to suppliers in respect of goods for resale and showed $89,400 revenue in the statement of profit or loss. There was no change in the figures for inventory and trade payables in the statements of financial position as at 30 June 20X6 and 20X7.

What was Plym's gross profit for the year ended 30 June 20X7?

A $4,900
B $16,500
C $19,800
D $31,400 (2 marks)

23.12 Muse commences trading on 1 January 20X6 and has zero inventories at that date. During 20X6 it has purchases of $455,000, incurs carriage inwards of $24,000, and carriage outwards of $29,000. Inventories at 31 December 20X6 are valued at $52,000.

Which of the following is the cost of sales figure for the year ended 31 December 20X6?

A $427,000
B $432,000
C $456,000
D $531,000 (2 marks)

23.13 Sunil started business on 1 December 20X5 with cash of $5,000. He has not yet prepared a full set of financial statements. As at the end of his first year of trading he has cash at bank of $1,726. He made sales of $33,498 during the year and paid expenses in cash of $19,385. He has no outstanding liabilities at the end of the period and has no non-current assets or inventory, but one customer owes him $2,387.

Sunil made no other capital contributions but withdraw cash amounting to $15,000 in the period.

What is Sunil's profit for the year to 30 November 20X6 and his net assets at the end of the period?

	Profit	*Net assets*
A	$11,726	$1,726
B	$14,113	$4,113
C	$11,726	$4,113
D	$14,113	$1,726

(2 marks)

23.14 Randolph started a trading business on 1 May 20X6 with capital of $40,000. In his first year of trading he made a profit of $117,000, selling goods at a mark-up on cost of 60%. He injected additional capital of $30,000 in the year and withdrew a monthly amount of $3,200 for his living expenses. At the end of the year he withdrew all remaining goods inventory with a resale value of $7,200 for his personal use.

What were Randolph's net assets at 30 April 20X7?

A $141,400
B $144,100
C $144,280
D $179,300 (2 marks)

23.15 Paul is a sole trader whose accounting records are incomplete. All the sales are cash sales and during the year $50,000 was banked, including $5,000 from the sale of a business car. He paid out $12,000 wages in cash and withdrew $2,000 per month for his living expenses. Cash in hand at the beginning and end of the year was $300 and $400 respectively.

What were Paul's sales for the year?

A $80,900
B $81,000
C $81,100
D $86,100 (2 marks)

23.16 **Which one of following formulae may be used to calculate the profit of a business?**

A Opening capital – drawings + capital introduced – closing capital
B Closing capital + drawings – capital introduced – opening capital
C Opening capital + drawings – capital introduced – closing capital
D Closing capital – drawings + capital introduced – opening capital (2 marks)

23.17 Bob used the following balances to prepare his final accounts as at 30 April 20X7:

	$	$
Receivables	6,000	
Bank loan		3,000
Bank overdraft		2,500
Drawings	4,100	
Capital		12,500
Revenue		22,000
Purchases	19,200	
Rent	5,400	
Bank interest	825	
Heat and light	4,475	
	40,000	40,000

The business does not hold inventory. No further adjustments were required.

What is Bobs' opening capital figure as at 1 May 20X7?

A $12,500
B $8,400
C $16,300
D $500 (2 marks)

23.18 Jay sells fruit and all sales are for cash. The takings are banked at the end of each week and a cash float of $50 is maintained. During the week commencing 25 March, the following payments were made from cash:

	$
Payments to suppliers	340
Wages	150
Rent	70

Jay banked $600 at the end of the week.

What were the cash takings for the week commencing 25 March?

A $1,110
B $1,160
C $600
D $560 (2 marks)

(36 marks)

Question 24 LAMORGAN

You are preparing a statement of profit or loss and statement of financial position for Lamorgan, a sole trader who does not keep adequate accounting records.

The following information is available to you to calculate the figures for inclusion in the accounts for sales revenue, purchases and closing inventory for the year ended 30 June 20X7:

(a) Sales revenue

		$
Cash received from credit customers		218,500
Cash sales receipts paid into bank		114,700
Expenses paid out of cash sales before banking		9,600
Trade receivables:	30 June 20X6	41,600
	30 June 20X7	44,200
Refunds to customers		800
Irrecoverable debts written off		4,100
Amount due from credit customer deducted by Lamorgan in paying supplier's account		700

Required:

Calculate the sales revenue figure from this information. (5 marks)

(b) Purchases

		$
Payments to suppliers		114,400
Trade payables:	30 June 20X6	22,900
	30 June 20X7	24,800
Cost of items taken from inventory by Lamorgan for personal use		400
Amount due from credit customer deducted by Lamorgan in settling supplier's account		700

Required:

Calculate the purchases figure from this information. (3 marks)

(c) Closing inventory

Cost of inventory obtained from physical count on 30 June 20X7 $77,700

This figure does NOT include any amounts for the two items below:

(i) An inventory line which had cost $1,800 was found to be damaged. Remedial work costing $300 is needed to enable the items to be sold for $1,700. Selling expenses of $100 would also be incurred in selling these items.

(ii) Goods sent to a customer on approval in May 20X7 were not included in the inventory. The sale price of the goods was $4,000 and the cost $3,000. The customer notified his acceptance of the goods in July 20X7. Note: No adjustment to the sales figure in (a) above is required for this item.

Required:

Calculate the adjusted closing inventory figure from this information. (2 marks)

(10 marks)

Question 25 ALTESE, SENJI & ALUKI

(a) The net assets of Altese, a trader, at 1 January 20X6 amounted to $128,000.

During the year to 31 December 20X6 Altese introduced a further $50,000 of capital and made drawings of $48,000.

At 31 December 20X6 Altese's net assets totalled $184,000.

Required:

Using this information calculate Altese's total profit for the year ended 31 December 20X6. (3 marks)

(b) Senji does not keep proper accounting records, and it is necessary to calculate her total purchases for the year ended 31 January 20X7 from the following information:

		$
Trade payables	31 January 20X6	130,400
	31 January 20X7	171,250
Payment to suppliers		888,400
Cost of goods taken from inventory by Senji for her personal use		1,000
Refunds received from suppliers		2,400
Discounts received		11,200

Required:

Calculate the figure for purchases for inclusion in Senji's financial statements. (3 marks)

(c) Aluki fixes prices to make a standard gross profit percentage on sales of $33^{1}/_{3}$%.

The following information for the year ended 31 January 20X7 is available to calculate her sales total for the year.

		$
Inventory:	1 February 20X6	243,000
	31 January 20X7	261,700
Purchases		595,400
Purchases returns		41,200

Required:

Calculate the sales figure for the year ended 31 January 20X7. (3 marks)

(9 marks)

Question 26 HASTA

Hasta is an antique dealer operating from rented premises. He keeps few accounting records. All his sales and purchases are for cash, except for some sales to other dealers which are made on credit.

The following information is available to prepare his statement of profit or loss for the year ended 31 December 20X6:

	As at 31 December	
	20X6	*20X5*
Assets and liabilities	$	$
Equipment	2,000	1,200
Inventory	88,500	85,000
Trade receivables	6,400	4,800
Payable for expenses	1,400	1,100

Cash summary

		$			$
1 Jan	Balance – float	100	31 Dec	Wages for assistant	15,600
				Sundry expenses	8,300
31 Dec	Cash from customers	191,400		Purchases of new equipment	2,000
	Proceeds of sale of equipment	700		Purchases	?
				Drawings	?
				Balance – float	150
		192,200			192,200

Hasta keeps cash that is in hand at the end of each week as drawings, subject to the retention of the float. No record has been made of payments for purchases of goods for sale. He fixes his selling price for all items by doubling their cost. He allowed a trade discount of $9,000, representing 30% on selling price, for sales to dealers with a normal price of $30,000.

All the equipment held at the beginning of the year was sold for $700, and new equipment purchased for $2,000.

A full year's depreciation is to be charged on the new equipment at 20%, with no depreciation on the items sold.

Required:

(a) **Prepare Hasta's statement of profit or loss for the year ended 31 December 20X5.** (9 marks)

(b) **Calculate Hasta's drawings for the year ended 31 December 20X6.** (2 marks)

(11 marks)

Question 27 MCQs REGULATORY FRAMEWORK

27.1 **Whose needs are general purpose financial statements intended to meet?**

A Shareholders of incorporated entities
B The general public
C Users of financial statements
D Regulatory authorities (2 marks)

27.2 Which body develops International Financial Reporting Standards?

A IASB
B IFRS Foundation
C IFRS IC
D IFRS Advisory Council (2 marks)

27.3 According to the International Accounting Standards Board, in whose interests are financial reporting standards issued?

A Company directors
B The public
C Company auditors
D The government (2 marks)

27.4 Which of the following are roles of the IASB?

(1) Responsibility for all IFRS technical matters
(2) Publication of IFRSs
(3) Overall supervision and governance of the IFRS Advisory Council
(4) Final approval of interpretations by the IFRS Interpretations Committee

A 2 only
B 1 and 2 only
C 1, 2 and 3
D 1, 2 and 4 (2 marks)

27.5 The issue of a new IFRS means that:

(1) An existing standard may be partially or completely withdrawn
(2) Issues that are not in the scope of an existing standard are covered
(3) Issues raised by users of existing standards are explained and clarified
(4) Current financial reporting practice is modified

Which combination of the above will most likely be the result of issuing a new IFRS?

A 1, 2 and 3
B 2, 3 and 4
C 1, 3 and 4
D 1, 2 and 4 (2 marks)

27.6 Which of the following are stages in the due process of developing a new International Financial Reporting Standard?

(1) Issuing a discussion paper that sets out the possible options for a new standard
(2) Publishing clarification on the interpretation of an IFRS
(3) Drafting an IFRS for public comment
(4) Analysing the feedback received on a discussion paper

A 1, 2 and 3
B 2, 3 and 4
C 1, 3 and 4
D 1, 2 and 4 (2 marks)

27.7 Which one of the following sentences is NOT a distinction between financial accounts and management accounts?

A Financial accounts are primarily for external users and management accounts are primarily for internal users

B Financial accounts are normally produced annually and management accounts are normally produced monthly

C Financial accounts are mandatory whereas management accounts are voluntary

D Financial accounts are audited by management whereas management accounts are audited by external auditors (2 marks)

27.8 Which of the following bodies has responsibility for encouraging global convergence of international financial reporting standards?

A The International Financial Reporting Standards Interpretations Committee
B The International Financial Reporting Standards Foundation
C The International Accounting Standards Board
D The International Accounting Standards Committee (2 marks)

(16 marks)

Question 28 IASB

(a) **State the objectives of the International Accounting Standards Board (IASB).** (3 marks)

(b) As well as developing International Accounting Standards, the IASB has published a *Conceptual Framework for Financial Reporting*.

Required:

State the purposes of the Framework. (5 marks)

(8 marks)

Question 29 MCQs QUALITATIVE CHARACTERISTICS AND ACCOUNTING CONCEPTS

29.1 Which of the following most closely describes the meaning of relevance in the IASB's "Conceptual Framework for Financial Reporting"?

A It makes information provided in the financial statements useful to primary users
B It ensures that accounting records and financial statements are free from bias
C It provides a predictive or confirmatory value that can make a difference in a decision
D It ensures that financial statements comply with all accounting standards and legal requirements (2 marks)

29.2 Which of the following statements about accounting concepts and the characteristics of financial information is correct?

(1) The concept of substance over form means that the legal form of a transaction must be reflected in financial statements, regardless of the economic substance

(2) Under the recognition concept only items capable of being measured in monetary terms can be recognised in financial statements

(3) It may sometimes be necessary to exclude information that is relevant and reliable from financial statements because it is too difficult for some users to understand

A 1 only
B 2 only
C 3 only
D None of these statements (2 marks)

29.3 Which of the following statements about accounting concepts are correct?

(1) The entity concept requires that a business is treated as being separate from its owners

(2) The prudence concept means that the lowest possible values should be applied to income and assets and the highest possible values to expenses and liabilities

(3) The money measurement concept means that only assets capable of being reliably measured in monetary terms can be included in the financial statements

A 1 and 2 only
B 1 and 3 only
C 2 and 3 only
D 1, 2 and 3 (2 marks)

29.4 Which of the following statements about accounting concepts are correct?

(1) The money measurement concept requires all assets and liabilities to be accounted for at original (historical) cost

(2) The substance over form convention means that the economic substance of a transaction should be reflected in the financial statements, not necessarily its legal form

(3) The realisation concept means that profits or gains cannot normally be recognised in profit or loss until realised

(4) The application of the prudence concept means that assets must be understated and liabilities must be overstated in preparing financial statements

A 1 and 3
B 1 and 4
C 2 and 3
D 2 and 4 (2 marks)

29.5 A sole trader is $5,000 overdrawn at her bank. She receives $1,000 from a credit customer.

Which elements of the financial statements will change due to this transaction?

A Assets and liabilities only
B Liabilities only
C Assets only
D Assets, liabilities and equity (2 marks)

29.6 A company includes in inventory goods received before the year end for which invoices are not received until after the year end.

Which of the following concepts is the company applying?

A Historical cost
B Accruals
C Going concern
D Substance over form (2 marks)

29.7 Which one of the following best describes the objective of management's stewardship of a company?

A Profit maximisation
B Safeguarding cash
C Accountability for company' assets
D High dividends for shareholders (2 marks)

29.8 What is the primary objective of general purpose financial statements?

A To provide financial information to the users of such information
B To maintain records of assets and liabilities
C To show the results of management's stewardship
D To fulfil statutory requirements (2 marks)

29.9 Which of the following are necessary characteristics of "faithful representation" of information?

(1) Information is free from bias
(2) Information is complete within the bounds of materiality and cost
(3) Information is free from material error

A 1 and 2 only
B 1 and 3 only
C 2 and 3 only
D 1, 2 and 3 (2 marks)

29.10 The IASB's *Conceptual Framework for Financial Reporting* (the *Conceptual Framework*) sets out the concepts that underlie the preparation and presentation of financial statements for external users.

According to the Conceptual Framework, which of the following describes the inclusion of an amount in the financial statements"?

A Disclosure
B Faithful presentation
C Measurement
D Recognition (2 marks)

29.11 Which of the following statements is correct?

A Profit is the amount by which the value of assets only have increased during the year
B Profit is the amount by which the value of liabilities only have decreased during the year
C Profit is not related to changes in the value of assets and liabilities
D Profit is the amount by which the increase in the value of assets exceeds the increase in the value of liabilities during the year (2 marks)

29.12 Which of the following is the basis on which allowance for depreciation is charged to the statement of profit or loss?

A Accruals
B Going concern
C Prudence
D Historical cost (2 marks)

29.13 In the last financial year, Cuchabee issued an invoice for $28,900 for the sale of a non-current asset with a carrying amount of $27,600.

What was the effect of this transaction on the company's assets, liabilities and equity?

	Assets	*Liabilities*	*Equity*	
A	Unchanged	Reduced	Increased	
B	Increased	Unchanged	Increased	
C	Increased	Reduced	Increased	
D	Reduced	Unchanged	Reduced	(2 marks)

29.14 The IASB's *Conceptual Framework for Financial Reporting* identifies four qualitative characteristics that enhance the usefulness of information that is relevant and faithfully represented.

Which of the following are examples of those characteristics?

(1) Consistency
(2) Cost constraint
(3) Timeliness
(4) Understandability

A 1 and 2
B 2 and 3
C 3 and 4
D 1 and 4 (2 marks)

29.15 Following the preparation of the financial statements, the accountant of Tamore has discovered that the depreciation charge has been overstated.

When the depreciation charge is corrected, how are the elements of the financial statements affected?

	Assets	*Liabilities*	*Equity*	
A	Increased	Decreased	Unchanged	
B	Decreased	Increased	Increased	
C	Decreased	Unchanged	Decreased	
D	Increased	Unchanged	Increased	(2 marks)

29.16 Consider the following statements:

(1) Items are reported in the statement of financial position based on the presumption that the entity will not be required to significantly reduce the scale of its operations

(2) Non-current assets are always valued at historical cost in the statement of financial position

Which of the following is correct?

	Statement (1)	*Statement (2)*	
A	Describes the accruals concept	Is true	
B	Describes the going concern concept	Is true	
C	Describes the accruals concept	Is false	
D	Describes the going concern concept	Is false	(2 marks)

29.17 Which of the following is represented by the residual interest in the assets of the entity after deducting all its liabilities?

A Income
B Profit
C Gains
D Equity (2 marks)

29.18 Consider the following statements about the IASB's *Conceptual Framework for Financial Reporting*:

(1) It will not be changed because it sets out underlying concepts
(2) It is intended to assist users in preparing financial statements
(3) It is an International Financial Reporting Standard

Which of the above statements is/are true?

A 1 only
B 2 only
C 1 and 2
D 2 and 3 (2 marks)

29.19 What is defined by the following statement?

"A resource controlled by an entity as a result of past events and from which future economic benefits are expected to flow to the entity."

A Income
B An expense
C A liability
D An asset (2 marks)

(38 marks)

Question 30 FOUR CONCEPTS

Required:

Define the following accounting concepts and explain for each their implications for the preparation of financial statements:

(a) **Business entity concept;** (3 marks)
(b) **Going concern;** (3 marks)
(c) **Materiality;** (3 marks)
(d) **Fair presentation.** (3 marks)

(12 marks)

Question 31 MATERIALITY

The International Accounting Standards Board's "Conceptual Framework for Financial Reporting" sets out among other things the qualitative characteristics of financial statements, and states that information in them needs to have the fundamental characteristics of relevance and faithful representation. IAS 1 "Presentation of Financial Statements" also contains important provisions relating to financial statements.

Required:

(a) **Define "materiality" in relation to financial statements, and state two factors affecting the assessment of materiality.** (2 marks)

(b) **Briefly explain what makes information in financial statements relevant to users.** (2 marks)

(c) **Two characteristics contributing to faithful representation are "neutrality" and "completeness".**

- **(i)** **Explain the meaning of these two terms;**
- **(ii)** **Give an example of a possible conflict between qualitative characteristics.** (4 marks)

(d) **One of the requirements of the Framework is that financial statements should be free from material error. Suggest THREE safeguards which may exist, inside or outside a company, to ensure that the financial statements are in fact free from material error.** (3 marks)

(11 marks)

Question 32 COMPARABILITY

Comparability is a characteristic which adds to the usefulness of financial statements.

Required:

(a) **Explain what is meant by the term "comparability" in financial statements, referring to TWO types of comparison that users of financial statements may make.** (3 marks)

(b) **Briefly explain TWO ways in which the IASB's *Conceptual Framework for Financial Reporting* and the requirements of accounting standards aid the comparability of financial information.** (2 marks)

(5 marks)

Question 33 MCQs IAS 1

33.1 **Which of the following could appear as separate items in the statement of changes in equity required by IAS 1 *Presentation of Financial Statements* as part of a company's financial statements?**

(1) Transfer to retained earnings
(2) Loss on sale of investments
(3) Proceeds of an issue of equity shares
(4) Dividends proposed after the year end

A 1 and 3
B 1 and 4
C 2 and 3
D 2 and 4 (2 marks)

33.2 Which of the following items must be disclosed in a company's published financial statements (including notes) if material, according to IAS 1 *Presentation of Financial Statements*?

(1) Finance costs
(2) Staff costs
(3) Depreciation and amortisation expense
(4) Movements on share capital

A 1 and 3 only
B 1, 2 and 4 only
C 2, 3 and 4 only
D 1, 2, 3 and 4

(2 marks)

33.3 Which of the following items may appear in a company's statement of changes in equity, according to IAS 1 *Presentation of Financial Statements*?

(1) Revaluation surplus
(2) Dividends proposed
(3) Proceeds of equity share issue
(4) Total comprehensive income for the period

A 1, 2 and 3
B 1, 2 and 4
C 1, 3 and 4
D 2, 3 and 4

(2 marks)

33.4 Which of the following should NOT appear in a company's statement of profit or loss and other comprehensive income?

A A loss after taxation for the financial year
B Dividends received from investments
C Gain on revaluation of a non-current asset
D Dividends paid to shareholders during the year

(2 marks)

33.5 DT's final dividend for the year ended 31 October 20X6 of $150,000 was declared on 1 February 20X7 and paid on 1 April 20X7. The financial statements were approved on 31 March 20X7.

Which TWO of the following statements describe the correct treatment of the dividend in DT's financial statements?

(1) The payment settles an accrued liability in the statement of financial position as at 31 October 20X6

(2) The dividend is shown as a deduction in the statement of profit or loss for the year ended 31 October 20X7

(3) The dividend is shown as an accrued liability in the statement of financial position as at 31 October 20X7

(4) The dividend is disclosed in the notes to the financial statements at 31 October 20X6

(5) The dividend is presented in the statement of changes in equity for the year ended 31 October 20X7

A 1 and 2
B 1 and 4
C 3 and 5
D 4 and 5 (2 marks)

33.6 Which of the following most accurately defines "going concern" in accordance with IAS°1 *Presentation of Financial Statements*?

A The directors do not intend to liquidate the entity or to cease trading in the foreseeable future

B The entity is able to pay its debts as and when they fall due

C The directors expect the entity's assets to yield future economic benefits

D Financial statements have been prepared on the assumption that the entity is solvent and would be able to settle all liabilities in full in the event of being wound up (2 marks)

33.7 According to IAS 1 *Presentation of Financial Statements*, compliance with International Financial Reporting Standards will normally ensure which one of the following?

A The entity's inventory is valued at net realisable value

B The entity's assets are valued at their break-up value

C The entity's financial statements are prepared on the assumption that it is a going concern

D The entity's financial position, financial performance and cash flows are "presented fairly" (2 marks)

33.8 Monksford is preparing its financial statements for the year ended 31 December 20X6. Its draft trial balance shows the following balances:

	$
Income tax payable at 1 January 20X6	2,091
Income tax paid in full settlement of 20X5 liability	1,762

Income tax due for the year ended 31 December 20X6 is estimated to be $2,584.

What is Monksford's income tax expense in its statement of profit or loss for the year ended 31 December 20X6?

A $1,269
B $2,255
C $2,584
D $2,913 (2 marks)

33.9 In the current financial year, Natamo has raised a loan for $3 million. The loan is repayable in 10 equal half-yearly instalments. The first instalment is due six months after the loan was received.

How should the loan be reported in Natamo's next financial statements?

A As a current liability
B As a long term liability
C As part of equity
D As both a current and a long term liability (2 marks)

33.10 When reporting profit for a period, companies are required to ensure that income and expenses are correctly classified.

Which one of the following items will NOT be included in profit or loss for the period?

A Interest payable
B Dividend paid to equity shareholders
C Depreciation charge for the year
D Income tax expense (2 marks)

33.11 When reviewing the draft financial statements, the Finance Director of Harlequin discovered that no provision had been made for consultancy fees incurred in respect of a proposed investment.

How will the profit and net assets reported in the financial statements be affected when the provision is made?

	Profit	*Net assets*
A	Increase	Increase
B	Increase	Decrease
C	Decrease	Increase
D	Decrease	Decrease

(2 marks)

33.12 Garden has a 30 November reporting date. On 10 November 20X6 Garden bought a machine for $85,000. $5,000 cash was paid to the supplier and the balance of the purchase price was financed by taking out a loan for $80,000. The loan will be repaid in 10 equal half-yearly instalments, with the first instalment falling due on 10 May 20X7.

How should this transaction be reported in Garden's statement of financial position at 30 November 20X6?

A A non-current asset of $85,000, a current liability of $64,000 and a non-current liability of $16,000

B A non-current asset of $85,000 and a non-current liability of $80,000

C A non-current asset of $85,000, a current liability of $16,000 and a non-current liability of $64,000

D A non-current asset of $85,000 and a current liability of $80,000 (2 marks)

33.13 **Which of the following should be recognised in other comprehensive income as an unrealised gain?**

(1) Interest earned but not yet credited
(2) Rental income received for a future period
(3) An increase in the value of a non-current asset
(4) A gain on the sale of shares held in a quoted company

A 3 only
B 3 and 4 only
C 2, 3 and 4 only
D 1, 2, 3 and 4 (2 marks)

33.14 The draft 20X6 statement of financial position of Vale reported retained earnings of $1,644,900 and net assets of $6,957,300. It was then discovered that several items in opening inventory had been valued at selling price. This resulted in a $300,000 overstatement of opening inventory. The closing inventory had been correctly valued in the draft 20X6 financial statements.

What are the correct figures for retained profit and net assets in the statement of financial position for 20X6?

	Retained earnings	*Net assets*	
A	$1,644,900	$6,657,300	
B	$1,644,900	$6,957,300	
C	$1,944,900	$6,657,300	
D	$1,944,900	$6,957,300	(2 marks)

33.15 The accountant of Verse is preparing the company's draft financial statements and must decide how the following items should be reported:

(1) Gain on revaluation of property
(2) Interest charge on long-term borrowings

Which items should be included in the calculation of total comprehensive income for the year?

A 1 only
B 2 only
C 1 and 2
D Neither 1 nor 2 (2 marks)

33.16 Fudge Co's statement of profit or loss for the year ended 31 March 20X7 shows a profit for the year of $575,000. During the year, a dividend of $130,000 was paid to equity shareholders and land costing $600,000 was revalued to $640,000.

What was the total comprehensive income for the year?

A $40,000
B $485,000
C $575,000
D $615,000 (2 marks)

(32 marks)

Question 34 ARBALEST

The summarised statement of financial position of Arbalest at 30 September 20X5 was as follows:

	Cost	*Aggregate depreciation*	*Carrying amount*
	$000	$000	$000
Non-current assets			
Land	2,000	nil	2,000
Buildings	1,500	450	1,050
Plant and equipment	2,800	1,000	1,800
	6,300	1,450	4,850
Current assets			3,180
Total assets			8,030
Equity and liabilities			
Equity shares ($0.50 each)			1,500
Share premium account			400
Retained earnings			4,060
			5,960
Current liabilities			2,070
Total equity and liabilities			8,030

During the year ended 30 September 20X6 the company had the following transactions:

(1) 1 November 20X5: The company made an issue to its members of one share for every three held (a rights issue) at a price of $1.50 per share. All the rights issue shares were taken up.

(2) 1 December 20X5: Sale for $70,000 of a plant and equipment which had cost $1,000,000 and a carrying amount of $200,000.

(3) 1 March 20X6: A bonus (capitalisation) issue of one share for every one held at that date, using the share premium account as far as possible for the purpose.

(4) 1 June 20X6: Purchased a new factory block for $3,000,000 (including land $600,000).

(5) 1 July 20X6: Purchased plant and equipment for $1,600,000.

(6) 30 September 20X6: The company decided to revalue the land held at 30 September 20X5 from $2,000,000 to $2,500,000. The company depreciation policies are:

Land	no depreciation
Buildings	2% per annum on cost, straight-line basis
Plant and equipment	10% per annum on cost, straight-line basis

Proportionate depreciation is allowed for in the year of purchase of an asset, with none in the year of disposal.

Profit for the year was $370,000.

Required:

(a) **Prepare a statement of changes in equity (as required by IAS 1 *Presentation of Financial Statements*) for the year ended 30 September 20X6.** (6 marks)

(b) **Prepare for the company's statement of financial position at 30 September 20X6, a note showing movements on non-current assets (as required by IAS 16 *Property, Plant and Equipment*).** (9 marks)

(15 marks)

Question 35 PERSEUS

The list of account balances of Perseus contains the following items at 31 December:

	Dr	*Cr*
	$	$
Opening inventory	3,432,000	
Accounts receivable ledger balances	2,980,000	1,970
Accounts payable ledger balances	14,300	1,210,400
Prepayments	770,000	
Cash at bank A	940,000	
Overdraft at bank B		360,000

In the course of preparing the financial statements at 31 December, the need for a number of adjustments emerged, as detailed below:

(1) Closing inventory amounted to $4,190,000 before allowing for the adjustments required by the following:

(i) Some items included in closing inventory at cost of $16,000 were found to be defective and were sold after the reporting period for $10,400. Selling costs amounted to $600.

(ii) Goods with a sales value of $88,000 were delivered to the wrong customer on 28 December. The goods were returned, in good condition, in January and subsequently dispatched to the correct customer. The cost of the goods was $66,000.

(2) Accounts receivable amounting to $92,000 are to be written off.

(3) A loss allowance for irrecoverable debts is to be made for 5% of accounts receivable.

(4) The manager of the main selling outlet of Perseus is entitled to a commission of 2% of the company's profit *after* charging that commission. The profit amounted to $1,101,600 *before* including the commission, and after adjusting for items (1) to (4) above. The manager has already received $25,000 on account of the commission due for the year to 31 December.

Required:

Show how the final figures for current assets should be presented in the statement of financial position at 31 December.

(15 marks)

Question 36 CRONOS

The following items have been extracted from the trial balance of Cronos as at 30 September 20X6:

	Reference to notes	$	$
Opening inventory		186,400	
Purchases		1,748,200	
Carriage inwards		38,100	
Carriage outwards	(2)	47,250	
Sales			3,210,000
Trade receivables		318,000	
Wages and salaries	(2 & 3)	694,200	
Sundry administrative expenses	(2)	381,000	
Loss allowance for trade receivables, at 1 October 20X5	(4)		18,200
Irrecoverable debts written off during the year	(4)	14,680	
Office equipment as at 1 October 20X5:	(5)		
Cost		214,000	
Accumulated depreciation			88,700
Office equipment: additions during year		48,000	
proceeds from sale			12,600
Interest paid	(2)	30,000	

Notes

(1) Closing inventory amounted to $219,600.

(2) Prepayments and accruals:

	Prepayments	*Accruals*
	$	$
Carriage outwards		1,250
Wages and salaries		5,800
Sundry administrative expenses	4,900	13,600
Interest payable		30,000

(3) Wages and salaries cost is to be allocated:

– cost of sales	10%
– distribution costs	20%
– administrative expenses	70%

(4) Further irrecoverable debts totalling $8,000 are to be written off, and the closing loss allowance is to amount to 5% of the final trade receivables figure. All irrecoverable debt expenses are to be included in administrative expenses.

(5) Office equipment:

Depreciation is to be provided at 20% per annum on the straight line basis, with a full year's charge in the year of purchase and none in the year of sale.

During the year equipment which had cost $40,000, with accumulated depreciation of $26,800, was sold for $12,600.

Required:

(a) Prepare the company's statement of profit or loss in accordance with IAS 1 *Presentation of Financial Statements.* (12 marks)

(b) Which of the following list must be presented in the statement of profit or loss in accordance with IAS 1? Select all that apply.

Item	*Description*
A	Gross profit
B	Revenue
C	Finance costs
D	Cost of sales
E	Dividend paid
F	Share of profit or loss from associate

(3 marks)

(15 marks)

Question 37 ABRADOR

(a) At 31 December 20X6 the following balances existed in the accounting records of Abrador:

	Reference to notes	$000
Equity shares, $0.50	(1)	1,000
Share premium account	(1)	400
Suspense account	(1)	800
Retained earnings	(2)	7,170
Deferred development costs		570
Property, plant and equipment – cost		5,000
depreciation at 31 December 20X5	(3)	1,000
Inventory at 31 December 20X6		3,900
Trade receivables	(4)	3,400
Overdraft at bank		100
Trade payables		1,900
Loss allowance for trade receivables at 31 December 20X5	(4)	100
6% Loan notes	(5)	400

Notes

(1) On 31 December 20X6 the company issued for cash 1,000,000 equity shares at a premium of $0.30 per share. The proceeds have been debited to cash and credited to the suspense account.

(2) The profit for the year is included in the figure of $7,170,000 above but does not include adjustments for Notes (3) and (4) below.

(3) Depreciation is to be provided at 25% per year on the reducing balance basis, on the property, plant and equipment.

(4) Debts totalling $400,000 are to be written off and the loss allowance for trade receivables is to be adjusted to 3% of accounts receivable.

(5) The 6% loan notes are due for redemption on 31 December 20X7 and the obligation is not to be refinanced. All interest due to 31 December 20X6 has been paid.

Required:

Prepare Abrador's statement of financial position as at 31 December 20X6 for publication, using the format in IAS 1 *Presentation of Financial Statements*.

Note: The information in (b) below is not relevant for this part of the question. (10 marks)

(b) The deferred development costs of $570,000 in (a) above are made up as follows:

	$	$
Project A		
Completed by 31 December 20X5		
Balance of costs as at 31 December 20X5	400,000	
Amortised 20X6	(100,000)	300,000
Project B		
In progress		
Total costs as at 31 December 20X5	150,000	
Further costs in 20X6	120,000	270,000
Balance as at 31 December 20X6		570,000

The charge in profit or loss for 20X6 was $185,000 made up as follows:

	$
Project A Amortisation	100,000
Project C Research costs written off	85,000

Required:

State the figures for the disclosure note summarising this information required by IAS 38 *Intangible Assets*. A statement of the company's policy for research and development expenditure is NOT required. (5 marks)

(15 marks)

Question 38 MINICA

The following balances have been extracted from the accounting records of Minica at 31 December 20X6:

	Reference to notes	$
Revenue	*2*	3,845,000
Opening inventory		360,000
Purchases	*3*	2,184,000
Carriage inwards		119,000
Carriage outwards		227,000
Office equipment at 1 January 20X6	*2, 3 and 4*	
Cost		460,000
Accumulated depreciation		92,000
Trade receivables		620,000
Loss allowance for receivables at 1 January 20X6	*5*	20,000
Irrecoverable debts written off during the year		15,000
Sundry administrative expenses		416,000

The following further information is available:

(1) Closing inventory amounts to $450,000.

(2) Some office equipment, which had cost $20,000, with accumulated depreciation at 1 January 20X6 of $14,000, was sold for $15,000 during the year. The sale proceeds were included in the sales figure of $3,845,000.

(3) The cost of new equipment purchased on 1 July 20X6 for $60,000 has been included in the purchases figure of $2,184,000

(4) The company depreciates its office equipment at 20 % per year on the straight line basis, with proportionate depreciation in the year of purchase but none in the year of sale. None of the equipment held at 1 January 20X6 was more than three years old.

(5) The loss allowance for trade receivables at 31 December 20X6 is to be 5% of accounts receivable.

(6) Accruals and prepayments on sundry administrative expenses at 31 December 20X6 were:

	$
Accrued expenses	28,700
Prepaid expenses	14,400

(7) The directors propose a dividend of 6c per share on the equity shares (4,000,000 shares of $0.25 each) to be paid in July 20X7.

No dividends were paid in 20X6.

Required:

(a) Prepare Minica's statement of profit or loss for the year ended 31 December 20X6 for internal use. (13 marks)

(b) Calculate the total amount of the proposed dividend and state how it should be dealt with in Minica's published financial statements. (2 marks)

(15 marks)

Question 39 SHUSWAP

The draft statement of financial position shown below has been prepared for Shuswap as at 31 December 20X6:

	Cost	*Accumulated depreciation*	*Carrying amount*
Assets	$000	$000	$000
Non-current assets			
Land and buildings	9,000	1,000	8,000
Plant and equipment	21,000	9,000	12,000
	30,000	10,000	20,000
Current assets			
Inventories			3,000
Receivables			2,600
Cash at bank			1,900
Total assets			27,500
Equity and liabilities			
Equity			
Equity shares ($0.50 each)			6,000
Retained earnings			12,400
Non-current liabilities: Loan notes (redeemable 20Y0)			2,000
Current liabilities: Trade payables			2,100
			22,500
Suspense account			5,000
			27,500

The following further information is available:

(1) It has been decided to revalue the land and buildings to $12,000,000 at 31 December 20X6.

(2) Trade receivables totalling $200,000 are to be written off.

(3) During the year there was a contra settlement of $106,000 in which an amount due to a supplier was set off against the amount due from the same company for goods sold to it. No entry has yet been made to record the set-off.

(4) Some inventory items included in the draft statement of financial position at cost $500,000 were sold after the reporting period for $400,000, with selling expenses of $40,000.

(5) The suspense account is made up of two items:

(a) The proceeds of issue of 4,000,000 $0.50 shares at $1·10 per share, credited to the suspense account from the cash book.

(b) The balance of the account is the proceeds of sale of some plant on 1 January 20X6 with a carrying amount at the date of sale of $700,000 and which had originally cost $1,400,000. No other accounting entries have yet been made for the disposal apart from the cash book entry for the receipt of the proceeds. Depreciation on plant has been charged at 25% (straight line basis) in preparing the draft statement of financial position without allowing for the sale. The depreciation for the year relating to the plant sold should be adjusted for in full.

Required:

(a) **Prepare Shuswap's statement of financial position as at 31 December 20X6, complying as far as possible with IAS 1 *Presentation of Financial Statements.*** (13 marks)

(b) **Calculate Shuswap's gearing ratio as at 31 December 20X6 and briefly state its meaning.** (2 marks)

(15 marks)

Question 40 MCQs CAPITAL STRUCTURE AND FINANCE COSTS

40.1 A company has issued 50,000 equity shares of $0.25 each at a premium of $0.50 per share. The cash received was correctly recorded but the full amount was credited to the equity share capital account.

Which of the following journal entries is needed to correct this error?

		Debit	*Credit*
		$	$
A	Share premium account	25,000	
	Share capital account		25,000
B	Share capital account	25,000	
	Share premium account		25,000
C	Share capital account	12,500	
	Share premium	25,000	
	Cash		37,500
D	Share capital account	37,500	
	Share premium account		37,500

(2 marks)

40.2 **Which of the following journal entries could correctly record a bonus (capitalisation) issue of shares?**

		Debit	*Credit*
		$	$
A	Cash	100,000	
	Equity share capital		100,000
B	Equity share capital	100,000	
	Share premium		100,000
C	Share premium	100,000	
	Equity share capital		100,000
D	Retained earnings	100,000	
	Equity share capital		60,000
	Share premium		40,000

(2 marks)

40.3 **Which of these statements about limited liability companies is/are correct?**

(1) A company might make a bonus (capitalisation) issue to raise funds for expansion

(2) Both realised and unrealised gains and losses are included in the statement of comprehensive income required by IAS 1 *Presentation of Financial Statements*

A 1 only
B 2 only
C Both 1 and 2
D Neither 1 nor 2 (2 marks)

40.4 Which of the following statements about financial accounting for a limited liability company is true?

A A revaluation surplus arises when a non-current asset is sold at a profit

B The market value of an equity share is not recorded

C The notes to the financial statements must contain details of all adjusting events as defined in IAS 10 *Events after the Reporting Period*

D The dividend paid in the year cannot exceed the profits of that year (2 marks)

40.5 Evon issued 1,000,000 equity shares of $0.25 each at a price of $1·10 per share, all received in cash.

What should be the accounting entries to record this issue?

A	Debit:	Cash	$1,100,000	
	Credit:	Share capital		$250,000
		Share premium		$850,000
B	Debit:	Share capital	$250,000	
		Share premium	$850,000	
	Credit:	Cash		$1,100,000
C	Debit:	Cash	$1,100,000	
	Credit:	Share capital		$1,100,000
D	Debit:	Cash	$1,100,000	
	Credit:	Share capital		$250,000
		Retained earnings		$850,000

(2 marks)

40.6 At 1 July 20X6 a limited liability company's capital structure was as follows:

	$
Equity share capital (of $0.50 each)	500,000
Share premium account	400,000

In the year ended 30 June 20X7 the company made the following share issues:

1 January 20X7: A bonus issue of one share for every four in issue at that date, using the share premium account.

1 April 20X7: A rights issue of one share for every ten in issue at that date, at $1·50 per share.

What will be the balances on the company's share capital and share premium accounts at 30 June 20X7 as a result of these issues?

	Share capital	*Share premium*
	$	$
A	687,500	650,000
B	675,000	375,000
C	687,500	400,000
D	687,500	150,000

(2 marks)

40.7 Which of the following statements are correct?

(1) A company might make a rights issue if it wished to raise more equity capital

(2) A rights issue might increase the share premium account whereas a bonus issue is likely to reduce it

(3) A rights issue will always increase the number of shareholders in a company whereas a bonus issue will not

A 1 and 2 only
B 1 and 3 only
C 2 and 3 only
D 1, 2 and 3

(2 marks)

40.8 Where should dividends paid to equity shareholders be shown in a company's published financial statements?

A In other comprehensive income
B In the statement of financial position
C In the statement of changes in equity
D In the statement of profit or loss

(2 marks)

40.9 At 30 June 20X6 a company had $1m 8% loan notes in issue. Interest is paid half-yearly on 30 June and 31 December.

On 30 September 20X6 the company redeemed $250,000 of these loan notes at par, and paid the interest due to that date.

On 1 April 20X7 the company issued $500,000 7% loan notes at par. Interest is payable half-yearly on 31 March and 30 September.

What figure should appear in the company's statement of profit or loss for finance costs for the year ended 30 June 20X7?

A $88,750
B $82,500
C $73,750
D $65,000

(2 marks)

40.10 Diamond issues 250,000 equity shares with a nominal value of $2 each at a price of $3.55 each for cash.

Which of the following sets of entries would be made to record this transaction?

A Cr Bank $887,500, Dr Share capital $500,000, Dr Share premium $387,500
B Dr Bank $887,500, Cr Share capital $250,000, Cr Share premium $637,500
C Dr Bank $887,500, Cr Share capital $500,000, Cr Share premium $387,500
D Cr Bank $887,500, Dr Share capital $250,000, Dr Share premium $637,500

(2 marks)

40.11 The following balances have been extracted from Saracen's trial balance at 31 December 20X6:

	Debit	*Credit*
	$	$
Retained earnings at 1 January 20X6		4,695,600
10% Loan notes issued in 20X3		1,300,000
Loan note interest paid	65,000	

Profit for the year ended 31 December 20X6 is $520,000. Income tax for the year has been estimated at $156,000.

What is the figure for retained earnings in Saracen's statement of financial position as at 31 December 20X6?

A $4,929,600
B $4,994,600
C $5,059,600
D $5,215,600 (2 marks)

40.12 Floyd made a rights issue of 150,000 $1 equity shares at price of $1.20 per share.

What is the correct journal to record this?

		Dr	*Cr*
		$	$
A	Bank	180,000	
	Share capital		150,000
	Share premium		30,000
B	Bank	180,000	
	Share premium		180,000
C	Bank	180,000	
	Share capital		180,000
D	Bank	150,000	
	Share premium		30,000
	Share capital		120,000

(2 marks)

40.13 The following information is available about a company's dividends:

		$
20X6		
September	Paid final dividend for the year ended 30 June 20X6 (declared August 20X6)	600,000
20X7		
March	Paid interim dividend for the year ended30 June 20X7	250,000
September	Paid final dividend for the year ended 30 June 20X7 (declared August 20X7)	750,000

How should these dividends be recognised in the company's profit or loss for the year ended 30 June 20X7 and its statement of financial position as at that date?

	Profit or loss for the period	*Statement of financial position*
A	$1,000,000 deduction	$750,000 liability
B	$850,000 deduction	$nil
C	$nil	$750,000 liability
D	$nil	$nil

(2 marks)

40.14 Which TWO items in the statement of financial position would change immediately following an issue of redeemable preference shares?

(1) Cash
(2) Retained earnings
(3) Finance cost
(4) Equity
(5) Long-term debt

A 1 and 5
B 1 and 4
C 2 and 4
D 3 and 5

(2 marks)

40.15 Which of the following statements is/are correct in relation to a rights issue made by a company?

(1) A rights issue capitalises the company's reserves, which can be a disadvantage, as this can reduce the amount of reserves available for future dividends

(2) A rights issue is offered to the company's existing shareholders and is usually at a discounted price compared to the nominal value of a share

	Statement 1	*Statement 2*
A	Correct	Correct
B	Correct	Incorrect
C	Incorrect	Correct
D	Incorrect	Incorrect

(2 marks)

40.16 During the year to 30 September 20X6 K Co made the following payments:

(1) $40,000 interest on $800,000 10% loan notes issued on 1 January 20X6. Interest is payable on 30 June and 31 December

(2) $12,000 dividend on 200,000 $1 6% irredeemable preference shares

(3) $5,000 dividend on 100,000 $1 5% redeemable preference shares

What should be the finance cost in the statement of profit or loss for the year ended 30 September 20X6?

A $45,000
B $60,000
C $65,000
D $77,000

(2 marks)

40.17 Shane Co has the following share capital in issue at 31 March 20X7:

30,000 2% $1 irredeemable preference shares
20,000 4% $1 redeemable preference shares
100,000 $0.50 equity shares

What amount will be included as equity capital in the statement of financial position at 31 March 20X7?

A $130,000
B $70,000
C $80,000
D $100,000 (2 marks)

40.18 Problem Co makes a 1 for 5 bonus issue using the share premium account to the extent that it is possible. Immediately before the bonus issue, the company had the following equity balances:

	$
Share capital ($1 shares)	100,000
Share premium account	15,000
Retained earnings	460,000

What is the balance on the retained earnings account after the bonus issue has been recorded?

A $460,000
B $465,000
C $440,000
D $455,000 (2 marks)

(36 marks)

Question 41 RESERVES AND ISSUES

(a) The term "reserves" is frequently found in the statement of financial position of a company.

Required:

(i) Explain the meaning of "reserves" in this context.
(ii) Give two examples of reserves and explain how each of your examples comes into existence. (3 marks)

(b) A company's share capital may be increased by a bonus (capitalisation) issue or a rights issue.

Required:

Define "bonus issue" and "rights issue" and explain the fundamental difference between these two types of share issue. (3 marks)

(6 marks)

Question 42 ARMANI

At 31 December the capital structure of Armani was as follows:

	$000
Equity share capital ($0.50 each)	1,500
Share premium	300
Revaluation surplus	150
Retained earnings	75

The directors, none of whom is a qualified accountant, are considering the following proposals:

(a) To make a bonus issue of one equity share for every two held to raise $750,000. (4 marks)

(b) To pay a dividend of $0.05 per share. (1 mark)

(c) To increase the revaluation surplus to $500,000 by revaluing goodwill from $750,000 to $1,100,000. (1 mark)

(d) To combine all reserves into a single figure. (2 marks)

Required:

Comment on the validity of each of these proposals.

NOTE: The mark allocation is shown against each of the four proposals.

(8 marks)

Question 43 MCQs IAS 2

43.1 According to IAS 2 *Inventories*, which of the following costs should be included in valuing the inventories of a manufacturing company?

(1) Carriage inwards
(2) Carriage outwards
(3) Depreciation of factory plant
(4) General administrative overheads

A 1 and 3 only
B 1, 2 and 4
C 2 and 3 only
D 2, 3 and 4 (2 marks)

43.2 Which of the following costs should be included in valuing inventories of finished goods held by a manufacturing company, according to IAS 2 *Inventories*?

(1) Carriage inwards
(2) Carriage outwards
(3) Depreciation of factory plant
(4) Accounts department costs relating to wages for production employees

A 1 and 4 only
B 2 and 3 only
C 1, 3 and 4
D 2, 3 and 4 (2 marks)

43.3 IAS 2 *Inventories* defines the extent to which overheads are included in the cost of inventories of finished goods.

Which of the following statements about the IAS 2 requirements relating to overheads are true?

(1) Finished goods inventories may be valued on the basis of labour and materials cost only, without including overheads

(2) Factory management costs should be included in fixed overheads allocated to inventories of finished goods

A 1 only
B 2 only
C Both 1 and 2
D Neither 1 nor 2 (2 marks)

43.4 Which of the following statements about inventory valuation are correct?

(1) The carrying amount should be as close as possible to net realisable value

(2) The valuation of finished goods inventory must include production overheads

(3) Production overheads included in valuing inventory should be calculated by reference to the company's normal level of production during the period

(4) In assessing net realisable value, inventory items must be considered separately, or in groups of similar items, not by taking the inventory value as a whole

A 1 and 2 only
B 1 and 3 only
C 2, 3 and 4
D 3 and 4 only

(2 marks)

43.5 Woodpecker has produced an inventory list which, taking account of physical quantities, gives the following values:

	Cost	*Net realisable value*
	$	$
5 mm nuts	100	180
7 mm nuts	170	190
10 mm nuts	180	150
8 mm washers	120	160
15 mm bolts	190	170

What is the correct value of inventory to be included in the statement of financial position?

A $710
B $740
C $760
D $850

(2 marks)

43.6 Sculpart buys and sells original sculptures. An item in inventory at 31 March 20X7 had been bought four years ago at a cost of $15,000. It had originally been anticipated that this item would be sold for $22,000. To date the best offer which has been received is $17,500 from an overseas collector. This offer has been made on the basis that the item will be transported to the collector. It is estimated that the costs of shipping and insurance are $3,000.

At what amount should Sculpart include the item in inventory at 31 March 20X7?

A $14,500
B $15,000
C $17,500
D $22,000

(2 marks)

43.7 The price of a raw material used by Diska is volatile. At the close of business on 30 November 20X6, the company had 430 kg of the material in inventory. At 1 November there had been none of the material in inventory. The movements in November were as follows:

Date	*Receipts*	*Issues*
4 Nov	800 kg at $45 per kg	
12 Nov		650 kg
19 Nov	700 kg at $52 per kg	
23 Nov		720 kg
28 Nov	300 kg at $60 per kg	

Using the first in first out (FIFO) method of inventory valuation, what is the value of the inventory of the material at 30 November 20X6?

A $21,596
B $23,850
C $24,760
D $25,800 (2 marks)

43.8 Josh Franklin buys and sells art and jewellery. At 31 May 20X7 he had three items in inventory; a painting, a necklace and a pair of earrings. He had bought the painting for $3,500, believing it was an original by Graham Knuttel. He has since discovered that it is a good copy and it is unlikely that it would sell for more than $1,200. The necklace was bought several years ago for $900, while the earrings were bought for $800. The earrings and necklace are of the same style and could be sold as a set at a combined price of $3,500.

At figure for inventory should be reported in his statement of financial position at 31 May 20X7?

A $7,000
B $5,200
C $4,700
D $2,900 (2 marks)

43.9 Silur buys and restores items of exclusive vintage jewellery. At 31 May 20X7, there were three items in inventory as follows:

	Necklace	*Bracelet*	*Pendant*
	$	$	$
Purchase cost	12,000	31,000	45,000
Expected selling price	25,000	38,000	53,000
Restoration costs to date	6,000	5,000	2,000
Further costs before sale	2,000	3,000	1,000

What was the total value of Silur's inventory at 31 May 20X7?

A $88,000
B $100,000
C $106,000
D $107,000 (2 marks)

43.10 The following figures relate to inventory held at 31 March 20X6:

	Product A	*Product B*
Units held	2,000	5,000
Cost per unit	$14	$16
Selling price	$17	$20

Modifications costing $5 per unit would need to be made to product A to achieve the selling price of $17.

What is the value of inventory held at 31 March 20X6 in accordance with IAS 2 *Inventories*?

A $108,000
B $124,000
C $134,000
D $104,000 (2 marks)

(20 marks)

Question 44 SAMPI

Sampi is a manufacturer of garden furniture. The company has consistently used the FIFO (first in, first out) method in valuing inventory, but it is interested to know the effect on its inventory valuation of using the continuous weighted average method instead.

At 28 February the company had inventory of 4,000 standard plastic tables, and has calculated its value on each side of the three bases as:

Basis	*Unit cost* $	*Total value* $
FIFO	16	64,000
Weighted average	13	52,000

During March the movements on the inventory of tables were as follows:

Received from factory:

Date	*Number of units*	*Production cost per unit* $
8 March	3,800	15
22 March	6,000	18

Revenue:	*Number of units*
12 March	5,000
18 March	2,000
24 March	3,000
28 March	2,000

On a FIFO basis the inventory at 31 March was $32,400.

Required:

Calculate the value of the inventory at 31 March using the continuous weighted average cost.

Note: In arriving at the total inventory values you should make calculations to two decimal places (where necessary) and deal with each inventory movement in date order.

(5 marks)

Question 45 P, Q & R

(a) A firm buys and sells two models, P and Q. The following unit costs are available (all figures are in $s and all the costs are borne by the firm):

	P	*Q*
Purchase cost	100	200
Delivery costs from supplier	20	30
Delivery costs to customers	22	40
Coloured sales packaging costs	15	18
Selling price	150	300

Required:

Calculate the figure to be included in closing inventory for a unit of each model; according to IAS 2. (3 marks)

(b) A firm has the following transactions with its product R.

Year 1

Opening inventory:nil
Buys 10 units at $300 per unit
Buys 12 units at $250 per unit
Sells 8 units at $400 per unit
Buys 6 units at $200 per unit
Sells 12 units at $400 per unit

Year 2

Buys 10 units at $200 per unit
Sells 5 units at $400 per unit
Buys 12 units at $150 per unit
Sells 25 units at $400 per unit.

Required:

Calculate on an item by item basis for both year 1 and year 2:

(i) closing inventory;
(ii) sales revenue;
(iii) cost of sales;
(iv) gross profit;

using the FIFO method of inventory valuation. Present all workings clearly. (5 marks)

(8 marks)

Question 46 MCQs Revenue

46.1 Which TWO of the following statements regarding the accruals basis are correct?

(1) Income and expenses are recorded in the financial statements in the periods to which they relate

(2) All expenses but not income are recognised and accrued for

(3) The effects of transactions and other events are recognised when they occur

(4) Revenue is recognised when it can be matched with expenditure incurred

A 1 and 3
B 1 and 4
C 2 and 3
D 2 and 4 (2 marks)

46.2 IFRS 15 *Revenue from Contracts with Customers* sets out principles of revenue recognition.

Which of the following are indicators that revenue should be recognised for the sale of goods?

(1) The seller has transferred physical possession of the goods
(2) The customer has legal title to the asset
(3) The customer has paid for the goods
(4) The customer has the significant risks and rewards of ownership

A 1, 2 and 3
B 1, 2 and 4
C 1, 3 and 4
D 2, 3 and 4 (2 marks)

46.3 OC signed a contract to provide office cleaning services to PQ for one year from 1 October 20X6 for $500 per month. The contract required PQ to make a single payment to OC for all 12 months at the beginning of the contract.

OC received $6,000 on 1 October 20X6.

What amount of revenue should OC recognise in its statement of profit or loss for the year ended 31 March 20X7?

A $nil
B $300
C $3,000 profit
D $6,000 profit (2 marks)

46.4 LP received an order to supply a customer with 10,000 units of product A every month for two years. The customer had negotiated a low price of $200 per 1,000 units and agreed to pay $12,000 in advance every six months.

The customer made the first payment on 1 July 20X6 and LP supplied the goods each month from that date.

LP's year end is 30 September.

In addition to the effect of cash received, what is the effect of this order on LP's financial statements for the year ended 30 September 20X6, in accordance with IFRS 15 *Revenue from Contracts with Customers*?

	Revenue	*Statement of financial position*
A	$6,000	$36,000 trade receivable
B	$6,000	$6,000 current liability
C	$12,000	$36,000 trade receivable
D	$12,000	No effect

(2 marks)

46.5 On 31 March 20X7, DT received an order from a new customer, XX, for goods with a sales value of $900,000. XX enclosed a deposit with the order of $90,000.

On 31 March 20X7, DT had not dispatched any goods. DT is considering the following possible entries for the transaction in its financial statements for the year ended 31 March 20X7:

(1) Include $900,000 in revenue
(2) Include $90,000 in revenue
(3) Do not include any amount in revenue
(4) Recognise a trade receivable for $810,000
(5) Recognise a trade payable for $90,000

How should DT account for this transaction in its financial statements for the year ended 31 March 20X7 in accordance with IFRS?

A 1 and 4
B 2 and 5
C 3 and 4
D 3 and 5 (2 marks)

(10 marks)

Question 47 MCQs IAS 16

47.1 On 1 January 20X6 a company purchased some plant. The invoice showed:

	$
Cost of plant	48,000
Delivery to factory	400
One year warranty covering breakdown during 20X6	800
	49,200

Modifications to the factory building costing $2,200 were necessary to enable the plant to be installed.

What amount should be capitalised for the plant in the company's records in accordance with IAS 16 *Property, Plant and Equipment*?

A $48,000
B $48,400
C $50,600
D $51,400 (2 marks)

47.2 At 31 December 20X6 Cutie owned a building that had cost $800,000 on 1 January 2006. It was being depreciated at 2% per year.

On 31 December 20X6 a revaluation to $1,000,000 was recognised. At this date the building had a remaining useful life of 40 years.

Which of the following pairs of figures correctly reflects the effects of the revaluation?

	Depreciation charge for year ending 31 December 20X7	*Revaluation surplus as at 31 December 20X6*	
	$	$	
A	25,000	200,000	
B	25,000	360,000	
C	20,000	200,000	
D	20,000	360,000	(2 marks)

47.3 **Which of the following statements are correct?**

(1) All non-current assets must be depreciated

(2) If goodwill is revalued, the revaluation surplus appears in the statement of changes in equity

(3) If a tangible non-current asset is revalued, all tangible assets of the same class should be revalued

(4) In a company's published statement of financial position, tangible assets and intangible assets must be shown separately

A 1 and 2
B 1 and 4
C 2 and 3
D 3 and 4 (2 marks)

47.4 Which of the following should be recognised as an asset under IAS 16 *Property, Plant and Equipment*?

A The cost of repainting a building
B The replacement of broken windows in a building
C The purchase of a car by a car dealer for re-sale
D Legal fees incurred on the purchase of a building (2 marks)

47.5 Gilmore purchased a machine for $15,000. The transportation costs were $1,500 and installation costs were $750. The machine broke down at the end of the first month in use and cost $400 to repair. Gilmore depreciates machinery at 10% each year on cost, assuming no residual value.

What is the carrying amount of the machine after one year in accordance with IAS 16 *Property, Plant and Equipment*?

A $13,500
B $14,850
C $15,525
D $15,885 (2 marks)

47.6 Groomers took delivery of a machine on 1 May 20X6. The invoice shows the following:

	$
Model XY54	124,760
Delivery	1,250
Installation	3,750
Maintenance 1 May 20X6 – 30 April 20X7	2,400

What is the cost of the machine in accordance with IAS 16 *Property, Plant and Equipment*?

A $124,760
B $126,010
C $129,760
D $132,160 (2 marks)

47.7 Resol owns three properties which are revalued at each reporting date. Relevant information on 30 November 20X6 is as follows:

	Head office	*Warehouse*	*Factory*
Carrying amount	$700,000	$400,000	$1,200,000
Market value	$740,000	$405,000	$1,100,000

At 1 December 20X5, equity included a revaluation surplus of $294,000 which comprised the following:

Head office	*Warehouse*	*Factory*
$186,000	$68,000	$40,000

What amount of revaluation surplus should appear in Resol's statement of financial position at 30 November 20X6?

A $254,000
B $294,000
C $299,000
D $339,000 (2 marks)

47.8 During the year, Clonadde made a profit on the sale of a machine and recognised a surplus on the revaluation of a building.

Which of the following is correct?

A Both the profit and the surplus are recognised gains
B Both the profit and the surplus are realised gains
C Only the sale of the machine is a recognised gain
D Only the increase in value of the building is a recognised gain (2 marks)

47.9 At 1 May 20X6, Bloxden had a revaluation surplus of $1,257,000 in respect of the revaluation of its head office.

During the year to 30 April 20X7, the value of the head office was increased by a further $82,000. In the same period, the value of the company's factory fell by $90,000.

What amount of revaluation surplus should appear in Bloxden's statement of financial position at 30 April 20X7?

A $1,167,000
B $1,249,000
C $1,257,000
D $1,339,000 (2 marks)

47.10 At 30 April 20X6, Mixtures had recognised a revaluation gain of $30,000 in respect of one of its properties. In the year to 30 April 20X7, the value of another of its properties fell by $45,000, due to the announcement of a plan to build a new road. The second property had not previously been revalued.

How are Mixture's profit for the year and the revaluation surplus as at 30 April 20X7 affected by these valuations?

	Profit or loss	*Revaluation surplus*
A	Not affected	Not affected
B	Not affected	Reduced by $45,000
C	Reduced by $15,000	Reduced to $nil
D	Reduced by $45,000	Not affected

(2 marks)

47.11 During the last financial year, a building owned by Mountain has increased in value. The directors wish to recognise this increase.

In which components of the financial statements will the increase be reflected?

(1) Statement of profit or loss
(2) Other comprehensive income
(3) Statement of financial position
(4) Statement of changes in equity

A 1 and 4 only
B 2 and 3 only
C 2 and 4 only
D 2, 3 and 4 (2 marks)

47.12 On 1 April 20X5, F Co revalued a property. As a result, the annual depreciation charge increased by $20,000 as compared to depreciation based on historical cost. F Co wishes to make the allowed transfer of excess depreciation between the revaluation surplus and retained earnings in accordance with IAS 16 *Property, Plant and Equipment.* Immediately before the transfer was made, retained earnings and the revaluation surplus were as follows:

	$
Retained earnings	875,000
Revaluation surplus	200,000

What should be the balance on the retained earnings and revaluation surplus accounts after the transfer?

	Retained earnings	*Revaluation surplus*
	$	$
A	855,000	20,000
B	855,000	180,000
C	895,000	220,000
D	895,000	180,000

(2 marks)

47.13 On 1 October 20X1, X Co purchased a property for $400,000. The property had a useful life of 40 years and was depreciated on a straight-line basis. On 1 October 20X5, the property was revalued to $432,000. The remaining useful life at that date was 36 years. The company wishes to make the allowed transfer of excess depreciation between the revaluation surplus and retained earnings.

Which of the following correctly records the transfer at 30 September 20X6?

	Debit	*Credit*
A	Retained earnings $2,000	Revaluation surplus $2,000
B	Revaluation surplus $2,000	Retained earnings $2,000
C	Retained earnings $12,000	Revaluation surplus $12,000
D	Revaluation surplus $12,000	Retained earnings $12,000

(2 marks)

(26 marks)

Question 48 NON-CURRENT ASSETS

(a) **Explain the following terms as used by accountants:**

(i) asset;
(ii) current asset;
(iii) non-current asset; and
(iv) depreciation.

(7 marks)

(b) **Explain which of the following may be recognised as an asset of a business for accounting purposes.**

(i) a screwdriver bought some years ago;
(ii) a machine hired by the business;
(iii) the good reputation of the business with its customers.

(5 marks)

(c) The non-current assets in the statement of financial position of a limited liability company have been summarised as follows:

			$m
Land at valuation			3
Buildings at cost			1
Plant and equipment –	cost	2	
	depreciation	(1.5)	0.5
			4.5

Required:

Explain the meaning of this $4.5 million figure to one of the company's shareholders and comment on its relevance from a shareholder's point of view. (5 marks)

(17 marks)

Question 49 MCQs IAS 38

49.1 IAS 38 *Intangible Assets* governs the accounting treatment of expenditure on research and development. The following statements about the provisions of IAS 38 may or may not be correct:

(1) Capitalised development expenditure must be amortised over a period not exceeding five years

(2) If all the conditions specified in IAS 38 are met, development expenditure may be capitalised if the directors decide to do so

(3) Capitalised development costs are shown in the statement of financial position under the heading of Non-current Assets

(4) Amortisation of capitalised development expenditure will appear as an item in a company's statement of changes in equity

Which of these statements is/are true?

A 1 and 3
B 1 and 4
C 2 and 3
D 3 only (2 marks)

49.2 **Which of the following statements about goodwill is correct?**

A Goodwill may only be revalued to a figure in excess of cost if there is relevant and reliable evidence to support the revaluation

B Internally-generated goodwill may be capitalised if certain criteria are met

C Purchased goodwill is the difference between the cost of acquiring an entity and the fair value of its identifiable net assets

D The period over which goodwill is amortised must be disclosed in a note to the financial statements (2 marks)

49.3 Which of the following statements about intangible assets in company financial statements is true according to International Financial Reporting Standards?

A Internally-generated goodwill should not be capitalised
B Development expenditure may be capitalised if certain conditions are met
C Research costs must be capitalised if certain conditions are met
D An entity can choose not to recognise purchased goodwill (2 marks)

49.4 Which of the following statements about intangible assets are correct?

(1) If certain criteria are met, research expenditure must be recognised as an intangible asset

(2) Goodwill may not be revalued upwards

(3) Internally-generated goodwill should not be capitalised

A 1 and 2 only
B 1 and 3 only
C 2 and 3 only
D 1, 2 and 3 (2 marks)

49.5 Resdev incurred the following expenditure on research and development in the year to 30 November 20X6:

Project 175	\$2.5 million
Project 254	\$1.6 million
Project 393	\$4.8 million

Project 175 is investigating the link between vitamin deficiency and emotional well-being. If a link is proven the company may produce a food additive to improve well-being.

Project 254 was completed during the year after a period of 15 months. It has achieved its aim of reducing the material cost of a new product. Production of the product commenced on 1 September 20X6. The first sales are expected in February 20X7 and the expected life of the product is four years. The project meets the capitalisation criteria of IAS 38 *Intangible Assets.*

Project 393 is a joint research project with a leading University.

What amount of research and development expenditure should appear in Resdev's statement of profit or loss for the year to 30 November 20X6?

A \$2.5 million
B \$7.3 million
C \$7.4 million
D \$8.9 million (2 marks)

49.6 Which of the following statements about intangible assets is/are true?

(1) All intangible assets should be reported in the statement of financial position
(2) Only purchased intangible assets can be reported in the statement of financial position
(3) Goodwill can only be carried in the statement of financial position at cost

A None of the statements
B 2 only
C 1 and 3
D 2 and 3 (2 marks)

49.7 Which of the following correctly state the accounting treatment for research costs and development expenditure, assuming that any relevant criteria are met?

	Research	*Development*
A	May be capitalised	May be capitalised
B	Must be written off	May be capitalised
C	May be capitalised	Must be capitalised
D	Must be written off	Must be capitalised

(2 marks)

49.8 Prior to 30 April 20X6 Marley had paid $300,000 to fund a research project. Following positive results, it was decided in May 20X6 to spend a further $600,000 to develop the new product, and production also commenced in May 20X6. The product is expected to have a commercial life of eight years. The development expenditure meets the criteria for capitalisation in accordance with IAS 38 *Intangible Assets*.

What amount should be expensed to profit or loss for the year to 30 April 20X7?

A $nil
B $37,500
C $75,000
D $112,500

(2 marks)

(16 marks)

Question 50 LION

Lion manufactures medicinal drugs. At 1 April 20X6 the following balances existed in the records:

Deferred development expenditure $1,200,000

Project Q. $800,000 is the balance remaining of expenditure totalling $1,000,000 on a completed project which is being amortised on the straight line basis over 10 years.

Project R. $400,000 is the accumulated costs to 31 March 20X6 of developing a new drug. The project was completed in January 20X7 and sales of the drug are expected to begin in July 20X7.

Equipment used in research $300,000 (cost $500,000, depreciation to date $200,000).

During the year ended 31 March 20X7 the following costs were incurred:

Project R Costs to complete $250,000
Project S (a research project) $140,000
Purchase of testing equipment for use in the research department $180,000.

All equipment has an estimated useful life of five years, and a full year's depreciation is charged in the year of acquisition.

Required:

(a) **Calculate the figures to be included in Lion's statement of profit or loss for the year ended 31 March 20X7 and statement of financial position as at that date, and state the headings under which they will appear.** (6 marks)

(b) **Prepare the disclosure notes required by IAS 38 *Intangible Assets*. (An accounting policy note for research and development expenditure is NOT required.)** (6 marks)

(12 marks)

Question 51 AIRCRAFT

A company manufacturing aircraft engages in a number of research and development projects.

At 1 January 20X6 the company's records showed total capitalised development costs of $18 million made up as follows:

	$000
Project A17:	14,000
This project was completed in 20X5 at a total cost of $16 million and is being amortised over eight years on the straight line basis, beginning on 1 January 20X5.	
Project J9:	4,000
This project began in 20X4 and the $4 million balance represents expenditure qualifying for capitalisation to 31 December 20X5 This project is due to be completed in 20X9	
	18,000

During the year ended 31 December 20X6 the following further expenditure was incurred:

	$000
Project J9: Further expenditure qualifying for capitalisation	$1,500
Project A20: Investigation into new materials for aircraft construction	$3,000

Required:

(a) **Calculate the amounts for research and development to be included in the company's statement of profit or loss and statement of financial position for the year ended 31 December 20X6.** (4 marks)

(b) **Discuss the principle accounting concepts applicable to the accounting treatment of development expenditure. You are NOT required to provide the criteria for recognition of an intangible asset arising from development in IAS 38 *Intangible Assets*.** (6 marks)

(10 marks)

Question 52 MCQs IAS 37

52.1 **Which of the following statements about provisions, contingencies and events after the reporting period is correct?**

A A company expecting future operating losses should make provision for those losses as soon as it becomes probable that they will be incurred

B Details of all adjusting events after the reporting period must be disclosed by note in a company's financial statements

C A contingent asset must be recognised as an asset in the statement of financial position if it is probable that it will arise

D Contingent liabilities must be treated as actual liabilities and provided for when it is probable that they will arise, if they can be measured with reliability (2 marks)

52.2 Which of the following statements about contingent assets and contingent liabilities is true?

(1) A contingent asset should be disclosed by note if an inflow of economic benefits is probable

(2) A contingent liability should be disclosed by note if it is probable that a transfer of economic benefits to settle it will be required, with no provision being made

(3) No disclosure is required for a contingent liability if it is less than probable that a transfer of economic benefits to settle it will be required

A 1 only
B 2 only
C 3 only
D None of these statements (2 marks)

52.3 Which of the following statements are correct?

(1) Contingent assets are included as assets in financial statements if it is probable that they will arise

(2) Contingent liabilities must be provided for in financial statements if it is probable that they will arise

(3) Details of all adjusting events after the reporting period must be given in notes to the financial statements

(4) Material non-adjusting events are disclosed by note in the financial statements

A 1 and 2
B 1 and 3
C 2 and 4
D 3 and 4 (2 marks)

52.4 The following items have to be considered in finalising the financial statements of Borgen:

(1) Borgen offers three-month warranties on all its products. Previous experience shows that about 5% of sales give rise to a warranty claim

(2) Borgen has guaranteed the overdraft of another company. The likelihood of a liability arising under the guarantee is assessed as possible

What is the correct treatment of these items in Borgen's financial statements under International Financial Reporting Standards?

	Item (1)	*Item (2)*
A	Recognise a provision	Disclose by note only
B	Disclose by note only	No treatment
C	Recognise a provision	Recognise a provision
D	Disclose by note only	Disclose by note only

(2 marks)

52.5 On 20 November 20X6, Clifdan received a letter from a customer claiming $250,000 in compensation for damage caused by one of Clifdan's products. Clifdan replied to the customer accepting liability and offering $100,000 in compensation. The customer refused the offer and is now taking legal action against Clifdan.

Clifdan's legal advisors have indicated that the case is unlikely to be heard in court for at least nine months and that the court is likely to award $150,000 in compensation.

What amount should be provided for the claim in the financial statements of Clifdan for the year to 31 December 20X6?

A $nil
B $100,000
C $150,000
D $250,000

(2 marks)

52.6 Brouha manufactures animal feed. The company accountant is preparing the 20X7 financial statements and considering the effect of a claim for damages of $50,000 received during the year. The company has offered the claimant $5,000 to settle the claim. The customer has declined the offer and made a claim to the court. The company's legal advisors have noted that a similar claim was recently rejected in court.

How should the claim be reported in the 20X7 financial statements?

A No disclosure
B Disclosure as a contingent liability
C As a provision of $5,000
D As a provision of $50,000

(2 marks)

52.7 A customer of Pern claims that, on 22 March 20X6, a fault in a product sold by Pern caused damage to its production line. The customer is seeking damages of $85,000. Pern has accepted liability and offered to pay $40,000 to repair the damage. The customer has refused this offer. The matter will be settled in a court case which is scheduled for July 20X7. Pern's legal representative has indicated that the court is almost certain to accept the customer's claim for $85,000.

How should this matter be dealt with in Pern's financial statements for the year to 30 April 20X6?

A As a current liability of $40,000
B As a non-current liability of $40,000
C As a current liability of $85,000
D As a non-current liability of $85,000

(2 marks)

52.8 At the reporting date, future obligations to transfer economic benefits may be classified as:

(1) liabilities;
(2) provisions; or
(3) contingent liabilities.

Which of the above are recognised in the statement of financial position?

A 1 and 2 only
B 2 and 3 only
C 1 and 3 only
D 1, 2 and 3

(2 marks)

(16 marks)

Question 53 RESERVES

Required:

For each of the following pairs of concepts, carefully explain the distinction between the first item of each pair and the second:

(a) Reserves; cash in hand.
(b) Ownership interest; capital employed.
(c) Liability; expense.
(d) Contingent liability; provision.

(12 marks)

Question 54 MCQs IAS 10 AND IAS 37

54.1 The draft financial statements of a limited liability company are under consideration. The accounting treatment of the following material events after the reporting period needs to be determined:

(1) The bankruptcy of a major customer, with a substantial debt outstanding at the end of the reporting period

(2) A fire destroying some of the company's inventory (the company's going concern status is not affected)

(3) An issue of shares to finance expansion

(4) Sale for less than cost of some inventory held at the end of the reporting period

According to IAS 10 *Events after the Reporting Period*, which of the above events require an adjustment to the figures in the draft financial statements?

A 1 and 4
B 1, 2 and 3
C 2 and 3 only
D 2 and 4

(2 marks)

54.2 **In finalising the financial statements of a company for the year ended 30 June 20X7, which of the following material matters should be adjusted for?**

(1) A customer who owed $180,000 at the 30 June 20X7 went bankrupt in July 20X7

(2) The sale in August 20X7 for $400,000 of some inventory items carried in the statement of financial position at $500,000

(3) A factory with a value of $3,000,000 was seriously damaged by a fire in July 20X7. The factory was back in production by August 20X7 but its value was reduced to $2,000,000

(4) The company issued 1,000,000 equity shares in August 20X7

A 1 and 2
B 1 and 4
C 2 and 3
D 3 and 4

(2 marks)

54.3 Which of the following events occurring after the reporting period are classified as adjusting, if material?

(1) The sale of inventories valued at cost at the end of the reporting period for a figure in excess of cost

(2) A valuation of land and buildings providing evidence of an impairment in value at the year end

(3) The issue of shares and loan notes

(4) The insolvency of a customer with a balance outstanding at the year end

A 1 and 3
B 1 and 4
C 2 and 3
D 2 and 4 (2 marks)

54.4 Which of the following events between the end of the reporting period and the date the financial statements are authorised for issue must be adjusted in the financial statements?

(1) Declaration of equity dividends
(2) Decline in market value of investments
(3) The announcement of changes in tax rates
(4) The announcement of a major restructuring

A 1 only
B 2 and 4
C 3 only
D None of them (2 marks)

54.5 Which TWO of the following events after the reporting period would normally qualify as adjusting events according to IAS 10 *Events after the Reporting Period*?

(1) The bankruptcy of a credit customer with a balance outstanding at the end of the reporting period

(2) A decline in the market value of investments

(3) The declaration of a dividend on equity shares

(4) The determination of the cost of assets purchased before the end of the reporting period

A 1 and 2
B 1 and 4
C 2 and 3
D 3 and 4 (2 marks)

54.6 On 7 November 20X6 there was a fire in the warehouse of Yorkfab, in which inventory valued at $120,000 was destroyed. This represented 30% of the company's inventory. Under the terms of the insurance contract, the insurance company has stated that it will only pay out the first $30,000 of the claim.

How should this be reported in the financial statements for the year to 31 October 20X6?

	Statement of profit or loss	*Disclosure in the notes*
A	$nil	None
B	$nil	A loss of $90,000
C	$120,000	A receivable of $30,000
D	$90,000 loss	None

(2 marks)

54.7 On 20 May 20X7 the finance director of Orajee reported to the board of directors that the company's financial statements for the year to 31 March 20X7 reported a profit of $3,528,650.

On 26 May 20X7 the directors were informed of the following:

(1) A flood on 25 May 20X7 in one of Orajee's warehouses damaged inventory valued at $330,000. All inventory was uninsured against flood damage. It will cost $20,000 to dispose of the damaged items and clear up the affected part of the warehouse

(2) An insurance claim in respect of inventory which was stolen on 2 April 20X7 was settled for $250,000. The finance director had anticipated that the claim would be settled for $270,000

What is Orajee's reported profit for the year to 31 March 20X7 when these events have been accounted for?

A $3,198,650
B $3,178,650
C $3,428,650
D $3,528,650 (2 marks)

54.8 On 1 December 20X6, after Flower's draft financial statements for the year to 30 September 20X6 had been prepared, the accountant received a letter regarding an accident which had taken place on 14 September 20X6.

The accident had destroyed a machine with a carrying amount of $275,000. The first $30,000 of any claim is not covered under the company's insurance policy. The accountant had treated this correctly when drafting the financial statements.

The letter now informs Flower that as the accident was due to negligence, the entire loss is uninsured.

How does the information in the letter affect the draft financial statements?

A $245,000 loss should be disclosed in a note
B $275,000 loss should be disclosed in a note
C $245,000 should be expensed to profit or loss
D $275,000 should be expensed to profit or loss (2 marks)

54.9 On 6 March 20X7, there was a fire in Tingle's factory. Tingle incurred $125,000 in repairing the damage. As Tingle had insurance cover, $125,000 was reported as a receivable in the draft financial statements for the year to 30 April 20X7. In May 20X7, the insurance company advised that due to non-compliance with the terms of the insurance contract, only $12,500 of the repair costs would be reimbursed.

Which of the following is the correct accounting treatment for the repair costs in the financial statements for the year to 30 April 20X7?

A Only a disclosure note is required
B Only an expense of $112,500 should be recognised
C Only a receivable for $12,500 should be recognised
D Both an expense of $112,500 and a receivable for $12,500 should be recognised
(2 marks)

(18 marks)

Question 55 ALUKI

The directors of Aluki, a fashion wholesaler, are reviewing the company's draft financial statements for the year ended 30 September 20X6, which show a profit of $900,000 before tax. The following matters require consideration:

(a) Closing inventory includes:

(i) 3,000 skirts at cost $40,000. Since the year end they have all been sold for $65,000, with selling expenses of $3,000.

(ii) 2,000 jackets at cost $60,000. Since the year end half the jackets have been sold for $25,000 (selling expenses $1,800) and the remainder are expected to sell for $20,000 with selling expenses of $2,000. (2 marks)

(b) An employee dismissed in August 20X6 began an action for damages for wrongful dismissal in October 20X6. She is claiming $100,000 in damages. Aluki is resisting the claim and the company's lawyers have advised that the employee has a 30% chance of success in her claim.

The financial statements currently include a provision for the $100,000 claim. (4 marks)

(c) In October 20X6 a fire destroyed part of the company's warehouse, with an uninsured loss of inventory worth $180,000 and damage to the building, also uninsured, of $228,000. The going concern status of the company is not affected.

The financial statements currently make no mention of the fire losses. (3 marks)

Required:

Explain to the directors how these matters should be treated in the financial statements for the year ended 30 September 20X6, stating the relevant accounting standards.

(9 marks)

Question 56 QUAPAW

The directors of Quapaw are reviewing the company's draft financial statements for the year ended 31 December 20X6.

The following material matters are under discussion:

(a) During the year the company has begun selling a product with a one-year warranty under which manufacturing defects are rectified without charge. Some claims have already arisen under the warranty. (3 marks)

(b) During the inventory count on 31 December, some goods which had cost $80,000 were found to be damaged. In February 20X7 the damaged goods were sold for $85,000 by an agent who received a 10% commission out of the sale proceeds. (3 marks)

Required:

Advise the directors on the correct treatment of these matters, stating the relevant accounting standard which justifies your answer in each case.

(6 marks)

Question 57 UMBRIA

The directors of Umbria are reviewing the company's draft financial statements for the year ended 30 June 20X7. The following material matters are under discussion:

(1) After the end of the reporting period one of the company's factories was seriously damaged by fire. Insurance will only cover part of the loss suffered. The company's going concern status is not affected.

(2) Umbria guaranteed the overdraft of another company in 20X5. No disclosure has been made in previous financial statements, but events in the latter part of the year ended 30 June 20X7 suggest that it is probable that a liability will fall on Umbria in 20X8.

(3) One of the company's directors was dismissed in March 20X7 for disclosing confidential information to a competitor. Umbria then commenced an action against this director, and the company has been advised that it is probable that substantial damages will be awarded.

(4) One of the company's buildings was revalued during the year. The directors are uncertain how the revaluation gain should be included in the financial statements. The gain has been separately disclosed as an item in the draft statement of profit or loss.

Required:

Explain how each of these four matters should be dealt with in the financial statements for the year ended 30 June 20X7, stating in each case the relevant accounting standard.

(10 marks)

Question 58 MCQs STATEMENT OF CASH FLOWS

58.1 An extract from a statement of cash flows prepared by a trainee accountant is shown below:

	$m
Profit before taxation	28
Adjustments for:	
Depreciation	(9)
Operating profit before working capital changes	19
Decrease in inventories	3
Increase in receivables	(4)
Increase in payables	(8)
Cash generated from operations	10

Which of the following criticisms of this extract are correct?

(1) Depreciation charges should have been added, not deducted
(2) Decrease in inventories should have been deducted, not added
(3) Increase in receivables should have been added, not deducted
(4) Increase in payables should have been added, not deducted

A 1 and 3
B 1 and 4
C 2 and 3
D 2 and 4

(2 marks)

58.2 Which of the following items could appear in a company's statement of cash flows?

(1) Proposed dividends
(2) Rights issue of shares
(3) Bonus issue of shares
(4) Repayment of loan

A 1 and 3
B 1 and 4
C 2 and 3
D 2 and 4 (2 marks)

58.3 A draft statement of cash flows contains the following calculation of net cash inflow from operating activities:

	$m
Operating profit	13
Depreciation	2
Decrease in inventories	(3)
Decrease in trade and other receivables	5
Decrease in trade payables	4
Net cash inflow from operating activities	21

Which of the following corrections need to be made to the calculation?

(1) Depreciation should be deducted, not added
(2) Decrease in inventories should be added, not deducted
(3) Decrease in receivables should be deducted, not added
(4) Decrease in payables should be deducted, not added

A 1 and 3
B 1 and 4
C 2 and 3
D 2 and 4 (2 marks)

58.4 A company sold a building at a profit.

How should this transaction be treated in the company's statement of cash flows?

	Proceeds of sale	*Profit on sale*
A	Cash inflow under Financing activities	Added to profit in calculating cash flow from operating activities
B	Cash inflow under Investing activities	Deducted from profit in calculating cash flow from operating activities
C	Cash inflow under Investing activities	Added to profit in calculating cash flow from operating activities
D	Cash inflow under Financing activities	Deducted from profit in calculating cash flow from operating activities

(2 marks)

58.5 APM provides the following note property, plant and equipment in its statement of financial position:

	Cost	*Depreciation*	*Carrying amount*
	$000	$000	$000
Opening balance	25	12	13
Additions	15		15
Depreciation		4	(4)
Disposals	(10)	(8)	(2)
Closing balance	30	8	22

There was a gain on disposal of $3,000.

What is the net cash outflow for investing activities relating to property, plant and equipment?

A $10,000
B $12,000
C $13,000
D $15,000 (2 marks)

58.6 The following information was extracted from the statements of financial position of Abacus at 31 December 20X6 and 31 December 20X5:

	20X6	*20X5*
	$000	$000
Inventory	120	100
Receivables	175	140
Trade payables	215	175

What is the overall effect of the above on Abacus's cash flows in the year ended 31 December 20X6?

A $25,000 outflow
B $15,000 outflow
C $15,000 inflow
D $25,000 inflow (2 marks)

58.7 The following extract is from the financial statements of Pompeii at 31 October:

	20X6	*20X5*
	$000	$000
Equity and liabilities		
Share capital	120	80
Share premium	60	40
Retained earnings	85	68
	265	188
Non-current liabilities		
Bank loan	100	150
	365	338

What is the cash inflow from financing activities to be disclosed in the statement of cash flows for the year ended 31 October 20X6?

A $10,000
B $27,000
C $60,000
D $110,000 (2 marks)

58.8 Greenfinch has an operating profit which exceeds the net cash inflow from operating activities.

Which of the following changes over the year could have caused this difference?

A Trade payables increased
B Inventory decreased
C Prepayments decreased
D Trade receivables increased (2 marks)

58.9 During the year to 30 April 20X7 Jaunty had purchased non-current assets which cost $687,000. The company financed the purchases by taking out loans totalling $597,000, and paying the balance in cash. In addition, non-current assets with a carrying amount of $75,000 were sold at a loss of $15,000.

What figure should appear for net cash used in investing activities in the statement of cash flows for the year to 30 April 20X7?

A $537,000
B $627,000
C $672,000
D $687,000 (2 marks)

58.10 At 1 November 20X5 the non-current assets of Field had a carrying amount of $2,758,940. During the year to 31 October 20X6, assets with a carrying amount of $273,790 were sold at a loss of $15,850, and new assets costing $568,900 were purchased.

What figure should appear for net cash used in investing cash flows in the statement of cash flows for the year to 31 October 20X6?

A $257,940
B $295,110
C $310,960
D $568,900 (2 marks)

58.11 The statements of financial position of Jurric at 30 April 20X7 and 20X6 include the following:

	20X7	*20X6*
	$	$
Inventory	193,885	164,843
Payables	62,887	87,996

How should the changes in these amounts be reflected in the statement of cash flows for the year to 30 April 20X7?

	Change in inventory	*Change in payables*
A	Inflow	Inflow
B	Outflow	Outflow
C	Inflow	Outflow
D	Outflow	Inflow

(2 marks)

58.12 At 31 May 20X7 and 20X6 Dron had the following balances:

	20X7	*20X6*
	$000	$000
Property, plant and equipment	2,110	1,945
Equity shares, $1	1,200	800
Share premium	760	500
Non-current loans	174	550

The depreciation charge for the year to 31 May 20X7 was $270,000. There were no disposals of non-current assets during the year.

What figure should appear as the net cash flow from investing activities in the statement of cash flows for the year to 31 May 20X7?

A $179,000
B $435,000
C $601,000
D $719,000 (2 marks)

(24 marks)

Question 59 CRASH

The statements of financial position of Crash at 31 March 20X7 and 31 March 20X6 were as follows:

	Reference to notes	*20X7* $000	$000	*20X6* $000	$000
Assets					
Non-current assets	*(1)*				
Cost		10,950		9,000	
Accumulated depreciation		(3,600)	7,350	(3,300)	5,700
Current assets					
Inventories		1,350		1,215	
Trade and other receivables		1,290		1,350	
Cash		105	2,745	60	2,625
Total assets			10,095		8,325
Equity and liabilities					
Equity					
Share capital		3,000		2,250	
Share premium account		1,200		750	
Revaluation surplus		750		–	
Retained earnings		3,045	7,995	2,640	5,640
Non-current liabilities					
10% Loan notes	*(2)*		750		1,500
Current liabilities					
Trade and other payables		1,080		990	
Bank overdraft		270	1,350	195	1,185
Total equity and liabilities			10,095		8,325

Notes:

(1) Non-current assets

(i) During the year non-current assets, which had cost $1,500,000 and which had a carrying amount of $300,000 at 31 March 20X6, were sold for $375,000.

(ii) Land acquired in 20X3 was revalued upwards by $750,000 in preparing the statement of financial position at 31 March 20X7.

(2) Loan notes

Interest is due half-yearly on 30 September and 31 March and was paid on the due dates. The company repaid $750,000 loan notes on 31 March 20X7.

(3) Profit after interest for the year ended 31 March 20X7 was $405,000. No dividends were paid during the year.

Required:

(a) Prepare a statement of cash flows for Crash for the year ended 31 March 20X7 using the indirect method, complying as far as possible with the requirements of IAS 7 *Statement of Cash Flows.* (11 marks)

(b) Calculate the gearing ratio and the current ratio for Crash for the two years ended 31 March 20X6 and 20X7. (4 marks)

(15 marks)

Question 60 MARMOT

The following information is available about the transactions of Marmot for the year ended 31 December:

	$000
Depreciation	880
Cash paid for expenses	2,270
Increase in inventories	370
Cash paid to employees	2,820
Decrease in receivables	280
Cash paid to suppliers	4,940
Decrease in payables	390
Cash received from customers	12,800
Profit before taxation*	2,370

*Marmot has no interest payable or investment income.

Required:

Calculate Marmot's net cash flow from operating activities for the company's statement of cash flows for the year ended 31 December using:

(a) the direct method;
(b) the indirect method.

(10 marks)

Question 61 RENADA

The summarised financial statements of Renada at 31 October 20X6 and 31 October 20X5 are given below:

Statements of financial position

	Reference to notes	20X6 $000	20X6 $000	20X5 $000	20X5 $000
Assets					
Non-current assets					
(at carrying amount)	(1), (2), (3)		1,800		1,000
Current assets					
Inventories		1,600		600	
Receivables		1,800		1,270	
Cash		–	3,400	140	2,010
Total assets			5,200		3,010
Equity and liabilities					
Equity					
Equity share capital	(4)	600		500	
Share premium account	(4)	820		420	
Revaluation surplus	(5)	300		–	
Retained earnings		1,080		920	
			2,800		1,840
Current liabilities					
Bank overdraft		260		–	
Income tax		40		120	
Trade payables		2,100	2,400	1,050	1,170
Total equity and liabilities			5,200		3,010

Statements of profit or loss

	31 October 20X6 $000	31 October 20X5 $000
Gross profit	1,800	2,100
Operating expenses	(1,600)	(1,500)
Profit before tax	200	600
Income tax expense	(40)	(120)
Profit for the year	160	480

Notes

(1) On 1 November 20X5 office equipment that had cost $240,000, with a carrying amount of $80,000, was sold for $30,000.

(2) The purchase of new non-current assets took place near the end of the year.

(3) The depreciation charge for the year ended 31 October 20X6 was $120,000.

(4) The equity share issue was on 31 October 20X6.

(5) Some of the non-current assets were revalued upwards by $300,000 on 1 November 20X5.

Required:

(a) **Prepare a statement of cash flows for Renada for the year ended 31 October 20X6 in accordance with IAS 7 *Statement of Cash Flows*.** (11 marks)

(b) **Calculate the ROCE ratio and the quick ratio for Renada for the two years ended 31 October 20X5 and 20X6.** (4 marks)

(15 marks)

Question 62 SIOUX

The following information is available for Sioux:

Statements of financial position at 31 December

		20X6		*20X5*
	$000	$000	$000	$000
Assets				
Non-current assets				
Cost or valuation		11,000		8,000
Accumulated depreciation		(5,600)		(4,800)
Carrying amount		5,400		3,200
Current assets				
Inventories	3,400		3,800	
Receivables	3,800		2,900	
Cash at bank	400	7,600	100	6,800
		13,000		10,000
Equity and liabilities				
Equity				
Equity share capital	1,000		1,000	
Revaluation surplus	1,500		1,000	
Retained earnings	3,100	5,600	2,200	4,200
Non-current liabilities				
10% Loan notes		3,000		2,000
Current liabilities				
Trade payables	3,700		3,200	
Income tax	700	4,400	600	3,800
		13,000		10,000

Summarised statements of profit or loss for the year ended 31 December 20X6

	$000
Profit from operations	2,650
Finance cost (loan note interest)	(300)
	2,350
Income tax expense	(700)
Profit for the year	1,650

Notes

(1) During the year non-current assets which had cost $800,000, with a carrying amount of $350,000, were sold for $500,000.

(2) The revaluation surplus arose on the revaluation of some land that was not being depreciated.

(3) The 20X5 income tax liability was settled at the amount provided for at 31 December 20X5.

(4) The additional loan notes were issued on 1 January 20X6. Interest was paid on 30 June and 31 December 20X6.

(5) Dividends paid during the year amounted to $750,000.

Required:

(a) Prepare Sioux's statement of cash flows for the year ended 31 December 20X6, using the indirect method, adopting the format in IAS 7 *Statement of Cash Flows.* (12 marks)

(b) Calculate the current ratio, quick ratio and gearing ratio for Sioux for the year ended 31 December 20X6 if the following transactions occurred on that date:

(i) Customers paid $1,000,000;
(ii) A further $1,000,000 10% loan notes were issued;
(iii) Suppliers were paid $2,000,000. (3 marks)

(15 marks)

Question 63 JOYCE

The statements of financial position of Joyce at 30 June 20X7 and 20X6 are as follows:

	Reference to notes	*30 June 20X7* $000	$000	*30 June 20X6* $000	$000
Non-current assets (carrying amount)	1		148,000		130,000
Current assets					
Inventories		14,000		9,100	
Receivables		21,400		12,500	
Cash at bank		–		4,600	
			35,400		26,200
			183,400		156,200
Equity share capital			110,000		109,000
Share premium account			5,000		4,000
Revaluation surplus			14,000		2,000
Retained earnings	1		28,000		18,000
Total equity			157,000		133,000
Non-current liabilities 8% Loan notes	3		10,000		8,000
Current liabilities					
Payables		7,100		9,200	
Current tax payable	2	8,000		6,000	
Bank overdraft		1,300		–	
			16,400		15,200
			183,400		156,200

Notes

(1) The depreciation charge for the year was $13,000,000

(2) $6,200,000 was paid during the year to settle the income tax liability at 30 June 20X6.

(3) The additional loan notes were issued on 1 January 20X7. All interest due was paid on 31 December 20X6 and 30 June 20X7.

(4) Dividends paid during the year totalled $4,000,000.

Required:

Prepare a statement of cash flows for Joyce for the year ended 30 June 20X7, using the indirect method, complying as far as possible with the requirement of IAS 7 *Statement of Cash Flows.*

(15 marks)

Question 64 MCQs CONSOLIDATED FINANCIAL STATEMENTS

64.1 At 1 January Barley acquired 100% of the share capital of Corn for $1,400,000. At that date the share capital of Corn consisted of 600,000 equity shares of $0.50 each and its reserves were $50,000. On acquisition Corn had some assets whose carrying amount was $230,000 but the fair value was $250,000.

What was goodwill on acquisition?

A $730,000
B $750,000
C $1,030,000
D $1,050,000

(2 marks)

64.2 Gonzo acquired 80% of the share capital of Bamboo a number of years ago. Bamboo has issued 200,000 $1 shares which had a market price of $3.10 on acquisition. The carrying amount of Bamboo's net assets today is $650,000; this is $50,000 higher than it was on acquisition.

What amount should be shown for non-controlling interest in Gonzo's consolidated statement of financial position today?

A $120,000
B $124,000
C $130,000
D $134,000

(2 marks)

64.3 **Which of the following statements is/are correct?**

(1) Dissimilar activities of a parent company and a subsidiary can be a reason for non-consolidation of the subsidiary

(2) A non-controlling interest must be presented in a consolidated statement of financial position as a separate line item within equity

A 1 only
B 2 only
C Both 1 and 2
D Neither 1 nor 2

(2 marks)

64.4 Salt owns 100% of Pepper. During the year Salt sold goods to Pepper for a sales price of $1,044,000, generating a margin of 25%. 40% of these goods had been sold on by Pepper to external parties at the end of the reporting period.

What adjustment for unrealised profit should be made in Salt's consolidated financial statements?

A $83,520
B $104,400
C $125,280
D $156,600 (2 marks)

The following information is relevant for questions 64.5 and 64.6:

On 1 January 20X6, Jarndyce acquired 80% of the equity share capital of Skimpole for $576,000. The statements of financial position of the two companies at 31 December 20X6 were as follows:

	Jarndyce	*Skimpole*
	$000	$000
Net assets	468	432
Investment in Skimpole	576	–
	1,044	432
Share capital	720	180
Retained earnings		
At 31 December 20X5	144	108
Profit for 20X6	180	144
	1,044	432

Non-controlling interest is valued at fair value on acquisition, which was $140,000. There has been no impairment of goodwill since the acquisition took place.

64.5 **What amount of goodwill should be included in the consolidated statement of financial position of Jarndyce as at 31 December 20X6?**

A $144,000
B $230,400
C $345,600
D $428,000 (2 marks)

64.6 **What is the non-controlling interest in the consolidated statement of financial position of Jarndyce as at 31 December 20X6?**

A $86,400
B $140,000
C $168,800
D $201,600 (2 marks)

64.7 On 1 April 20X1, Woolwich paid $816,000 for 80% of Malta's $408,000 share capital. Malta's retained earnings at that date were $476,000. At 31 March 20X7 the retained earnings of the companies are:

	$000
Woolwich	1,224
Malta	680

Woolwich's inventory includes goods purchased from Malta for $18,000. Malta makes a profit at 20% on the cost of all goods sold to Woolwich.

What are the retained earnings in the consolidated statement of financial position of Woolwich as at 31 March 20X7?

A $1,384,320
B $1,384,800
C $1,387,200
D $1,439,200

(2 marks)

64.8 During the year Subway invoiced $200,000 to its parent company for transfers of goods in inventory. Transfers were made at a 25% mark-up. At the end of the year the parent still held 60% of the goods in inventory.

What adjustment should be made for unrealised profit in the consolidated financial statements for the year?

A $16,000
B $24,000
C $30,000
D $40,000

(2 marks)

64.9 **Which of the following statements regarding the equity method of accounting is true?**

(1) An investment in an associate is always carried at cost
(2) An investor recognises its share of the associate's profit or loss in profit or loss

A Neither statement
B Statement 1 only
C Statement 2 only
D Both statements

(2 marks)

64.10 **Which of the following could provide evidence of "significant influence"?**

(1) 51% of the voting power of the investee
(2) interchange of management personnel
(3) participation in decisions about dividends
(4) provision of essential technical information

A 1, 2 and 3
B 1, 2 and 4
C 1, 3 and 4
D 2, 3 and 4

(2 marks)

64.11 **Which of the following statements regarding accounting for associates is true?**

(1) Any goodwill relating to an associate is included in the carrying amount of the investment

(2) An investment in an associate is accounted for using the equity method from the end of the reporting period in which the associate is acquired

A Neither statement
B Statement 1 only
C Statement 2 only
D Both statements (2 marks)

64.12 Which of the following statements apply when producing a consolidated statement of financial position?

(1) All intra-group balances should be eliminated
(2) Intra-group profit in year-end inventory should be eliminated
(3) Closing inventory held by subsidiaries needs to be included at fair value

A 1 only
B 1 and 2
C 2 and 3
D 3 only (2 marks)

64.13 At 1 July 20X6 Kipper acquired 25% of the equity share capital of Pike for $960,000 when the retained earnings of Pike were $1,080,000. Pike appointed two of Kipper's directors to the board of Pike.

Both companies prepare financial statements to 31 May each year. The summarised statement of financial position for Pike at 31 May 20X7 is as follows:

	$000
Share capital	1,200
Share premium account	675
Retained earnings	1,710
	3,585

Pike has not issued any new shares since Kipper acquired its holding.

What amount of investment in Pike will appear in the consolidated statement of financial position of Kipper at 31 May 20X7?

A $896,250
B $960,000
C $1,117,500
D $1,387,500 (2 marks)

64.14 Bram owns 70% of the shares in Stoker. Bram has payables of $244,000. Stoker has payables of $40,000 of which $6,000 is owed to Bram. Bram has receivables of $360,000 and Stoker has receivables of $150,000.

What amounts should be recorded for consolidated receivables and payables in the group financial statements of Bram?

	Payables	*Receivables*
A	$278,000	$504,000
B	$278,000	$516,000
C	$290,000	$504,000
D	$290,000	$516,000

(2 marks)

64.15 Venus acquired 75% of Mercury's 100,000 $1 equity share capital on 1 November 20X6. The consideration consisted of $2 cash per share and 1 share in Venus for every 1 share acquired in Mercury. Venus shares have a nominal value of $1 and a fair value of $1.75. The fair value of the non-controlling interest was $82,000 and the fair value of net assets acquired was $215,500.

What should be recorded as goodwill on acquisition of Venus in the consolidated financial statements?

A $16,500
B $63,375
C $91,500
D $147,750

64.16 On 30 June 20X3 Petra acquired 90% of the share capital of Sabu. The non-controlling interest had a fair value of $450,000.

Extracts from the statements of financial position of Sabu at 30 June 20X3 and 30 June 20X7 are shown below:

	30 June 20X3	*30 June 20X7*
	$	$
Equity share capital	800,000	800,000
Share premium account	200,000	200,000
Retained earnings	3,200,000	4,000,000

What figure for non-controlling interest should appear in the consolidated statement of financial position as at 30 June 20X7?

A $420,000
B $450,000
C $500,000
D $530,000

64.17 At 31 December 20X6 the following require inclusion in a company's separate financial statements:

(1) In January 20X7 the company received $6,000 for management charges from a subsidiary company covering the six months to 31 December 20X6

(2) On 1 January 20X6 the company made a loan of $9,000 to an associate, repayable on 1 January 20X7, charging interest at 3% per year. On the due date the loan, together with the whole of the interest due was repaid

(3) The company has paid $12,000 in 20X6 for software licences covering the year ending 31 July 20X7

For these items, what total figure should be included in current assets in the company's separate statement of financial position at 31 December 20X6?

A $13,270
B $19,270
C $22,270
D $27,270

64.18 During the last three years Harvert had held 400,000 equity shares in Jamee. Jamee has $500,000 shares of $0.50 each in issue. The finance director of Harvert is also a director of Jamee.

How should the investment in Jamee be treated in the consolidated financial statements of Harvert?

A As a non-current asset investment
B As a current asset investment
C As an associate
D As a subsidiary (2 marks)

64.19 **Which of the following statements regarding group accounting is/are correct?**

(1) Only the group's share of the assets of a subsidiary is included in the consolidated statement of financial position

(2) Only the group's share of the net assets of an associate is reflected in the consolidated statement of financial position

(3) Share capital in a consolidated statement of financial position includes the share capital of both the parent and the subsidiary

A 1 only
B 2 only
C 3 only
D None of the statements (2 marks)

64.20 During the last financial year, Orius acquired 44% of the equity shares of Eerus. Under the terms of the acquisition, the finance director of Orius was appointed to the board of directors of Eerus.

How should Orius account for its interest in Eerus in the consolidated financial statements?

A As a subsidiary, using acquisition accounting
B As a subsidiary, using equity accounting
C As an associate, using acquisition accounting
D As an associate, using equity accounting (2 marks)

64.21 Panther Co acquired 80% of the equity shares in Seal Co on 31 August 20X6. The statements of profit or loss of the two companies for the year ended 31 December 20X6 showed:

	Panther Co	*Seal Co*
	$	$
Revenue	100,000	62,000
Cost of sales	25,000	16,000

During October 20X6, sales of $6,000 were made by Panther Co to Seal Co. None of these items remained in inventory at the year end.

What is the consolidated revenue for Panther Group for the year ended 31 December 20X6?

A $156,000
B $118,667
C $144,800
D $114,667 (2 marks)

64.22 Honey Co acquired 75% of Bee Co on 1 April 20X6, paying $2 for each equity share acquired. The fair value of the non-controlling interest at 1 April 20X6 was $300. Bee Co's individual financial statements as at 30 September 20X6 included:

	$
Statement of financial position	
Equity share capital ($1 each)	1,000
Retained earnings	710
	1,710
Statement of profit or loss	
Profit after tax for the year	250

Profit accrued evenly throughout the year.

What is the goodwill on acquisition on 1 April 20X6?

A $715
B $90
C $517
D $215

(2 marks)

(44 marks)

Question 65 HAYDN & STRAUSS

Haydn acquired 75% of the share capital of Strauss on 1 January 20X3 when the balance on retained earnings was $24,000 and there was no revaluation surplus. Strauss has not issued or redeemed any share capital since 1 January 20X3.

Their respective statements of financial position as at 31 December 20X6 are as follows:

	Haydn	*Strauss*
	$	$
Non-current assets		
Tangible	131,500	144,000
Investment in Strauss	93,500	–
	225,000	144,000
Current assets	57,000	110,400
	282,000	254,400
Equity share capital, $1	50,000	36,000
Share premium	–	24,000
Revaluation surplus	50,000	12,000
Retained earnings	150,000	120,000
	250,000	192,000
Current liabilities	32,000	62,400
	282,000	254,400

Non-controlling interest is valued at fair value, which is based on the market price of Strauss's shares, which on 1 January 20X3 was $3.50.

At the year end the current liabilities of Strauss include an amount payable to Haydn of $3,000 which related to some goods purchased three months ago.

Required:

(a) **Prepare the consolidated statement of financial position for the Haydn group as at 31 December 20X6.** (11 marks)

(b) Haydn sold goods to Strauss during the year, at a profit, and Strauss still held one quarter of these goods at the year end.

Consolidated revenue should be calculated using which of the following formulae?

A Haydn + 75% Strauss – 100% intra-group revenue
B Haydn + 100% Strauss – 25% intra-group revenue
C Haydn + 100% Strauss – 100% intra-group revenue
D Haydn + 75% Strauss – 25% intra-group revenue (2 marks)

(c) Haydn is considering acquiring a number of equity shares in Bach.

Which TWO of the following would indicate that Haydn has significant influence over Bach?

(1) Haydn has the ability to dictate strategic policy
(2) There is an interchange of managerial personnel between the two companies
(3) Haydn provides essential technical assistance to Bach
(4) Haydn has control of the board of directors

A 1 and 2
B 1 and 4
C 2 and 3
D 3 and 4 (2 marks)

(15 marks)

Question 66 DUBLIN & BELFAST

The following are the draft statements of financial position of Dublin and its subsidiary Belfast as at 31 December 20X6:

	Dublin		Belfast	
Assets	$	$	$	$
Non-current assets				
Tangible assets		157,000		82,000
Investments: Belfast		58,000		
Others		12,000		
Current assets				
Cash at bank and in hand	8,000		25,150	
Trade receivables	96,800		46,900	
Inventory	73,200		35,200	
		178,000		107,250
		405,000		189,250
Equity and liabilities				
Equity				
Share capital ($1 shares)		250,000		50,000
Share premium account				6,250
Revaluation surplus				15,000
Retained earnings		32,000		40,000
		282,000		111,250
Non-current liabilities: 6% Loan				20,000
Current liabilities				
Trade payables		123,000		58,000
		405,000		189,250

Notes:

(1) Dublin acquired 40,000 shares in Belfast on 1 January 20X5 for a cost of $58,000 when the balances on Belfast's reserves were:

	$
Share premium account	6,250
Revaluation surplus	–
Retained earnings	10,000

(2) Non-controlling interest is valued at fair value, which was $14,500 on 1 January 20X5.

(3) At 31 December 20X6 Belfast's inventory included $12,000 of goods purchased from Dublin. Dublin earns a gross profit of 25% on sales.

(4) At 31 December 20X6 Dublin's trade receivables include $28,000 due from Belfast and Belfast's trade payables include $28,000 due to Dublin.

Required:

Prepare the consolidated statement of financial position as at 31 December 20X6 of Dublin.

(15 marks)

Question 67 HELIOS AND LUNA

Helios acquired 80% of the equity share capital of Luna for $700,000 on 1 July 20X4, when the retained profits of Luna amounted to $60,000. There have been no movements on Luna's share capital or share premium account since that date.

At 30 June 20X7 the summary statements of financial position of the two companies were as follows:

	Helios	*Luna*
	$000	$000
Tangible non-current assets	280	490
Investment in Luna	700	
Net current assets	130	260
	1,110	750
Share capital	600	400
Share premium account	350	200
Retained earnings	160	150
	1,110	750

Net current assets include intra-group account balances that have been agreed between Helios and Luna. At 30 June 20X7 $27,000 was due from Helios to Luna.

Luna has some land whose fair value is $20,000 greater than its carrying amount on acquisition.

Non-controlling interest is valued at fair value on acquisition, which was $179,000.

Required:

(a) **Prepare the consolidated statement of financial position of Helios and its subsidiary as at 30 June 20X7.** (11 marks)

(b) The following table shows factors to be considered when determining whether a parent-subsidiary relationship exists.

Factor	*Description*
A	Greater than 50% of equity shares held by investor
B	Ability to control board of directors
C	Participation in policy-making processes
D	Material transactions between the two entities
E	Interchange of managerial personnel
F	Non-controlling interest
G	Provision of essential technical assistance
H	100% of equity shares held by investor

Required:

Which of the above factors A to H illustrate the existence of a parent-subsidiary relationship? (4 marks)

(15 marks)

Question 68 BRADSHAW & MARTIN

You are presented with the following information for Bradshaw and its subsidiary, Martin:

Statements of profit or loss for the year ended 31 October 20X6

		Bradshaw	*Martin*
		$000	$000
Revenue		125,000	77,900
Cost of sales		(65,000)	(38,500)
Gross profit		60,000	39,400
Distribution costs		(6,750)	(8,050)
Administrative expenses		(17,500)	(9,780)
Finance costs		–	(20)
Income from Martin:	Loan note interest	15	–
	Dividends	5,200	–
Profit before tax		40,965	21,550
Income tax expense		(19,250)	(10,850)
Profit for the year		21,715	10,700

The following information is also available:

(i) Bradshaw purchased 80% of the share capital of Martin on 1 November 20X5 for $34,000,000. At that date, Martin's equity consisted of 23,150,000 $1 equity shares and retained earnings of $5,338,000.

(ii) It is group policy to value the non-controlling interest at fair value. The fair value of the non-controlling interest at the acquisition date was $7,408,000.

(iii) Bradshaw owns $150,000 of Martin's $200,000 loan notes. The annual interest rate on the loan notes is 10%.

(iv) During the year ended 31 October 20X6 Bradshaw sold goods to Martin for $15,000,000. Bradshaw made a profit on these goods of $2,500,000. Martin still has all of these goods in inventory at 31 October 20X6.

(v) All Martin's dividends of $6,500,000 were paid in the financial year ended 31 October 20X6.

Required:

(a) Calculate the goodwill arising on the acquisition of Martin as at 1 November 20X5.
(3 marks)

(b) Prepare the consolidated statement of profit or loss for the year ended 31 October 20X6.
(8 marks)

(c) The following table shows factors to be considered when determining whether a parent-associate relationship exists.

Factor	*Description*
A	Greater than 80% of equity shares held by investor
B	Holding six of eight positions on the board of directors
C	Participation in policy-making processes
D	Material transactions between the two entities
E	Interchange of managerial personnel
F	Existence of non-controlling interest
G	Provision of essential technical assistance
H	40% of preference shares held by investor

Required:

Which of the above factors A to H illustrate the existence of a parent-associate relationship? (4 marks)

(15 marks)

Question 69 MCQs INTERPRETATION OF FINANCIAL STATEMENTS

69.1 Which of the following are reasons why financial statement analysis is useful to investors?

(1) To monitor current investments or to plan future ones
(2) Because past performance is often a good indicator of future performance
(3) Because future trends can then be accurately predicted
(4) To assess the risk associated with their expected returns

A 1, 2 and 3
B 1, 2 and 4
C 1, 3 and 4
D 2, 3 and 4 (2 marks)

69.2 Which of the following will be of least concern to a company's providers of loan finance?

A Current share price
B Profitability
C Short-term liquidity
D Solvency (2 marks)

69.3 Which of the following are true of trend analysis?

(1) It uses changes in monetary amount and percentage terms to identify patterns
(2) It concentrates on the relative size of current assets
(3) It examines changes over time
(4) It examines the relationships of percentage changes to each other

A 1 and 3
B 1 and 4
C 2 and 3
D 2 and 4 (2 marks)

69.4 Which of the following are short-term liquidity ratios?

(1) Current ratio
(2) Inventory turnover
(3) Gearing ratio
(4) Quick ratio

A 1 and 3
B 1 and 4
C 2 and 3
D 2 and 4 (2 marks)

69.5 Gormenghast's current ratio has been calculated as 1.2. However, it has now been discovered that closing inventory has been understated by $24,000 and opening inventory has been overstated by $24,000.

What impact have these misstatements made on the calculations of Gormenghast's current ratio and inventory days?

	Current ratio	*Inventory days*
A	Higher	Higher
B	Higher	Lower
C	Lower	Higher
D	Lower	Lower

(2 marks)

69.6 In a period of rising prices Andreas has decided to value inventory at average cost rather than FIFO. Inventory levels remain unchanged.

What impact does this decision have on the gross margin and current ratio?

	Gross margin	*Current ratio*
A	Higher	Higher
B	Higher	Lower
C	Lower	Higher
D	Lower	Lower

(2 marks)

69.7 Which ONE of the following formulae correctly expresses the relationship between the return on capital employed (ROCE), net profit margin (NPM) and asset turnover (AT)?

A ROCE = NPM ÷ AT
B ROCE = NPM + AT
C ROCE = NPM × AT
D ROCE = NPM – AT (2 marks)

69.8 What is the effect on working capital of an increase in inventories of $500, a decrease in the bank balance of $600 and an increase in payables of $1,400?

A $1,500 decrease
B $1,300 decrease
C $1,300 increase
D $1,500 increase (2 marks)

69.9 The Statement of financial position of Jardino includes the following information:

	$
Non-current assets	219,650
Current assets	124,800
Current liabilities	64,290

What is the amount of working capital?

A $60,510
B $64,290
C $124,800
D $280,160 (2 marks)

69.10 Aeon uses the first in, first out (FIFO) method of inventory valuation; Baco uses the average cost (AVCO) method. Over the last year, the unit cost of items purchased has been falling. There are no other factors that may affect the inventory turnover ratio derived from the published financial statements.

Which of the following statements regarding the inventory turnover ratio is correct?

A Aeon will have a shorter inventory turnover period than Baco
B Baco will have a shorter inventory turnover period than Aeon
C The inventory turnover period for both companies will be the same
D The method of inventory valuation will not affect inventory turnover (2 marks)

69.11 The financial statements of a company show that during the past year the company has:

(1) Raised a long term loan to finance the purchase of non-current assets
(2) Reduced the value of closing inventory

How are the current ratio and gearing affected in comparison to last year?

	Current ratio	*Gearing*
A	Increased	Decreased
B	Decreased	Increased
C	Decreased	Decreased
D	Increased	Increased

(2 marks)

69.12 In the last financial year, the net profit margin of Grippa was 14.7% and asset turnover was 2.3 times.

What was the company's return on capital employed for the financial year?

A It cannot be calculated on the information given
B 17%
C 33.81%
D 6.39% (2 marks)

69.13 The following information relates to Light Co and Murky Co:

	Light Co	*Murky Co*
Equity	$1,500,000	$1,500,000
Profit before interest and tax	$100,000	$100,000
Gearing ratio	25%	35%

Both companies borrow money at an interest rate of 5% and no new loans have been taken out during the year.

Based on this information, which of the following statements is TRUE?

A Murky Co's interest cover is higher than Light Co's
B Light Co's interest cover is higher than Murky Co's
C Light Co and Murky Co have the same interest cover
D It is not possible to draw any conclusions regarding interest cover from the information provided (2 marks)

(26 marks)

Question 70 BETA

Beta is reviewing the financial statements of two companies, Zeta and Omega. The companies trade as wholesalers, selling electrical goods to retailers on credit. Their statements of profit or loss for the year ended 31 March 20X7 are as follows:

	Zeta		*Omega*	
	$000	$000	$000	$000
Sales revenue		4,000		6,000
Cost of sales				
Opening inventory	200		800	
Purchases	3,200		4,800	
Less: Closing inventory	400		800	
		3,000		4,800
Gross profit		1,000		1,200
Expenses:				
Distribution costs	200		150	
Administrative expenses	290		250	
Interest paid	10		400	
		500		800
Profit before tax		500		400
Taxation		120		90
Profit for the year		380		310

Statement of financial position as at 31 March 20X7

	Zeta		*Omega*	
	$000	$000	$000	$000
Assets				
Tangible non-current assets				
Warehouse and office buildings	1,200		5,000	
Equipment and vehicles	600		1,000	
		1,800		6,000
Current assets				
Inventories	400		800	
Trade receivables	800		900	
Other receivables	150		80	
Cash at bank			100	
		1,350		1,880
		3,150		7,880
Equity and liabilities				
Equity				
Share capital	1,000		1,600	
Revaluation surplus			500	
Retained earnings	950		790	
		1,950		2,890
Non-current liabilities				
Non-current loan (interest 10% per annum)				4,000
Current liabilities				
Trade payables	800		800	
Other payables	80		100	
Overdraft	200			
Taxation	120		90	
		1,200		990
		3,150		7,880

Required:

(a) **Calculate the following for Zeta and Omega:**

(i) Two measures of profitability;
(ii) Two short-term liquidity ratios;
(iii) Three efficiency ratios. (7 marks)

(b) **Based on the ratios you have calculated in (a), compare the profitability, liquidity and efficiency of the two companies.** (5 marks)

(c) Omega is much more highly geared than Zeta.

Explain the implications of this for the two companies. (3 marks)

(15 marks)

Question 71 WEDEN

The summarised financial statements of Weden, a manufacturing company, are shown below:

Statements of profit or loss

	Year ended 31 March 20X7		*Year ended 31 March 20X6*	
	$000	$000	$000	$000
Sales revenue		4,000		3,200
Cost of sales				
Opening inventory	300		800	
Purchases	3,200		1,800	
	3,500		2,600	
less: Closing inventory	500		300	
		(3,000)		(2,300)
Gross profit		1,000		900
Expenses		(450)		(400)
Interest paid		(200)		(100)
Profit		350		400

Statements of financial position

	31 March 20X7		*31 March 20X6*	
	$000	$000	$000	$000
Assets				
Non-current assets		4,000		1,970
Current assets				
Inventory	500		300	
Receivables – trade	800		600	
Prepayments	70		60	
Cash	10		50	
		1,380		1,010
		5,380		2,980
Equity and liabilities				
Equity				
Share capital		600		600
Share premium account		200		200
Retained earnings		1,100		750
		1,900		1,550
Non-current liabilities				
10% Loan notes		2,000		1,000
Current liabilities				
Payables – trade	1,400		380	
Accruals	80	1,480	50	430
		5,380		2,980

Required:

(a) Calculate the following five ratios for each of the two years:

(i) return on capital employed;
(ii) return on equity;
(iii) current ratio;
(iv) inventory turnover (use closing figures);
(v) number of days' purchases in trade payables. (5 marks)

(b) Comment briefly on the changes in the company's results and position between the two years, mentioning possible causes for the changes. (5 marks)

(10 marks)

Question 72 APILLON

Extracts from the financial statements of Apillon for the years ended 31 March 20X6 and 20X7 are given below:

	Year ended 31 March			
Statement of profit or loss	*20X7*		*20X6*	
	$000	$000	$000	$000
Revenue (Note 1)		3,800		3,100
Cost of sales				
Opening inventory	540		360	
Purchases (Note 2)	2,580		2,080	
	3,120		2,440	
Less: closing inventory	720		540	
		(2,400)		(1,900)
Gross profit		1,400		1,200
Expenses		(1,100)		(900)
Profit		300		300

	Year ended 31 March			
Statement of financial position	*20X7*		*20X6*	
	$000	$000	$000	$000
Current assets				
Inventory	720		540	
Trade receivables	700		450	
		1,420		990
Current liabilities				
Trade payables	690		410	
Bank overdraft	170	860	20	430

Notes:

(1) Revenue includes cash sales $100,000 in 20X7 ($300,000 in 20X6).
(2) All purchases are on credit.

Required:

(a) Calculate the following for each of the two years:

- **(i) Current ratio;**
- **(ii) Quick ratio (acid test);**
- **(iii) Inventory turnover period (use closing inventory);**
- **(iv) Average period of credit allowed to customers;**
- **(v) Average period of credit taken from suppliers.**

Calculate items (iii), (iv) and (v) in days. (5 marks)

(b) Make four brief comments on the changes in the position of the company as revealed by the changes in these ratios and/or in the given figures from the financial statements.
(4 marks)

(9 marks)

SPECIMEN EXAM

Section A – ALL 35 questions are compulsory and MUST be attempted

1 Which of the following calculates a sole trader's net profit for a period?

A Closing net assets + drawings – capital introduced – opening net assets
B Closing net assets – drawings + capital introduced – opening net assets
C Closing net assets – drawings – capital introduced – opening net assets
D Closing net assets + drawings + capital introduced – opening net assets

2 Which of the following explains the imprest system of operating petty cash?

A Weekly expenditure cannot exceed a set amount
B The exact amount of expenditure is reimbursed at intervals to maintain a fixed float
C All expenditure out of the petty cash must be properly authorised
D Regular equal amounts of cash are transferred into petty cash at intervals

3 Which of the following statements are TRUE of limited liability companies?

(1) The company's exposure to debts and liability is limited
(2) Financial statements must be produced
(3) A company continues to exist regardless of the identity of its owners

A 1 and 2 only
B 1 and 3 only
C 2 and 3 only
D 1, 2 and 3

4 Annie is a sole trader who does not keep full accounting records. The following details relate to her transactions with credit customers and suppliers for the year ended 30 June 20X6:

	$
Trade receivables, 1 July 20X5	130,000
Trade payables, 1 July 20X5	60,000
Cash received from customers	686,400
Cash paid to suppliers	302,800
Discounts allowed	1,400
Discounts received	2,960
Contra between payables and receivables ledgers	2,000
Trade receivables, 30 June 20X6	181,000
Trade payables, 30 June 20X6	84,000

What figure should appear for purchases in Annie's statement of profit or loss for the year ended 30 June 20X6?

A $325,840
B $330,200
C $331,760
D $327,760

5 **Which TWO of the following errors would cause the total of the debit column and the total of the credit column of a trial balance not to agree?**

(1) A transposition error was made when entering a sales invoice into the sales day book

(2) A cheque received from a customer was credited to cash and correctly recognised in receivables

(3) A purchase of non-current assets was omitted from the accounting records

(4) Rent received was included in the trial balance as a debit balance

A 1 and 2
B 1 and 3
C 2 and 3
D 2 and 4

6 At 31 December 20X5 the following require inclusion in a company's financial statements:

(1) On 1 January 20X5 the company made a loan of $12,000 to an employee, repayable on 1 January 20X6, charging interest at 2% per year. On the due date she repaid the loan and paid the whole of the interest due on the loan to that date.

(2) The company paid an annual insurance premium of $9,000 in 20X5, covering the year ending 31 August 20X6.

(3) In January 20X6 the company received rent from a tenant of $4,000 covering the six months to 31 December 20X5.

For these items, what total figures should be included in the company's statement of financial position as at 31 December 20X5?

A	Current assets $10,000	Current liabilities $12,240
B	Current assets $22,240	Current liabilities $nil
C	Current assets $10,240	Current liabilities $nil
D	Current assets $16,240	Current liabilities $6,000

7 A company's statement of profit or loss for the year ended 31 December 20X5 showed a net profit of $83,600. It was later found that $18,000 paid for the purchase of a motor van had been debited to the motor expenses account. It is the company's policy to depreciate motor vans at 25% per year on the straight line basis, with a full year's charge in the year of acquisition.

What would the net profit be after adjusting for this error?

A $106,100
B $70,100
C $97,100
D $101,600

8 Xena has the following working capital ratios:

	20X9	*20X8*
Current ratio	1·2:1	1·5:1
Receivables days	75 days	50 days
Payables days	30 days	45 days
Inventory turnover	42 days	35 days

Which of the following statements is correct?

A Xena's liquidity and working capital has improved in 20X9
B Xena is receiving cash from customers more quickly in 20X9 than in 20X8
C Xena is suffering from a worsening liquidity position in 20X9
D Xena is taking longer to pay suppliers in 20X9 than in 20X8

9 **Which of the following statements is/are correct?**

(1) A statement of cash flows prepared using the direct method produces a different figure to net cash from operating activities from that produced if the indirect method is used

(2) Rights issues of shares do not feature in a statement of cash flows

(3) A surplus on revaluation of a non-current asset will not appear as an item in a statement of cash flows

(4) A profit on the sale of a non-current asset will appear as an item under cash flows from investing activities in the statement of cash flows

A 1 and 3 only
B 3 and 4 only
C 2 and 4 only
D 3 only

10 A company receives rent from a large number of properties. The total received in the year ended 30 April 20X6 was $481,200.

The following were the amounts of rent in advance and in arrears at 30 April 20X5 and 20X6:

	30 April 20X5	*30 April 20X6*
	$	$
Rent received in advance	28,700	31,200
Rent in arrears (all subsequently received)	21,200	18,400

What amount of rental income should appear in the company's statement of profit or loss for the year ended 30 April 20X6?

A $486,500
B $460,900
C $501,500
D $475,900

11 **Which of the following are differences between sole traders and limited liability companies?**

(1) A sole trader's financial statements are private and never made available to third parties; a company's financial statements are sent to shareholders and may be publicly filed

(2) Only companies have share capital

(3) A sole trader is fully and personally liable for any losses that the business might make

(4) Drawings would only appear in the financial statements of a sole trader

A 1 and 4 only
B 2, 3 and 4
C 2 and 3 only
D 1, 3 and 4

12 **Which of the following statements is true?**

A The interpretation of an entity's financial statements using ratios is only useful for potential investors

B Ratios based on historical data can predict the future performance of an entity

C The analysis of financial statements using ratios provides useful information when compared with previous performance or industry averages

D An entity's management will not assess an entity's performance using financial ratios

13 A company's motor vehicles cost account at 30 June 20X6 is as follows:

Motor vehicles – cost

	$		$
Balance b/f	35,800	Disposal	12,000
Additions	12,950	Balance c/f	36,750
	48,750		48,750

What opening balance should be included in the following period's trial balance for Motor vehicles – cost at 1 July 20X6?

A $36,750 Dr
B $48,750 Dr
C $36,750 Cr
D $48,750 Cr

14 **Which TWO of the following items must be disclosed in the note to the financial statements for intangible assets?**

(1) The useful lives of intangible assets capitalised in the financial statements
(2) A description of the development projects that have been undertaken during the period
(3) A list of all intangible assets purchased or developed in the period
(4) Impairment losses written off intangible assets during the period

A 1 and 4
B 2 and 3
C 3 and 4
D 1 and 2

15 **Which of the following statements are correct?**

(1) Capitalised development expenditure must be amortised over a period not exceeding five years

(2) Capitalised development costs are shown in the statement of financial position under the heading of non-current assets

(3) If certain criteria are met, research expenditure must be recognised as an intangible asset

A 2 only
B 2 and 3
C 1 only
D 1 and 3

16 The following transactions relate to Rashid's electricity expense ledger account for the year ended 30 June 20X9:

	$
Prepayment brought forward	550
Cash paid	5,400
Accrual carried forward	650

What amount should be charged to the statement of profit or loss in the year ended 30 June 20X9 for electricity?

A $6,600
B $5,400
C $5,500
D $5,300

17 At 30 June 20X5 a company's allowance for receivables was $39,000. At 30 June 20X6 trade receivables totalled $517,000. It was decided to write off debts totalling $37,000 and to adjust the allowance for receivables to the equivalent of 5% of the trade receivables based on past events.

What figure should appear in the statement of profit or loss for the year ended 30 June 20X6 for receivables expense?

A $61,000
B $52,000
C $22,000
D $37,000

18 The total of the list of balances in Valley's payables ledger was $438,900 at 30 June 20X6. This balance did not agree with Valley's payables ledger control account balance. The following errors were discovered:

(1) A contra entry of $980 was recorded in the payables ledger control account, but not in the payables ledger

(2) The total of the purchase returns daybook was undercast by $1,000

(3) An invoice for $4,344 was posted to the supplier's account as $4,434

What amount should Valley report in its statement of financial position for accounts payable at 30 June 20X6?

A $436,830
B $438,010
C $439,790
D $437,830

19 **According to IAS 2 *Inventories*, which TWO of the following costs should be included in valuing the inventories of a manufacturing company?**

(1) Carriage inwards
(2) Carriage outwards
(3) Depreciation of factory plant
(4) General administrative overheads

A 1 and 4
B 1 and 3
C 3 and 4
D 2 and 3

20 Prisha has not kept accurate accounting records during the financial year. She had opening inventory of $6,700 and purchased goods costing $84,000 during the year. At the year end she had $5,400 left in inventory. All sales are made at a mark up on cost of 20%.

What is Prisha's gross profit for the year?

A $13,750
B $17,060
C $16,540
D $20,675

21 At 31 December 20X4 a company's capital structure was as follows:

	$
Ordinary share capital	125,000
(500,000 shares of 25c each)	
Share premium account	100,000

In the year ended 31 December 20X5 the company made a rights issue of 1 share for every 2 held at $1 per share and this was taken up in full. Later in the year the company made a bonus issue of 1 share for every 5 held, using the share premium account for the purpose.

What was the company's capital structure at 31 December 20X5?

	Ordinary share capital	*Share premium account*
A	$450,000	$25,000
B	$225,000	$250,000
C	$225,000	$325,000
D	$212,500	$262,500

22 **Which of the following should appear in a company's statement of changes in equity?**

(1) Total comprehensive income for the year
(2) Amortisation of capitalised development costs
(3) Surplus on revaluation of non-current assets

A 1, 2 and 3
B 2 and 3 only
C 1 and 3 only
D 1 and 2 only

23 The plant and machinery account (at cost) of a business for the year ended 31 December 20X5 was as follows:

Plant and machinery – cost

20X5	$	20X5	$
1 Jan Balance b/f	240,000	31 Mar Transfer to disposal account	60,000
30 Jun Cash purchase of plant	160,000	31 Dec Balance c/f	340,000
	400,000		400,000

The company's policy is to charge depreciation at 20% per year on the straight line basis, with proportionate depreciation in the years of purchase and disposal.

What should be the depreciation charge for the year ended 31 December 20X5?

A $68,000
B $64,000
C $61,000
D $55,000

24 The following extracts are from Hassan's financial statements:

	$
Profit before interest and tax	10,200
Interest	(1,600)
Tax	(3,300)
Profit after tax	5,300
Share capital	20,000
Reserves	15,600
	35,600
Loan liability	6,900
	42,500

What is Hassan's return on capital employed?

A 15%
B 29%
C 24%
D 12%

25 **Which of the following statements about sales tax is/are true?**

(1) Sales tax is an expense to the ultimate consumer of the goods purchased
(2) Sales tax is recorded as income in the accounts of the entity selling the goods

A 1 only
B 2 only
C Both 1 and 2
D Neither 1 nor 2

26 Q's trial balance failed to agree and a suspense account was opened for the difference. Q does not keep receivables and payables control accounts. The following errors were found in Q's accounting records:

(1) In recording an issue of shares at par, cash received of $333,000 was credited to the ordinary share capital account as $330,000

(2) Cash of $2,800 paid for plant repairs was correctly accounted for in the cash book but was credited to the plant asset account

(3) The petty cash book balance of $500 had been omitted from the trial balance

(4) A cheque for $78,400 paid for the purchase of a motor car was debited to the motor vehicles account as $87,400.

Which of the errors will require an entry to the suspense account to correct them?

A 1, 2 and 4 only
B 1, 2, 3 and 4
C 1 and 4 only
D 2 and 3 only

27 Prior to the financial year end of 31 July 20X9, Cannon Co has received a claim of $100,000 from a supplier for providing poor quality goods which have damaged the supplier's plant and equipment. Cannon Co's lawyers have stated that there is a 20% chance that Cannon will successfully defend the claim.

Which of the following is the correct accounting treatment for the claim in the financial statements for the year ended 31 July 20X9?

A Cannon should neither provide for nor disclose the claim
B Cannon should disclose a contingent liability of $100,000
C Cannon should provide for the expected cost of the claim of $100,000
D Cannon should provide for an expected cost of $20,000

28 Gareth, a sales tax registered trader purchased a computer for use in his business. The invoice for the computer showed the following costs related to the purchase:

	$
Computer	890
Additional memory	95
Delivery	10
Installation	20
Maintenance (1 year)	25
	1,040
Sales tax (17·5%)	182
Total	1,222

How much should Gareth capitalise as a non-current asset in relation to the purchase?

A $1,193
B $1,040
C $1,222
D $1,015

29 The following bank reconciliation statement has been prepared by a trainee accountant:

	$
Overdraft per bank statement	3,860
Less: Unpresented cheques	9,160
	5,300
Add: Outstanding lodgements	16,690
Cash at bank	21,990

What should be the correct balance per the cash book?

A $21,990 balance at bank as stated
B $3,670 balance at bank
C $11,390 balance at bank
D $3,670 overdrawn

30 The IASB's *Conceptual Framework for Financial Reporting* identifies characteristics which make financial information faithfully represent what it purports to represent.

Which of the following are examples of those characteristics?

(1) Accruals
(2) Completeness
(3) Going concern
(4) Neutrality

A 1 and 2
B 2 and 4
C 2 and 3
D 1 and 4

31 The following control account has been prepared by a trainee accountant:

Receivables ledger control account

	$		$
Opening balance	308,600	Cash	147,200
Credit sales	154,200	Discounts allowed	1,400
Cash sales	88,100	Interest charged on overdue accounts	2,400
Contras	4,600	Irrecoverable debts	4,900
		Allowance for receivables	2,800
		Closing balance	396,800
	555,500		555,500

At the point of sale, customers are not expected to take advantage of settlement discounts.

What should the closing balance be when all the errors made in preparing the receivables ledger control account have been corrected?

A $395,200
B $304,300
C $309,500
D $307,100

32 **Which of the following material events after the reporting date and before the financial statements are approved are adjusting events?**

(1) A valuation of property providing evidence of impairment in value at the reporting date

(2) Sale of inventory held at the reporting date for less than cost

(3) Discovery of fraud or error affecting the financial statements

(4) The insolvency of a customer with a debt owing at the reporting date which is still outstanding

A 1, 2 and 4 only
B 1, 2, 3 and 4
C 1 and 4 only
D 2 and 3 only

33 A company values its inventory using the FIFO method. At 1 May 20X5 the company had 700 engines in inventory, valued at $190 each. During the year ended 30 April 20X6 the following transactions took place:

20X5
1 July Purchased 500 engines at $220 each
1 November Sold 400 engines for $160,000

20X6
1 February Purchased 300 engines at $230 each
15 April Sold 250 engines for $125,000

What is the value of the company's closing inventory of engines at 30 April 20X6?

A $188,500
B $195,500
C $166,000
D $106,000

34 Amy is a sole trader and had assets of $569,400 and liabilities of $412,840 on 1 January 20X8. During the year ended 31 December 20X8 she paid $65,000 capital into the business and she paid herself wages of $800 per month.

At 31 December 20X8, Amy had assets of $614,130 and liabilities of $369,770.

What is Amy's profit for the year ended 31 December 20X8?

A $32,400
B $23,600
C $22,800
D $87,800

35 Bumbly Co extracted the trial balance for the year ended 31 December 20X7. The total of the debits exceeded the credits by $300.

Which of the following could explain the imbalance?

A Sales of $300 were omitted from the sales day book
B Returns inward of $150 were extracted to the debit column of the trial balance
C Discounts received of $150 were extracted to the debit column of the trial balance
D The bank ledger account did not agree with the bank statement by a debit of $300

(70 marks)

Section B – BOTH questions are compulsory and MUST be attempted

1 Keswick Co acquired 80% of the share capital of Derwent Co on 1 June 20X5. The summarised draft statements of profit or loss for Keswick Co and Derwent Co for the year ended 31 May 20X6 are shown below:

	Keswick Co	*Derwent Co*
	$000	$000
Revenue	8,400	3,200
Cost of sales	(4,600)	(1,700)
Gross profit	3,800	1,500
Operating expenses	(2,200)	(960)
Profit before tax	1,600	540
Tax	(600)	(140)
Profit for the year	1,000	400

During the year Keswick Co sold goods costing $1,000,000 to Derwent Co for $1,500,000. At 31 May 20X6, 30% of these goods remained in Derwent Co's inventory.

Required:

(a) **Prepare the Keswick group consolidated statement of profit or loss for the year ended 31 May 20X6.**

Note: The statement should stop once the consolidated profit for the year has been determined. The amounts attributable to the non-controlling interest and equity owners of Keswick are not required. Show all workings as credit will be awarded to these as appropriate. (7 marks)

(b) **Which of the following formulas describes the amount to be entered in the consolidated statement of profit or loss as *"Profit attributable to: Equity owners of Keswick Co"*?**

A Group profit after tax – non-controlling interest
B Group profit after tax + non-controlling interest
C Keswick Co's profit after tax
D Group profit after tax (2 marks)

(c) **What amount should be shown in the consolidated statement of profit or loss for the non-controlling interest?** (2 marks)

(d) The following table shows factors to be considered when determining whether a parent–subsidiary relationship exists.

Factor	*Description*
A	Significant influence
B	Control
C	Non-controlling interest
D	Greater than 50% of the equity shares being held by an investor
E	100% of the equity shares being held by an investor
F	Greater than 50% of the preference shares being held by an investor
G	50% of all shares and all debt being held by an investor
H	Greater than 50% of preference shares and debt being held by an investor

Required:

Which of the above factors A to H illustrate the existence of a parent–subsidiary relationship? (4 marks)

(15 marks)

2 Malright, a limited liability company, has an accounting year end of 31 October. The accountant is preparing the financial statements as at 31 October 20X7 and requires your assistance. The following trial balance has been extracted from the general ledger

Account	*Dr*	*Cr*
	$000	$000
Buildings at cost	740	
Buildings accumulated depreciation, 1 November 20X6		60
Plant at cost	220	
Plant accumulated depreciation, 1 November 20X6		110
Bank balance		70
Revenue		1,800
Net purchases	1,140	
Inventory at 1 November 20X6	160	
Cash	20	
Trade payables		250
Trade receivables	320	
Administrative expenses	325	
Allowance for receivables at 1 November 20X6		10
Retained earnings at 1 November 20X6		130
Equity shares, $1		415
Share premium account		80
	2,925	2,925

The following additional information is also available:

- The allowance for receivables is to be increased to 5% of trade receivables. The allowance for receivables is treated as an administrative expense.
- Plant is depreciated at 20% per annum using the reducing balance method and buildings are depreciated at 5% per annum on their original cost. Depreciation is treated as a cost of sales expense.
- Closing inventory has been counted and is valued at $75,000.
- An invoice of $15,000 for energy costs relating to the quarter ended 30 November 20X7 was received on 2 December 20X7. Energy costs are included in administrative expenses.

Required:

Prepare the statement of profit or loss and the statement of financial position of Malright Co as at 31 October 20X7.

(15 marks)

Answer 1 MCQs ACCRUALS AND PREPAYMENTS

Item	*Answer*	*Justification*
1.1	B	$(^{7}/_{12} \times 8,400) + (^{5}/_{12} \times 12,000) = 9,900$ income; 1,000 paid in advance in sundry payables (a customer's advance payment is a liability)
1.2	D	$(2 \times 5,000) + (10 \times 6,000) = \$70,000$
1.3	C	

Rent received account

	$		$
Balance	16,900	Balance	24,600
Income (balancing figure)	316,200	Cash	318,600
Balance	28,400	Balance	18,300
	361,500		361,500

1.4 C

Insurance account

	$		$
Prepayment	8,200	Expense	**36,700**
Paid	38,000	Prepayment $(38,000 \times ^{3}/_{12})$	9,500
	46,200		46,200

1.5 C

Rent receivable account

	$		$
Arrears b/f	3,800	Prepaid b/f	2,400
Income for the year	**84,000**	Received	83,700
Prepaid c/f	3,000	Arrears c/f	4,700
	90,800		90,800

Item	*Answer*	*Justification*
1.6	D	$^{5}/_{12} \times 24,000 + ^{7}/_{12} \times 30,000 = 27,500$; $^{2}/_{3} \times 7,500 = \$5,000$
1.7	A	Profit or loss: $^{12}/_{18} \times 60,000 = \$40,000$; Prepayment: $^{3}/_{12} \times 40,000 = \$10,000$
1.8	B	Opening prepayment of rent increases (i.e. debit)office expenses and closing prepayment decreases (i.e. credit). Total office expenses is $\$89,100 + \$9,500 - (^{2}/_{3} \times \$15,300) = \$88,400$
1.9	A	

Rent account

	$		$
Advances	7,720	Receipts received	22,850
Profit or loss (balancing figure)	19,620	Arrears	4,490
	27,340		27,340

1.10	C	$\$1,800 \times ^{9}/_{12} + \$2,000 \times ^{3}/_{12} = \$1,850$

1.11 C $2,400 × $^{7}/_{12}$ = $1,400 charge to profit or loss
$2,400 × $^{5}/_{12}$ = $1,000 prepayment in statement of financial position

1.12 C Charge to profit or loss = opening prepayment + ($^{5}/_{12}$ × 36,000). Closing prepayment = $^{7}/_{12}$ × 36,000 = $21,000

1.13 C **Tutorial note:** *The adjustment for prepayment of an expense increases profit and creates a current asset in the statement of financial position. Conversely, the adjustment for deferred income (i.e. income received but not yet earned) will decrease profit and create a current liability.*

	$
Prepaid insurance expense ($12,000 × $^{3}/_{12}$)	3,000
Prepaid rental income ($6,000 × $^{2}/_{3}$)	(4,000)
	(1,000)

The net effect is a reduction in profit and net assets (i.e. assets less liabilities).

Answer 2 MCQs DEPRECIATION AND DISPOSALS

Item	*Answer*	*Justification*
2.1	A	Difference between 20,000 and (20,000 – 4,000) × 20% × $^{6}/_{12}$ = $18,400
2.2	B	(160,000 × 20%) + (40,000 × 20% × ¾) + (50,000 × 20% × ½) = $43,000
2.3	D	(240,000 × 20%) + (160,000 × 20% × $^{6}/_{12}$) – (60,000 × 20% × $^{9}/_{12}$) = $55,000
2.4	B	83,600 + 18,000 – 4,500 = $97,100
2.5	A	(280,000 × 20%) + (48,000 × 20% × $^{9}/_{12}$) + (36,000 × 20% × $^{4}/_{12}$) – – (14,000 × 20% × $^{6}/_{12}$) = $64,200

2.6 B

	$
Draft net profit	83,600
Add: purchase price	18,000
Less: additional depreciation (18,000 × 25%)	(4,500)
Adjusted profit	97,100

2.7 C The internal administration costs cannot be treated as part of the asset's cost, so in the first two years' depreciation of 2 × $^{1}/_{5}$($96,720 + $3,660) = $40,152 was charged. This means that the whole of the remaining carrying amount of $60,228 must be expensed on the revision of the asset's useful life.

2.8 B

Disposal

	$		$
Cost	23,500	Accumulated depreciation 23,500 – (23,500 × 70% × 70%)	11,985
		Part-exchange (28,200 – 19,350)	8,850
		Loss on disposal (balancing figure)	**2,665**
	23,500		23,500

2.9 B

The carrying amount is $626,000 – $368,165 = $257,835.

Cost

	$		$
B/fwd	614,500		
Additions	11,500	C/fwd	626,000
	626,000		626,000

Accumulated depreciation

	$		$
		B/fwd (614,500 – 399,960)	214,540
C/fwd	368,165	Charge (614,500 × 25%)	153,625
	368,165		368,165

Tutorial note: *There is no depreciation charged in the year to 31 March 20X7 for the asset acquired at the year end.*

2.10 B

	$
Cost	12,000
Accumulated depreciation ($12,000 × 20% × 3 years)	7,200
Carrying amount	4,800
Trade-in value = disposal proceeds	5,000
Profit on disposal	200

Tutorial note: *There is no depreciation in the year of sale according to the company's depreciation policy.*

2.11 D

Annual depreciation = ($52,000 – $4, 000) ÷ 8 = $6,000
Carrying amount after five years = $52,000 – (5 × $6,000) = $22,000
Gain on disposal = $35,000 – $22,000 = $13,000

2.12 C

Fall in carrying amount of machine = $40,000 – $15,000 = $25,000

2.13 B

31 December

20X3	80,000 × 75% = 60,000
20X4	60,000 × 75% = 45,500
20X5	45,000 × 75% = 33,750
20X6	33,750 × 75% = 25,312

2.14 D

	$
Carrying amount after four years' depreciation $200,000 \times (100\% - 25\%)^4$	63,281
Proceeds	90,000
Profit	26,719

Alternative (long-hand) calculation of carrying amount

Cost	*200,000*
Year 1 depreciation @ 25%	*(50,000)*
Carrying amount	*150,000*
Year 2 depreciation @ 25%	*(37,500)*
Carrying amount	*112,500*
Year 3 depreciation @ 25%	*(28,125)*
Carrying amount	*84,375*
Year 4 depreciation @ 25%	*(21,094)*
Carrying amount	*63,281*

2.15 B The depreciation charge in the first year on both the reducing balance and straight line bases is $22,000. Using the reducing balance basis, the charge in the second year is $16,500 (W). The accountant incorrectly charged $22,500 (i.e. $5,500 more than it should have been). Correction of the error will therefore increase profit.

WORKING

	$
Cost	88,000
Year 1 depreciation @ 25%	(22,000)
Carrying amount	66,000
Year 2 depreciation @ 25%	(16,500)
Carrying amount	49,500

2.16 B Depreciation for the year is $427,400 (W) × 25% = $106,850.

WORKING

	$
Initial cost	680,500
Add: Cost of asset purchased in year	32,800
Less: Accumulated depreciation	(285,900)
Carrying amount	427,400

Answer 3 MCQs RECEIVABLES AND PAYABLES

Item	*Answer*	*Justification*
3.1	A	28,500 + ((5% × (868,500 – 28,500) – 38,000) = $32,500
3.2	C	146,000 + 218,000 – 83,000 = $281,000
3.3	B	Statement of financial position: (864,000 – 13,000) – 5% × 851,000 = $808,450 Profit or loss: 13,000 – (48,000 – 42,550) = $7,550

3.4 B

Receivables ledger control account

	$		$
Opening balance	138,400	*Cash received from credit customers*	*78,420*
Credit sales	*80,660*	Contras against credit balances in payables ledger	1,000
Dishonoured cheques	*850*	Discounts allowed	1,950
		Irrecoverable debts written off	3,000
		Closing balance	**135,540**
	219,910		219,910

Tutorial note: *The debit for discounts allowed is to the revenue account.*

3.5 D The supplier (Beta) is owed $500 less than Alpha's books show, in respect of the credit note.

3.6 A

Allowance account

	$		$
Profit or loss	15,000	B/f	39,000
C/f (5% × (517,000 – 37,000)	24,000		
	39,000		39,000

Charge for year: Write-off $37,000 less reduction in allowance $15,000 = $22,000

3.7 A 3,980 – 270 – 180 – 320 = 3,210 Therefore, difference is 100.

3.8 A (430,000 × 5%) – 18,000 + 28,000 = $31,500

3.9 A

Payables ledger control account

	$		$
Cash paid to suppliers	*988,400*	Opening balance	384,600
Discounts received	12,600	*Purchases*	*963,200*
Contras with amounts receivable in receivables ledger	4,200		
Purchases returns	*17,400*		
Closing balance	**325,200**		
	1,347,800		1,347,800

3.10 A The allowance needs to be debited with $6,546 – $5,060 = $1,486 and $1,860 needs to be credited to trade receivables. The net debit to the irrecoverable debts expense account is therefore $1,860 – $1,486 = $374

Allowance for receivables

	$		$
Irrecoverable debts expense	1,486	Balance b/fwd	6,546
Balance c/fwd ($12,650 × 0.4)	5,060		
	6,546		6,546

Irrecoverable debt expense

	$		$
Write off	1,860	Allowance (decrease)	1,486
		Profit or loss	374
	1,860		1,860

3.11 A The expense is $2,251 (W2) and the figure for receivables is $578,645 – $250 = $578,395.

WORKINGS

(1) Allowance for receivables

	$		$
Irrecoverable debts expense	950	B/fwd (Cusack)	1,200
C/fwd (Dancer)	250		
	1,200		1,200

(2) Irrecoverable debts expense

	$		$
Expense before adjustments	3,290	Allowance	950
		Recovered debt	89
		Profit or loss	2,251
	3,290		3,290

3.12 C Carrying amount of closing inventory ($572,904 – $27,485 + $15,000) = $560,419.

Tutorial note: *This is debited and credited to the closing inventory account; the debit is for the statement of financial position and the credit is for the statement of profit or loss.*

3.13 A The correcting journals in full are:

	$	$
Dr Receivables	180	
Cr Cash		180
Dr Sales (2 × 12)	24	
Cr Receivables		24

So the net correcting journal is:

	$	$
Dr Receivables	156	
Dr Sales	24	
Cr Cash		180

3.14 B

	$
Opening balance	1,200
Goods received	1,700
Good returned	(100)
Payment	(1,615)
Discount received ($1,700 – $1,615 or 5% × $1,700)	(85)
Closing balance	1,100

3.15 A

Receivables = 4,000,000 × 7.5% = $300,000
Closing allowance for irrecoverable debts = 3% × $300,000 = $9,000
Opening allowance = 9,000 ÷ 125% = $7,200
Increase in allowance = $9,000 – $7,200 = $1,800 charge to profit or loss.

3.16 A

	$
Increase in allowances (W1)	8,966
Irrecoverable debt recovered	(2,000)
Receivables expense	6,966

WORKINGS

(1) **Allowance a/c**

	$		$
		Balance b/f	1,900
		Receivables expense	8,966
Balance c/f (W2)	10,866		
	10,866		10,866
		Balance b/f	10,866

(2) Allowance at the year end

	$
Specific	2,400
Further allowance (2% (425,700 – 2,400))	8,466
	10,866

Tutorial note: *Remember that any "general" allowance must be calculated on total receivables (as per the control a/c) LESS any account balances for which specific allowance has been made.*

3.17 A

	$
Balance as per the receivables ledger	633,700
Error (1) correction	(400)
Error (2) correction	(9)
Corrected balance (per control a/c)	633,291

Tutorial note: *A control a/c summarises the* ***totals*** *of large numbers of transactions in the general ledger. As part of the double entry bookkeeping system it is used to prove the accuracy of the ledger accounting system. A receivables ledger is a memorandum of* **individual** *transactions and amounts owed by each customer. (This helps with credit control and cash flow management.)*

To answer such questions, it is necessary to consider each error and decide if and how it affects the receivables ledger, then make the correct adjustment. In this case only errors (1) and (2) concern individual postings. Error (3) relates to a total which does not concern the receivables ledger.

3.18 B **Tutorial note:** *One way to approach this question is to consider each of the errors and determine to what extent they affect the payables control ledger, if at all. Remember that the balance on a control a/c is made up of postings of totals.*

	$
Balance as per the payables control a/c	147,000
Error (1) correction	(250)
Error (3) correction ($23,000 – $32,000)	(9,000)
Corrected balance (per list of payables ledger balances)	137,750

(1) An omission from a day book means that the transaction will be missing from the ledger (of individual a/c balances) and a total that is posted to the control a/c.

(2) A duplicate posting of an invoice to the supplier's (individual) a/c in the payables ledger will require correction to the list of balances. The payables control a/c is not affected.

(3) A transposition error in posting a total must be corrected in the control a/c.

Answer 4 MCQs INVENTORY

Item Answer *Justification*

4.1 A 386,400 – 3,800 (loss on (1) = $382,600

4.2 B 836,200 – 8,600 + 700 + (14,000 × 70%) = $838,100

4.3 B Opening inventory is expensed in the period and closing inventory is the current asset carried forward in the statement of financial position.

4.4 B

		Units	*Value* $	$
1 August	b/f	2,400	10	24,000
14 November	Sell	(900)	10	(9,000)
		1,500	10	15,000
28 January	Buy	1,200	16.75	20,100
		2,700	13	35,100
7 May	Sell	(1,800)	13	(23,400)
31 July	c/fwd	900	13	11,700

Answer 5 MCQs BOOKS OF PRIME ENTRY AND CONTROL ACCOUNTS

Item *Answer* *Justification*

5.1 C

Receivables ledger control account

	$		$
Opening	308,600	Cash received	147,200
Credit sales	154,200	Discounts allowed	1,400
Interest charged	*2,400*	Irrecoverable debts	4,900
		Contras	*4,600*
		Closing	**307,100**
	465,200		465,200

Tutorial note: *A receivables allowance is not recorded in the control account. The corresponding debit entry for the discounts allowed is to the revenue account.*

5.2 B C is also true of a non-imprest system.

5.3 A

Receivables ledger control account

	$		$
Balance	614,000	*Cash*	*311,000*
Sales	*301,000*	Discounts allowed	3,400
Interest	*1,600*	*Contras*	*8,650*
		Irrecoverable debts	32,000
		Balance	561,550
	916,600		916,600

5.4 B

Receivables ledger control account

	$		$
Balance	318,650	Cash	181,140
Credit sales	161,770	Irrecoverable debts	1,390
Interest	*280*	Sales returns	3,990
		Discounts allowed	*1,240*
		Balance	**292,940**
	480,700		480,700

5.5 A This describes the meaning of an imprest system.

Tutorial note: *(2) is a disadvantage of a non-imprest system. (3) is not true because the imprest balance should equal physical cash + petty cash vouchers at any point in time. (4) is a non-imprest system.*

5.6 D

Receivables ledger control account

	$		$
Opening receivables	148,200	*Cash received from customers*	*819,300*
Sales (balancing figure)	**880,600**	*Discounts allowed*	*16,200*
		Irrecoverable debts written off	*1,500*
		Returns from customers	*38,700*
		Closing receivables	153,100
	1,028,800		1,028,800

5.7 A When Marius buys goods on credit, Johan enters this in the sales day book. Contra entries are then made between the sales ledger and purchase ledger accounts.

5.8 C The transposition error is $17,150 – $11,750 = $5,400. As the understatement is in the purchase day book total it affects only the control account, which is understated by $5,400 and so should be increased by that amount.

5.9 B An overcast of the total of invoices in the sales day book means that $782 will be debited to the control account but not to the receivables ledger.

5.10 A

	$
1 July float	150
Cash received from staff	25
Cheque cashed for employee	(90)
Cash received from company bank account	500
Expenses paid from petty cash	**(385)**
1st August float	200

5.11 B

Sales ledger control account

	$		$
Sales	250,000	Bank	225,000
Dishonoured cheque	3,500	Returns inwards	2,500
		Irrecoverable debts	3,000
		Contra	4,000
		Closing balance	19,000
	253,500		253,500

5.12 B

	$
Opening float	300
Window cleaning	(20)
Stationery	(100)
Coffee and biscuits	(145)
Photocopying receipts	20
Miscellaneous sales receipt	60
From bank	**260**
Closing float	375

5.13 D Sales tax received from customers is $30,000 (15% × $200,000). Purchases made $161,000 inclusive of sales tax (i.e. gross) ⇒ $161,000 × $^{15}/_{115}$ = $21,000 sales tax charged by suppliers. $9,000 balance is a liability (i.e. credit).

5.14 B

Sales tax a/c

	$		$
Balance b/f (recoverable)	2,000	Sales (600,000 × $^{20}/_{120}$)	100,000
Purchases (450,000 × 20%)	90,000		
Balance c/f	8,000		
	100,000		100,000
		Balance b/f	**8,000**

Tutorial note: *A business that is registered for sales tax collects it on behalf of the tax authorities. It will usually pay over the tax calculated on its sales less the tax it can recover on its purchases. Care must be taken in the calculations to distinguish between "gross" amounts (i.e. including tax) and "net" amounts (i.e. excluding tax). As a collector of sales tax the business does not incur a sales tax expense nor earn sales tax income. A recoverable amount is an asset (i.e. a debit balance).*

5.15 D (1) is a transposition error in the individual ledger, therefore the adjustment must be made in the receivables ledger. (2) is a cash sale, so should not have been posted to individual receivables ledger and needs to be removed.

Answer 6 MCQs JOURNAL ENTRIES

Item	*Answer*	*Justification*
6.1	C	Debits and credits are the wrong way around in A and B, and discount received is a credit entry.
6.2	B	Debits and credits are the wrong way around in A, C and D.
6.3	B	Debit and credit are the wrong way round in A and D. Shares are $0.50 so amount should be $200,000.
6.4	A	Goods take for own use are a reduction in purchases.
6.5	C	As some goods have been taken by the owner the purchases figure should be reduced (credited) which will increase profit. There is no effect on assets of liabilities (the debit entry is to drawings which is a reduction in capital).

Tutorial note: *Understand that closing inventory (an asset) is not affected because this is based on measurement of goods held at the reporting date. If goods have been taken they cannot be in closing inventory.*

6.6 A In the absence mentioning a drawings account capital should be debited, since drawings reduce the amount of the owner's interest in the business. The amount of the correcting entry would be $76,200 (i.e. 2 × $38,100).

Tutorial note: *The error is an error of principle; the amount that should have been debited against capital (a balance in the statement of financial position) was debited as an expense (in the statement of profit or loss). Therefore there is no possibility of balance arising on a suspense account.*

6.7 D Expenses are recorded net (excluding the sales tax) but the gross amount (including sales tax) is owed to the supplier and is shown in payables.

Tutorial note: *The sales tax is not an expense as it will be recovered from the tax authority (e.g. as a deduction against the amount of sales tax collected on sales).*

Answer 7 ROOK

		Dr	*Cr*
		$	$
(a)	Salaries account	2,000	
	Suspense account		2,000
	Correction of error – undercasting of debit side of salaries account.		
(b)	Motor vehicles	6,000	
	Irrecoverable debts	1,500	
	Wren accounts receivable ledger account		7,500
	Acceptance of car in settlement for trade debt, and writing off of balance.		
(c)	Factory buildings	46,100	
	Purchases		27,600
	Wages		18,500
	Materials and labour used in constructing extension to factory.		
(d)	Motor vehicles	18,000	
	Plant and equipment	33,000	
	Purchases	20,000	
	Crow loan account		71,000
	Purchase of sundry assets from Crow with delayed settlement.		

			Dr	*Cr*
			$	$
(e)	*(i)*	Motor vehicles cost	20,000	
		Car Dealer		20,000
		Purchase of car on credit.		
	(ii)	Disposal account	18,000	
		Motor vehicles cost		18,000
		Transfer of cost of car given in part exchange.		
	(iii)	Accumulated depreciation	6,000	
		Disposal account		6,000
		Transfer of depreciation of car given in part exchange.		
	(iv)	Car Dealer	12,000	
		Disposal account		12,000
		Agreed part-exchange value of car.		

Tutorial note: *These entries could validly be combined into a single compound journal entry as follows:*

	Dr	*Cr*
	$	$
Motor vehicles cost	20,000	
Car Dealer – account payable		8,000
Motor vehicles cost		18,000
Accumulated depreciation	6,000	
Purchase of new car with old car given up in part exchange.		

Answer 8 ADDAX

(a) Plant and equipment – cost

Plant and equipment – cost

20X6	$	20X6	$
1 April Balance	840,000	10 Dec Transfer disposal	100,000
		20X7	
1 Oct Cash	180,000	31 Mar Balance	920,000
	1,020,000		1,020,000

Plant and equipment – depreciation

20X6	$	20X6	$
10 Dec Transfer – disposal	60,000	1 April Balance	370,000
20X7		20X7	
31 Mar Balance	393,000	31 Mar Profit or loss (74,000 + 9,000)	83,000
	453,000		453,000

Plant and equipment – disposal

20X6	$	20X6	$
10 Dec Transfer – cost	100,000	10 Dec Transfer – depreciation	60,000
20X7			
31 Mar Profit or loss	5,000	Cash	45,000
	105,000		105,000

(b) Addax

Statement of cash flows for the year ended 31 March 20X7 (extracts)

	$
Cash flow from operating activities	
Profit before taxation	
Adjustments for:	
Depreciation	83,000
Profit on sale of plant	(5,000)
Cash flows from investing activities	
Purchase of plant	(180,000)
Proceeds of sale of plant	45,000

Answer 9 RIFFON

Tutorial note: *The question only required that balances and events be recorded. It was not therefore necessary to balance the accounts for full marks to be awarded. The ledger accounts are balanced here for completeness.*

(a) Ledger accounts – Office building

Cost/valuation

20X6	$	*20X6*	$
1 July Balance	1,600,000		
Revaluation	400,000	30 June Balance	2,000,000
	2,000,000		2,000,000

Accumulated depreciation

20X6	$	*20X6*	$
1 July Revaluation surplus	320,000	1 July Balance	320,000
20X7		*20X7*	
30 June Balance	50,000	30 June Profit or loss (W1)	50,000
	370,000		370,000

Revaluation surplus

20X6	$	*20X6*	$
		1 July Office building – cost	400,000
30 June Balance	720,000	Office building – depreciation	320,000
	720,000		720,000

(b) Ledger accounts – Plant and equipment

Cost

20X6	$		$
1 July Balance	840,000	*20X7*	
1 Oct Cash	200,000	1 April Transfer disposal	240,000
		30 June Balance	800,000
	1,040,000		1,040,000
20X7			
1 July Balance	800,000		

Plant and equipment – accumulated depreciation

	$		$
		20X6	
		1 July Balance	306,000
20X7		*20X7*	
1 April Transfer – disposal	180,000	30 June Profit or loss (W2)	200,000
30 June Balance	326,000		
	506,000		506,000

Plant and equipment – disposal

20X7	$	*20X7*	$
1 April Transfer – cost	240,000	1 April Transfer – depreciation	180,000
30 June Profit or loss	10,000	Cash	70,000
	250,000		250,000

WORKINGS

(1) Depreciation of office building

$2m ÷ 40 years (remaining useful life) = $50,000

(2) Depreciation of plant and equipment

25% × ($840,000 – $240,000 + $200,000) = $200,000

Answer 10 UNITED

		Dr $000	*Cr* $000
(1)	Revenue	180	
	Receivables control		180
	Memorandum individual receivables account		180
(2)	Memorandum individual receivables account	800	
(3)	Revenue	70	
	Receivables control		70
	Memorandum individual receivables account		70
(4)	Revenue	198	
	Receivables control		198
	Memorandum individual receivables account		198
(5)	Payables (creditors) control	600	
	Receivables control		600
	Memorandum individual payables account	600	
	Memorandum individual receivables account		600
(6)	Memorandum individual receivables account		160

Answer 11 SCIMITAR

Accounts receivable ledger control account

		$			$
1 Sept	Balance brought down	188,360	1 Sept	Balance brought down	2,140
30 Sept	Revenue		30 Sept	Sales returns	9,160
	(101,260 + 1,360)	102,620		Cash from customers	92,700
	Cash refunds	300		Irrecoverable debts w/off	460
	Extra cash refund	20		Contras	980
	Balance carried down				
	(2,680 + 680 – 40)	3,320		Balance carried down	189,180
		294,620			294,620

Accounts payable ledger control account

		$			$
1 Sept	Balance brought down	120	1 Sept	Balance brought down	89,410
30 Sept	Purchases returns	4,280	30 Sept	Purchases	
	Cash to suppliers	71,840		(68,420 - 1,360)	67,060
	Cash discounts	880			
	Contras	980			
	Balance carried down	78,460		Balance carried down	90
		156,560			156,560

Answer 12 OTTER

Accounts receivable ledger control account

	$		$
Opening balances	386,430	Opening balances	190
Sales (163,194 + 1,386 ①)	164,580	Cash received	160,448
Cash refund ②	350	Returns inwards	590
		Contra ③	870
		Irrecoverable debts written off ④	1,360
Closing balances (370 – 350 ②)	20	Closing balances	387,922
	551,380		551,380

Accounts payable ledger control account

	$		$
Opening balances	520	Opening balances	184,740
Cash paid	103,040	Purchases	
Discounts received	990	(98,192 + (1,395 – 1,359) ⑥)	98,228
Returns out (1,370 + 2,000 ⑤)	3,370	Cash refund correction ②	350
Contra ③	870	Irrecoverable debt written off	420
Closing balances	175,048	Closing balances	100
	283,838		283,838

Answer 13 ATANGA

(a) Receivables ledger control account balance

		+	–	
		$	$	
	Original balance	487,600		
(1)	Sales day book overcast		2,000	1
(2)	Irrecoverable debt written off		8,550	1
(4)	Contras incorrectly entered		32,200	1
(5)	Credit note adjustment	1,100		1
		488,700	42,750	
		42,750		
	Revised balance	445,950		4

(b) Receivables ledger balances

		+	–	
		$	$	
	Original balance	455,800		
(2)	Irrecoverable debt written off		8,550	1
(3)	Credit note incorrectly entered		2,400	1
(5)	Credit note adjustment	1,100		1
		456,900	10,950	
		10,950		
	Revised balance	445,950		4

Answer 14 MCQs BANK RECONCILIATIONS

Item	*Answer*	*Justification*
14.1	D	The cash book position needs only to be adjusted for items (3) and (5).
14.2	C	Not (2) as timing differences do not require correction. Not (3) as it is the cash book that must be adjusted. (1) is correct as a dishonoured cheque must be written back, as worthless. (4) is correct as outstanding lodgements will increase cash in the bank/decrease an overdraft.
14.3	A	39,800 + 44,200 – 64,100 = $19,900 overdrawn
14.4	C	

Balance per bank statement	(38,600)
(1) Bank charges omitted	200
(2) Outstanding lodgements	14,700
(3) Unpresented cheques	(27,800)
(4) Payment recorded as receipt (2 × 4,200)	8,400
Per cash book	(43,100)

14.5	B	38,640 + 14,260 – 19,270 = $33,630

14.6 D

	$
Uncorrected cash book balance	42,510
Dishonoured cheque	(2,470)
Corrected cash book balance	40,040
Unpresented cheques	2,990
Outstanding lodgements	(10,270)
Bank statement balance	32,760

14.7 B

	$
Per bank statement	(825)
Unpresented cheques	(475)
Incorrect direct debit	160
Deposits not credited	600
Per statement of financial position	(540)

14.8 D (2) will require correction only by the bank. (3) and (4) are timing differences.

14.9 A

	$
Adjusted cash book balance per bank reconciliation	1,060
Outstanding lodgements	(5,000)
Unpresented cheques	2,800
Balance overdrawn at the bank	(1,140)

In the books of the bank and on the bank statement, an overdraft will appear as a **debit** balance.

Tutorial note: *To correctly answer this type of question, it is necessary to start with the adjusted cash book balance and reconcile it to the bank statement. Unfortunately, there are no shortcuts. It is therefore advisable to work an answer without reference to the options available. The cash book balance per the bank reconciliation ($1,060 debit) has already taken account of the bank charges ($125).*

Answer 15 GEORGE

(a) Adjusted cash book

George – cash book

	$		$
Balance	4,890	Bank charges (3)	320
Correction of error		Plant (4)	10,000
– interest (8)	320	Cheque dishonored (5)	980
		Correction of error in	
		entering cheque (6)	4,800
Balance	11,890	Error in addition (7)	1,000
	17,100		17,100

Tutorial note: *Although the dishonored cheque was returned by the bank after 31 March the funds were never available to George, so it should be adjusted in the cash book.*

(b) Bank reconciliation

	$
Balance per bank statement (overdrawn)	(12,800)
Less: Lodgements not credited (2)	2,890
	(9,910)
Add: Dishonoured cheque	(980)
Add: Outstanding cheque (1)	(1,000)
Balance per cash book – overdrawn	(11,890)

(c) Statement of effect on profit

	+	–
	$	$
Profit per draft accounts	81,208	
Bank charges (3)		320
Depreciation (4)		1,000
Irrecoverable debt (5)		980
Motor expenses (6)		2,400
Additional depreciation (6)		600
Purchases understated (7)		1,000
Interest adjustment (8)	320	
Repairs to premises (9)	870	
	82,398	6,300
	6,300	
Adjusted profit	76,098	

Answer 16 MCQs SUSPENSE ACCOUNTS

Item *Answer* *Justification*

16.1 D The excess is $7,182 debits over credits. Goods returned outwards should have been a $3,591 credit balance.

Tutorial note: *Discounts allowed should be debited to revenue but as there is no error in principle it does not give rise to a difference in the trial balance.*

16.2 B (1) has been correctly debited but to the wrong account (should be debited to revenue). (2) should have been credited. Omission on extraction (3) gives rise to a difference. (4) debit and credit are the wrong way around but the double-entry has been maintained.

16.3 A Suspense a/c (difference) = 398,580 – 384,030 = 14,550 excess credit
Would be cleared by:
Dr Cash 10,000
Dr Rent expense 4,550 (6,160 – 1,610)

16.4 D Although the amount in (1) is incorrect it does not create a difference on the extraction of a trial balance. Since (2) is an omission it does not create a difference. The arithmetic error in (4) results in a difference.

16.5 C 630,000 – 4,320 – 440 = $625,240

16.6 C (1) Discount received should have been credited to a profit or loss account and debited to payables. Since both sides of the entry were debits, the debit side of the trial balance would exceed the credit side and a suspense account with a credit balance would be opened. (2) Goods returned by a customer should have been debited to sales and credited to receivables. As they were debited to receivables the same situation arises, and a suspense account with a credit balance would be opened.

16.7 C A single journal to correct all these errors would be:

	$	$
Cr Receivables (90 + (2 × 33))		156
Dr Sales	110	
Dr Suspense (9,980 – 9,890) + (2 × 33) – 110	46	
	156	156

Tutorial note: *This question is not asking for the balance on the suspense account, but for the adjustment made to the suspense account by the correcting journal. The discount taken should have been credited to the customer's account (not debited and debited to revenue.*

16.8 C The difference in the amount at which the purchase of stamps was recorded is $120 – $12 = $108. As only $12 was recorded expenses have clearly been understated. Petty cash should have been topped up with ($36 + $60 + $120) = $216, so the $108 top-up is $216 – $108 = $108 too little.

16.9 A If the debit side of the trial balance is undercast by $692 this shortfall is a debit in the suspense account. When the payment of $905 was credited to cash it should have been debited to an expense account; so this too is a debit in the suspense account. Thus the suspense account has a debit balance of $692 + $905 = $1,597

16.10 C As a purchase ledger control account is maintained in the general ledger *totals* of purchases and payments (also refunds and contra entries) will be posted to this account. The individual items that make up the totals (e.g. all the different types of expenses) will be posted to relevant revenue and capital expense accounts. A transposition error in a total or the omission of a total will cause the trial balance not to balance. However, an error of principle (i.e. recording an item as revenue expense rather than capital expense, or vice versa) will affect only the individual accounts and not give rise to a difference.

16.11 B To correct the error of commission:

Dr Suspense account	$1,400	
Cr Receivables control (2 × $700)		$1,400

Suspense account

	$		$
		Balance b/f	560
Receivables control a/c	1,400	Balance c/f	840
	1,400		1,400
Balance (remaining) b/f	**840**		

Answer 17 ANDROMEDA

Suspense account

20X6		$	*20X6*		$
31 Dec	Jason loan account	40,000	31 Dec	Difference	42,130
31 Dec	Discounts received	2,130			
		42,130			42,130

		$	$
(1)	Suspense account	40,000	
	Jason loan account		40,000
	Correction of error – entry on wrong side of loan account		
(2)	Motor expenses	28,600	
	Motor vehicles asset account	28,600	
	Supplier account		57,200
	Correction of error in recording purchase of motor vehicle on credit.		
(3)	Irrecoverable debts recovered	800	
	A Smith accounts receivable ledger account		800
	Correction of mis-posting of cheque from A Smith, wrongly credited to irrecoverable debts recovered.		
(4)	Bank charges	380	
	Cash book		380
	Recording of bank charges not entered in cash book.		
(5)	Suspense account	2,130	
	Discount received		2,130
	Correction for December discount total not posted		
(6)	Plant	16,000	
	Plant repairs		16,000
	Depreciation expense	3,200	
	Allowance for depreciation		3,200
	Correction of error in posting cash paid for purchase of plant and insertion of necessary depreciation.		

Tutorial note: *The question states that control accounts are not maintained. You should appreciate that if control accounts had been maintained the error in (2), for example, would have been detected by the reconciliation of the payables ledger control account (and so corrected before the extraction of the list of balances).*

Answer 18 ARBADOS

	Debit	*Credit*
	$	$
Repairs to premises	8,700	
Premises asset		7,800
Suspense		900

Correction of error in posting cost of repairs to premises.

Suspense account	1,000	
Motor vehicle disposal		1,000

Entry for un-posted item.

Accumulated depreciation	6,000	
Depreciation expense		6,000

Reversal of depreciation charged in error for year of disposal.

Motor vehicle disposal (carrying amount)	24,000	
Motor vehicles – cost		30,000
Motor vehicle disposal		6,000

Transfer cost and depreciation of vehicle (i.e. carrying amount) to disposal account.

Profit or loss	23,000	
Motor vehicle disposal		23,000

Loss on destruction of car transferred.

Answer 19 LORCA

(a) Journal entries

		Dr	*Cr*	
		$	$	
(1)	Sales	70,000		
	Share capital		50,000	
	Share premium		20,000	1½
(2)	Suspense	16,000		
	Interest payable		8,000	
	Interest receivable		8,000	1½
(3)	Sales	16,000		
	Purchases	16,000		
	Suspense		32,000	3

	OR			
	Suspense	*48,000*		
	Sales		*48,000*	
	Purchases	*64,000*		
	Suspense		*64,000*	
	Sales	*64,000*		
	Suspense		*64,000*	
	Suspense	*48,000*		
	Purchases		*48,000*	
(4)	Suspense	36,000		
	Rent		36,000	1
				7

(b) Adjustment to profit

		–	+	
		$	$	
Profit per draft accounts			830,000	
Adjustments				
(1)	Sales	70,000		1
(2)	Interest		16,000	1
(3)	Sales/Purchases	32,000		1
(4)	Rent		36,000	1
		102,000	882,000	4
			102,000	
Revised profit			780,000	11

Answer 20 PRIDE

(a) Adjustment to profit statement

	$000	$000	$000
	–	+	
Profit per draft accounts			80
Profit on disposal (11 – 6)		5	
Depreciation			
– buildings (2% × 200)	4		
– plant (20% × ((318 – 18) – (88 – 12))	60		
Accruals and prepayments	4	8	
Increase in receivables allowance	2		
	70	13	57
Adjusted profit			23

(b) Statement of financial position as at 31 March 20X7

	$000	$000	$000
Assets			
Non-current assets			
Land	210		210
Buildings (120 + 4 (per (a))	200	124	76
Plant and equipment (318 – 18)/ (88 – 12 + 60 (per (a))	300	136	164
	710	260	450
Current assets			
Inventory		180	
Receivables (146 – 12)		134	
Prepayments		8	
Cash		50	372
Total assets			822
Equity and liabilities			
Equity shares ($0.50)		350	
Share premium account		240	
Retained earnings (11 b/fwd + 23 per (a))		34	
			624
Non-current liabilities 10% Loan notes (20Y1)			100
Current liabilities			
Payables		94	
Accrued expenses		4	98
Total equity and liabilities			822

Answer 21 CHOCTAW

		$	$
(1)	Profit or loss	8,000	
	Accumulated depreciation of motor vehicles		8,000
	Adjustment to depreciation from reducing balance basis to straight-line basis		
(2)	Petty cash	1,200	
	Rent receivable		1,200
	Rent received omitted from records		
(3)	Irrecoverable debts	8,400	
	Sundry receivables ledger accounts		8,400
	Irrecoverable debts written off		
(4)	Suspense account	3,310	
	Motor vehicle repairs		3,310
	Correction of error – opening balance not brought forward		

Profit adjustments

		$
Profit per draft financial statements		86,400
(a)	Depreciation adjustment	(8,000)
(b)	Rent receivable not recorded	1,200
(c)	Irrecoverable debts written off	(8,400)
(d)	Motor repairs adjustment	3,310
Adjusted profit		74,510

Answer 22 RAMPION

(a) Adjustment to profit statement

		$	
Profit per draft financial statements		684,000	
(1)	Inventory movement Adjustment for sales ($36,000 × 60%)	21,600	1
(2)	Duplicated sale Elimination of profit	(4,000)	1
(3)	Reduction in inventory: ($18,000 – ($13,500 – $500))	(5,000)	1
(4)	Debts written off	(8,000)	1
(5)	Increase in allowance for receivables ($11,500 – $10,000)	(1,500)	1
Revised profit		687,100	

(b) Effect on inventory and receivables

(i) Inventory

		$	
Inventories per draft financial statements		116,800	
(1)	Inventory movement – as (a) above	21,600	1
(2)	Duplicated sale cost of inventory returned	6,000	1
(3)	Reduction in inventory (a) above	(5,000)	1
	Revised closing inventory	139,400	

(ii) Receivables

		$	
Per draft financial statements		248,000	
(2)	Deduction for duplicated sale	(10,000)	1
(4)	Debts written off	(8,000)	1
		230,000	
(5)	*Less:* Loss allowance for receivables	(11,500)	1
		218,500	
			11

Answer 23 MCQs INCOMPLETE RECORDS

Item *Answer* *Justification*

23.1 C

Receivables ledger total account

Opening	130,000	Cash received	687,800
		Irrecoverable debts	4,160
Sales (Balancing figure)	**744,960**	Contra	2,000
		Closing	181,000
	874,960		874,960

23.2 D

Payables ledger total account

Cash paid	302,800	Opening	60,000
Discounts received	2,960		
Contra	2,000	Purchases (Balancing figure)	**331,760**
Closing	84,000		
	391,760		391,760

23.3 A $281{,}250 \times \frac{50}{150} - 53{,}050 = \$40{,}700$

23.4 B $38{,}000 + 637{,}000 - 45{,}000 = 630{,}000 \times {}^{10}/_{7} = \$900{,}000$

23.5 B Using the balance sheet equation: Profit = Change in net assets – capital introduced + drawings i.e. (400,000 – 210,000) – 100,000 + 48,000 = $138,000

23.6 B An overstatement in opening inventory will increase cost of goods sold (and reduce gross profit).

23.7 D Using the balance sheet equation: Profit = Change in net assets – capital introduced + drawings i.e. (274,000 – 186,000) – 50,000 + (68,000 + 20,000) = $126,000

23.8 B The amount of the overstatement in closing inventory (A) will reduce cost of sales in the current period, hence gross profit would increase. (B) will charge to profit costs that relate to the next period. (Note that the goods are not in inventory at the period end, hence cost of sales is overstated.) (C) would inflate sales and hence increase profit. (D) would cause the gross profit percentage to increase, as costs would be lower.

23.9 C

	$	%
Cost of sales:		
Opening inventory	138,600	
Add: Purchases	**716,100**	
Less: Closing inventory	(149,100)	
	705,600	70
Sales	1,008,000	100
Gross profit	302,400	30

23.10 B $77{,}000 + 763{,}000 - 945{,}000 \times {}^{100}/_{125} = \$84{,}000$

23.11 D

	$
Revenue (net of sales tax)	89,400
Purchases (69,600 × $^{100}/_{120}$)	(58,000)
Gross profit	31,400

23.12 A Cost of sales includes carriage inwards (a cost incurred in bringing inventories to their present location) but excludes carriage outwards (a distribution cost). Closing inventories should be deducted in arriving at cost of sales.

	$
Purchases	455,000
Carriage inwards	24,000
Closing inventories	(52,000)
Cost of sales	427,000

23.13 B

Using the accounting equation:	$
Closing net assets (1,726 + 2,387)	4,113
Drawings	15,000
Opening net assets	(5,000)
Profit	14,113

23.14 B

	$
Opening net assets	40,000
Profit	117,000
Capital injection	30,000
Drawings ($3,200 × 12)	(38,400)
Inventory withdrawn ($7,200 × $^{100}/_{160}$)	(4,500)
Closing net assets	144,100

23.15 C

	$
Banked	50,000
Wages paid from cash	12,000
Drawings	24,000
Increase in cash balance	100
Cash proceeds on disposal of car	(5,000)
Sales	81,100

23.16 B In accordance with the accounting equation

23.17 D Using the accounting equation: Opening capital* + Profit (or – Loss) – Drawings* = Closing capital = Opening capital for next period

$12,500 – $7,900 (W) – $4,100 = $500

* Are given in the list of balances so it is profit/(loss) needs to be calculated.

WORKING

	$
Revenue	22,000
Cost of sales **	(19,200)
Rent	(5,400)
Bank interest	(825)
Heat and light	(4,475)
Loss for the year	(7,900)

** Since the business does not hold inventory cost of sales = purchases.

23.18 B

As all the transactions are cash, one approach is to produce a petty cash book "T" account to derive the cash takings (sales) as the balancing amount:

Petty cash book

	$		$
Float b/f	50	Payment to suppliers	340
Cash takings (sales)	**1,160**	Wages	150
		Rent	70
		Paid into bank	600
		Float c/f	50
	1,210		1,210
Float b/f	50		

Answer 24 LAMORGAN

(a)

Sales revenue total account

	$		$
Opening receivables	41,600	Cash received from customers	218,500
Refunds to customers	800	Irrecoverable debts written off	1,500
Sales	225,100	Contra purchases	700
		Closing receivables	44,200
	267,500		267,500

	$
Credit sales as above	225,100
Cash sales $114,700 + $9,600	124,300
	349,400

(b)

Purchases total account

	$		$
Payments to suppliers	114,400	Opening payables	22,900
Contra sales	700	Lamorgan – goods taken	400
Closing payables	24,800	Purchases	116,600
	139,900		139,900

(c) Inventory

	$
Per inventory count	77,700
Damaged item: ($1,700 – $300 – $100)	1,300
Goods on approval	3,000
	82,000

Answer 25 ALTESE, SENJI & ALUKI

(a) Altese

	$
Opening capital	128,000
Capital introduced	50,000
	178,000
Less: Drawings	48,000
	130,000
Closing capital	184,000
Profit is therefore	54,000

(b) Senji

Purchases total account

	$		$
		Balance brought forward	130,400
Payments to suppliers	888,400	Goods taken by Senji	1,000
Discounts received	11,200	Refunds from suppliers	2,400
		Purchases	937,050
Balance carried forward	171,250		
	1,070,850		1,070,850

(c) Aluki

	$	$
Cost of sales:		
Opening inventory		243,000
Purchases	595,400	
Less: Returns	41,200	554,200
		797,200
Less: Closing inventory		261,700
		535,500

Sales figure is therefore $535,500 × $^3/_2$ = $803,250

Answer 26 HASTA

(a) Statement of profit or loss for the year ended 31 December 20X6

		$	$	
Sales ($191,400 – $4,800 + $6,400)			193,000	1
Less:	Cost of sales			
	Opening inventory	85,000		½
	Purchases (balancing figure)	104,500		method 1
		189,500		
Less:	Closing inventory	88,500		½
			101,000	
Gross profit (W)			92,000	2
Less:	Expenses			
	Wages	15,600		½
	Sundry expenses (8,300 – 1,100 + 1,400)	8,600		1½
	Loss on sale of equipment (1,200 – 700)	500		1
	Depreciation (2,000 × 20%)	400		1
			25,100	
Profit for the year			66,900	9

WORKING

	$	$	
Sales		193,000	
Gross profit			
½(193,000 – $21,000)	86,000		1
$21,000 – (½ × $30,000)	6,000		1
		92,000	
Cost of goods sold is therefore		101,000	

Alternative calculation of gross profit:

	$	
Sales	*193,000*	
Add: Trade discount	*9,000*	
	202,000	½
Gross profit if all sales at full price	*101,000*	*1*
Less: Trade discount	*9,000*	½
	92,000	

(b) Drawings

Cash not accounted for:		
($192,200 – $15,600 – $8,300 – $2,000 – $150)	166,150	1
Less: Purchases	104,500	as per (a) 1
Drawings	61,650	2

Answer 27 MCQs REGULATORY FRAMEWORK

Item	*Answer*	*Justification*
27.1	C	By definition. Shareholders and government are users of the financial statements but they are not the only ones (e.g. directors, employees, banks will also use them). The general public encompasses users, but a substantial majority of the general public will not be users of financial statements.
27.2	A	The International Accounting Standards Board (IASB) is the sole body having responsibility and authority to issue IFRS and is overseen by the IFRS Foundation. IFRS IC and the IFRS Advisory Board are separate bodies within the IFRS Foundation framework.
27.3	B	This is stated in the IASB's objectives ("to develop, in the public interest, ..."). Whilst only certain elements of the public may be users of the financial statements, the members of the public as a whole are affected by the activities of companies and users of financial statements. Financial information that is relevant and faithfully represents what it purports to represent underpins the economies of all jurisdictions.
27.4	D	The IFRS Advisory Council is supervised by the IFRS Foundation. (The IASB and the IFRS IC are also supervised by the Foundation.)
27.5	D	IFRSs are not issued to clarify users' issues concerning application of an IFRS. (This is the purpose of an IFRIC.)
27.6	B	This is the function of the IFRS Interpretations Committee.
27.7	D	Financial accounts are audited externally whereas management accounts are unaudited.
27.8	B	It is the IASB that is committed to developing, in the public interest, a single set of high-quality, understandable and enforceable global accounting standards (IFRSs) that require transparent and comparable information in general purpose financial statements. **Tutorial note:** *The IFRS Foundation is the independent body that oversees the IASB.*

Answer 28 IASB

(a) Objectives

- To formulate and publish in the public interest accounting standards to be observed in the presentation of financial statements and to promote their world-wide acceptance and observance.
- To promote the use and rigorous application of those standards.
- To work actively with national standard-setters to achieve convergence of national accounting standards and IFRS to provide high quality solutions.

(b) Conceptual Framework for Financial Reporting

The primary purposes of the Framework are to assist the IASB:

- in developing IFRSs and reviewing existing ones; and
- in harmonising regulations and accounting standards by providing a basis for reducing alternative treatments.

Other purposes are:

- To assist national standard setting bodies in developing national standards.
- To assist prepares of financial statements in applying IFRSs and in dealing with topics not yet covered by IFRSs.
- To assist auditors in forming an opinion as to whether financial statements comply with IFRSs.
- To assist users of financial statements in interpreting financial statements.
- To give those interested in the work of the IASB information about its approach to the formulation of IFRSs.

Answer 29 MCQs QUALITATIVE CHARACTERISTICS AND ACCOUNTING CONCEPTS

Item	*Answer*	*Justification*
29.1	C	Relevant financial information is capable of making a difference in decisions and has a predictive value, confirmatory value or both. A describes qualitative characteristics (which include not only relevance). B describes neutrality which is an aspect of faithful representation. D is also an aspect of faithful representation.
29.2	B	(1) is incorrect as concept is economic substance *over* legal form. Information should not be excluded merely on the grounds of difficulty (3).
29.3	B	Under prudence a liability is measured at a best estimate, not the highest possible amount.
29.4	C	Historical cost is not the only convention that requires money measurement (e.g. a revaluation model requires money measurement also). The exercise of prudence concept does not permit overstatement of liabilities/understatement of liabilities.
29.5	A	The overdraft liability will decrease and receivables will decrease by an equal amount.
29.6	B	Inventory should be recognised as an asset on the date it is delivered into the warehouse and the invoice accrued.
29.7	C	Management, as agents of the company, have a duty to safeguard all the company's assets entrusted to them (not only cash). (Accountability encompasses recording, controlling and safeguarding them).
29.8	A	*The Conceptual Framework for Financial Reporting*
29.9	D	Information must possess all three characteristics (neutrality, completeness and accurate) to faithfully represent what it is held out to represent *(Conceptual Framework for Financial Reporting*).

29.10 D Recognition means incorporating in the financial statements items that meet definitions and satisfy criteria. Disclosure means inclusion notes, etc, not in the financial statements – so not A. Faithful presentation is a qualitative characteristic, not a process – so not B. Measurement is determining the monetary amount only, not its depiction – so not C.

29.11 D This is based on the *Conceptual Frameworks* definition of asset, liabilities, income and expenses.

29.12 A Depreciation matches the cost of a non-current asset over its useful life against the profits that it generates.

29.13 B A profit on sale has been made and therefore assets will increase; the profit will also increase reserves. The sale has no effect on liabilities.

29.14 D The accrued expense will increase liabilities and therefore decrease net assets.

29.15 D Overstatement of depreciation will require assets to be increased with a corresponding increase in equity (as profit is increased by the reduction in depreciation expense). Liabilities are not affected.

29.16 D Statement (1) describes the going concern concept. Statement (2) is false as many non-current assets can be valued at fair value.

29.17 D The quote relates to the definition of equity according to the *Conceptual Framework.*

29.18 B The IASB's *Conceptual Framework for Financial Reporting* was amended in 2010 and the IASB is looking to update it again in the future. It is not a standard.

29.19 D This is the definition of an asset according to the *Conceptual Framework.*

Answer 30 FOUR CONCEPTS

(a) Business entity concept

In accounting, it is necessary to define the boundaries of the entity concerned. In the case of a limited liability company, only transactions of that company must be included. There must be no confusion between the transactions of the company and the transactions of its owners and managers.

If the entity concept is not followed, the profit, financial position and cash flow may all be distorted to the point where they become meaningless.

A limited liability company is therefore a separate entity which can sue and be sued in its own name.

(b) Going concern concept

The going concern is that financial statements are prepared on the basis that the entity will continue for the foreseeable future – that there is no intention or necessity to liquidate or curtail the scale of operations.

If the going concern concept is followed when it is not appropriate, assets may be overstated, liabilities may continue to be shown as non-current when the collapse of the going concern status of the entity renders them current liabilities, and the profit is likely to be overstated.

(c) Materiality

Information is material if its omission from, or misstatement in, the financial statements could influence the economic decisions of users. Materiality cannot always be measured in monetary or percentage terms, but a commonly used measure is 5% of normal pre-tax profit. Above that level, for example, an exceptional item would need to be disclosed by note or in the statement of profit or loss.

Materiality is not solely related to the size of a transaction; it would also be necessary to consider the nature of the transaction and the fact that the nature would give rise to an item being treated as material and require disclosure.

If the materiality concept is not followed, financial statements could become confused by the inclusion of unnecessary detail of trivial matters, or could be rendered misleading by the exclusion of reference to important matters.

(d) Fair presentation

Fair presentation really means that all figures in financial statements have been arrived at accurately when accuracy is possible (true) and that when judgement or estimation is needed it has been exercised without bias (fair). Compliance with generally accepted concepts and principles will normally result in fair presentation.

Failure to present information fairly will obviously mean that users may be misled by the financial statements.

Answer 31 MATERIALITY

(a) Materiality

Information is material if its omission or misstatement could influence the economic decisions of users taken on the basis of the financial statements.

Factors affecting materiality are:

- The size of the item;
- The nature of the item.

(b) What makes information relevant to users?

To be useful, information must be relevant to the decision-making needs of users. Information is relevant when it influences the economic decisions of users by helping them evaluate past, present or future events or confirming, or correcting their past evaluations.

(c) Neutrality and completeness

(i) Meaning of terms

- Neutrality means that the information in financial statements should be free from deliberate or systematic bias.
- Completeness means that, within bounds of materiality and cost, nothing has been omitted that could cause information to be false or misleading (and therefore unreliable).

Possible conflict

- Information will not be *relevant* if there is undue delay in preparing it. There is therefore a trade-off between the need for *timely* reporting and providing relevant information.
- *Timely* information may be less *accurate* or *complete*. So there is a trade-off between the need for timely reporting and providing complete and accurate information.

Tutorial note: *Only one example is required. Cost/benefit could also be mentioned.*

(d) Safeguards to ensure that a company's financial statements are free from material error

- The audit of financial statements by an independent professional.
- The existence of sound internal controls in the company.
- The existence of an internal audit function in the company.

Answer 32 COMPARABILITY

(a) Meaning and types

Comparability means that users are able to draw conclusions about the performance or financial position of a business by relating figures for a particular period to other relevant figures.

Possible types of comparison are with:

- figures for the same business for earlier periods;
- figures for other businesses for the same period;
- budgets or forecasts.

Tutorial note: *Two types only required for full marks.*

(b) Aid to comparability

The IASB's *Conceptual Framework* and the requirements of accounting standards aid comparability by:

- requiring the disclosure of accounting policies (IAS 1 *Presentation of Financial Statements)*;
- reducing or eliminating the number of possible alternative treatments for similar items available to businesses;
- requiring businesses to treat similar items in the same way within each period and from one period to the next (unless a change is required to comply with accounting standards or to ensure that a more appropriate presentation of events or transactions is provided).

Answer 33 MCQs IAS 1

Item	*Answer*	*Justification*
33.1	A	(2) would be in profit or loss (an expense) and (4) may only be disclosed. A transfer to retained earnings (e.g. for excess depreciation on a revalued asset) will be shown as a movement in the statement of changes in equity. Only dividends paid during the year and declared before the year end (i.e. a liability) are movements in equity.
33.2	D	
33.3	C	Dividends merely proposed are not an appropriation and merely disclosed (not accounted for).
33.4	D	Dividends paid are recognised in the statement of changes in equity.
33.5	D	Declaration of the dividend after the end of the reporting period but before the financial statements are approved (a non-adjusting event) is disclosed in the notes. As distributions, dividends are presented in the statement of changes in equity. **Tutorial note:** *The dividend is not a liability at either year end (so (1) and (3) are incorrect. A dividend is not an expense (so (2) is also incorrect).*
33.6	A	According to IAS 1 going concern relates to whether the entity will continue in operational existence without liquidating or ceasing trading.
33.7	D	**Tutorial note:** *A is clearly incorrect since inventory will only be valued at net realisable value if this is lower than cost (IAS 2). B is clearly incorrect since such a valuation basis will only be appropriate when an entity is not a going concern. When the going concern basis is not appropriate financial statements must be prepared on an alternative basis to comply with IFRS; so C is also incorrect.*
33.8	B	

Income tax account

	$		$
Cash	1,762	Balance b/fwd	2,091
Balance c/fwd	2,584	Profit or loss (balancing figure)	2,255
	4,346		4,346

33.9	D	As the loan is being repaid in six-monthly instalments some of the liability will be current and some will be non-current.
33.10	B	Dividends paid is a movement in retained earnings (in the statement of changes in equity). Interest (a finance cost), depreciation and income tax are items of expense.
33.11	D	The accruals principle requires the company to recognise the cost in the period in which it was incurred. Therefore, expenses increases (reducing profits) and the liability to pay the fees will be included in the statement of financial position (reducing net assets).
33.12	C	Under the terms of the loan, two repayments (total $16,000) fall due within the next 12 months (i.e. current liability), with the balance ($64,000) being due for repayment after more than one year.

33.13 A The increase in value of a non-current asset is not included in profit or loss but in other comprehensive as it is unrealised (until the asset is sold). All other items are recognised in profit or loss.

33.14 B As the error has been corrected (closing inventory is correct), both retained profit and net assets are correct as stated in the draft statement of financial position.

Tutorial note: *Correction of the error would reduce the retained profit brought forward at the beginning of the current year (and therefore the prior year net assets) and increase the profit for the current year. These adjustments cancel each other out.*

33.15 C The interest charge is an expense in profit or loss and the revaluation gain is a gain recognised in other comprehensive income. Profit or loss and other comprehensive income make up total comprehensive income.

33.16 D

	$
Profit from the statement of profit or loss	575,000
Unrealised gain on the land revaluation	40,000
Total comprehensive income	615,000

Tutorial note: *This question tests understanding of the difference between (1) the statement of profit or loss and (2) the statement of comprehensive income. (1) summarises the revenues earned and expenses incurred during the financial period. (2) is an extension of (1); "other comprehensive income" includes unrealised gains (e.g. on the revaluation of tangible assets). As a distribution of profit, equity dividends are recognised in the statement of changes in equity.*

Answer 34 ARBALEST

(a) Statement of changes in equity

	Share capital	*Share premium*	*Revaluation surplus*	*Retained earnings*	*Total*
	$000	$000	$000	$000	$000
At 1 October 20X5	1,500	400		4,060	5,960
Rights issue	500	1,000			1,500
Bonus issue	2,000	(1,400)		(600)	–
Total comprehensive income for the year			500	370	870
At 30 September 20X6	4,000	Nil	500	3,830	8,330

(b) Movements on non-current assets

	Land	*Building*	*Plant and equipment*	*Total*
	$000	$000	$000	$000
Cost				
At 1 October 20X5	2,000	1,500	2,800	6,300
Additions	600	2,400	1,600	4,600
Disposals			(1,000)	(1,000)
Revaluation	500			500
At 30 September 20X6	3,100	3,900	3,400	10,400
Depreciation				
At 1 October 20X5	Nil	450	1,000	1,450
Charge for the year	Nil	46	220	266
Disposals			(800)	(800)
At September 20X6	Nil	496	420	916
Carrying amount				
At 30 September 20X6	3,100	3,404	2,980	9,484

Calculation of depreciation charges

		$000
Buildings	2% × $1,500,000	30
	2% × $2,400,000 × $^4/_{12}$	16
		46
Plant and equipment	10% × $1,800,000	180
	10% × $1,600,000 × $^3/_{12}$	40
		220

Answer 35 PERSEUS

Current assets in the statement of financial position

	$
Inventory (W1)	4,249,800
Trade receivables (W2)	2,674,300
Prepayments	773,400
Cash at bank (Bank A only)	940,000

WORKINGS

(1) Inventory

		$	$
As originally stated			4,190,000
(i)	Reduction to net realisable value		
	Original cost	16,000	
	Net realisable value (10,400 – 600)	9,800	
			(6,200)
(ii)	Goods returned at cost		66,000
			4,249,800

(2) Trade receivables

As originally stated		
	Accounts receivable ledger	2,980,000
Less:	Goods returned	88,000
		2,892,000
Less:	Debts written off	92,000
		2,800,000
Less: Allowance (5% × $2,800,000)		140,000
		2,660,000
Accounts payable ledger balances		14,300
		2,674,300

Tutorial notes: *The delivery of goods to the wrong customer is not a sale in the current year. Revenue (and profit) can only be recognised in the following year, when the goods are transferred to the correct customer.*

Strictly speaking, where debit balances on accounts payable represent an asset (e.g. advance payments) they should be reclassified as trade receivables (as above) or prepayments. However, in practice (especially when such balances are immaterial) they would most likely be "netted off" against the credit balances. The same is true of credit balances on accounts receivable. Note that an overdraft, even with the same bank, can only be offset against cash at bank if there is a legal right to offset the liability against the asset.

(3) Prepayments

		$	$
As originally stated			770,000
Payments on account		25,000	
Less:	Commission due ($^{2}/_{102}$ × $1,101,600)	21,600	
			3,400
			773,400

Answer 36 CRONOS

(a) Statement of profit or loss for the year ended 30 September 20X6

	$
Sales	3,210,000
Cost of sales (W)	(1,823,100)
Gross profit	1,386,900
Distribution costs (W)	(188,500)
Administrative expenses (W)	(944,680)
Interest payable (30,000 + 30,000)	(60,000)
Profit for the year	193,720

WORKING

		Cost of sales	*Distribution costs*	*Administrative expenses*
		$	$	$
Opening inventory		186,400		
Purchases		1,748,200		
Carriage inwards		38,100		
Carriage outwards (47,250 + 1,250)			48,500	
Wages and salaries	694,200			
	5,800			
	700,000	70,000	140,000	490,000
Sundry administrative expenses (381,000 + 13,600 – 4,900)				389,700
Irrecoverable debts (14,680 + 8,000 – 2,700)				19,980
Depreciation of office equipment 20% × (214,000 – 40,000 + 48,000)				44,400
Loss on sale				600
Closing inventory		(219,600)		
		1,823,100	188,500	944,680

(b) Items appearing in profit or loss

B, C and F. Revenue, finance costs and income from associate must be presented in the statement of profit or loss.

Tutorial note: *Cost of sales and gross profit may be presented in the statement of profit or loss or disclosed in the notes. Dividends paid are a distribution of profit and therefore shown in the statement of changes in equity (not in the statement of profit or loss).*

Answer 37 ABRADOR

(a) Statement of financial position as at 31 December 20X6

	$000	$000
Assets		
Non-current assets		
Property, plant and equipment (W1)	3,000	
Development costs	570	3,570
Current assets		
Inventory	3,900	
Receivables (W2)	2,910	6,810
		10,380
Equity and liabilities		
Share capital		1,500
Share premium account		700
Retained earnings (W3)		5,780
		7,980
Current liabilities		
Trade payables	1,900	
Bank overdraft	100	
6% Loan notes	400	2,400
		10,380

WORKINGS

(1) Property, plant and equipment

	$000
Cost per list of balances	5,000
Less: Depreciation at 31 December 20X5	1,000
	4,000
Less: 25% × 4,000,000	1,000
	3,000

(2) Receivables

Per list of balances	3,400
Less: Written off	400
	3,000
Less: Allowance	90
	2,910

(3) Retained earnings

Per list of balances		7,170
Less: Depreciation	1,000	
Irrecoverable debts	400	
Allowance for trade receivables	(10)	1,390
		5,780

(b) IAS 38 disclosure

Movements on deferred development expenditure during year

	$000
Balance at 31 December 20X5	550
Expenditure in 20X6	120
	670
Amortisation for year	(100)
Balance at 31 December 20X6	570

Total expenditure on research and development charged to profit or loss

	$000
Current expenditure	85
Amortisation	100
	185

Answer 38 MINICA

(a) Statement of profit or loss for the year ended 31 December 20X6

		$	$
Revenue (3,845,000 – 15,000)			3,830,000
less:	Cost of sales		
	Opening inventory	360,000	
	Purchases (2,184,000 – 60,000)	2,124,000	
	Carriage inwards	119,000	
		2,603,000	
Less:	Closing inventory	450,000	2,153,000
Gross profit		1,677,000	
Less:	Expenses		
	Sundry administrative expenses (W1)	430,300	
	Carriage outwards	227,000	
	Irrecoverable debts (W2)	26,000	
	Depreciation (W3)	94,000	
	Profit on sale of office equipment (15,000 – 6,000)	(9,000)	
			768,300
Profit for the year			908,700

WORKINGS

(1)	Sundry administrative expenses 416,000 + 28,700 – 14,400		430,300
(2)	Irrecoverable debts		
	Written off	15,000	
	Allowance (31,000 – 20,000)	11,000	26,000
(3)	Depreciation		
	((460,000 – 20,000) × 20%)	88,000	
	(60,000 × 20% × $^{6}/_{12}$)	6,000	94,000

(b) Proposed dividend

The proposed dividend of $240,000 should be disclosed in a note in Minica's published financial statements, it is not included as a current liability or as a deduction from retained earnings in the current period's financial statements.

Answer 39 SHUSWAP

(a) Statement of financial position as at 31 December 20X6

	Cost or valuation	*Accumulated depreciation*	*Carrying amount*
Assets	$000	$000	$000
Non-current assets			
Land and buildings	12,000	–	12,000
Plant and equipment	19,600	7,950	11,650
	31,600	7,950	23,650
Current assets			
Inventories (3,000 – 140)		2,860	
Receivables (2,600 – 200 – 106)		2,294	
Cash at bank		1,900	7,054
			30,704
Equity and liabilities			
Share capital (6,000 + 2,000)		8,000	
Share premium account		2,400	
Revaluation surplus		4,000	
Retained earnings (W)		12,310	
			26,710
Non-current liabilities			
Loan notes			2,000
Current liabilities			
Trade payables (2,100 – 106)			1,994
			30,704

WORKING

Retained earnings balance

	$000
Per question	12,400
Irrecoverable debts written off	(200)
Loss on sale of plant	(100)
Depreciation adjustment	350
Inventory adjustment	(140)
	12,310

(b) Gearing ratio

Debt ÷ (Debt + Equity): $2,000 ÷ $28,710 6.96%

Or

Debt ÷ Equity: $2,000 ÷ 2$6,710 7.49%

Gearing is perceived to be a guide to the financial risk faced by a business. The higher the gearing then the higher the risk (although high risk could lead to high returns). The gearing of Shuswap is very low.

Answer 40 MCQs CAPITAL STRUCTURE AND FINANCE COSTS

Item	*Answer*	*Justification*
40.1	B	$0.50 × 50,000 = $25,000 (premium) credited to share capital account that should have been credited to share premium,
40.2	C	The increase in share capital does not involve cash.
40.3	B	A bonus issue converts reserves to shares so does not raise funds for investment. All gains and losses are shown in a statement of comprehensive income (e.g. realised gains/losses in profit and loss and unrealised gains in other comprehensive income).
40.4	B	
40.5	A	Of the $1,100,000 received 1,000,000 × $0.25 = 250,000 share capital and 1,000,000 × ($1.1 – $0.25) = 850,000 share premium
40.6	C	

	No. of shares	*Capital*	*Premium*
	000	$000	$000
1 January	1,000	500	400
1 April (1:4 Bonus)	250	125	(125)
1 October (1:10 Rights)	125	62.5	125
	1,375	687.5	400

Item	*Answer*	*Justification*
40.7	A	A rights issue: increases equity capital, may increase share premium and is to existing shareholders (so does not increase number).
40.8	C	Dividends on equity shares are an appropriation of profit to shareholders.
40.9	C	

	$
July – September (1,000,000 × 8% × $^3/_{12}$)	20,000
October – March (750,000 × 8% × $^6/_{12}$)	30,000
April – June (750,000 × 8% × $^3/_{12}$)	15,000
April – June (500,000 × 7% × $^3/_{12}$)	8,750
	73,750

Item	*Answer*	*Justification*
40.10	C	Cash raised is 250,000 × $3.55 = $887,500, which is debited to cash at bank. The credit to share capital is 250,000 × $2 = $500,000, while the credit to share premium is 250,000 × $1.55 = $387,500

40.11 A

	$
Retained earnings at 1 January	4,695,600
Operating profit	520,000
Loan notes interest ($1.3m × 10%)	(130,000)
Income tax	(156,000)
Retained earnings at 31December	4,929,600

40.12 A Bank is debited with the actual amount received. Share capital is credited with the nominal value ($1 per share) and the surplus above nominal value is credited to the share premium account.

40.13 D Dividends paid are never recognised in profit or loss. At the end of the reporting period the interim dividend has been paid (so no liability) and the final dividend is not declared (so no liability).

40.14 A On issue of redeemable preference shares, the two items affected would be cash (as money is coming in from the issue of shares) and long-term debt. This is because, although legally equity, redeemable preference shares are, in substance, debt (i.e. they have a fixed return and are repayable/redeemable in future).

40.15 D Both statements are incorrect.

(1) is describing a bonus issue and is therefore incorrect. A rights issue does not "capitalise company reserves"; it contributes cash resources, but just at a discounted amount.

(2) is correct in so far as a rights issue is offered to existing shareholders at a discount. However, it is a discount on the *market* value of a share. Shares cannot be issued at less than their nominal (par) value.

40.16 C

	$
10% Loan note interest ($800,000 × 10% × $^9/_{12}$)	60,000
Dividend paid on redeemable preference shares	5,000
	65,000

The substance of redeemable preference shares under IFRS is that of a loan. Therefore, the dividend on such shares is treated as a finance charge.

Tutorial note: *The treatment of dividends on* **irredeemable** *preference shares is the same as for dividends on equity shares (i.e. a distribution of retained earnings that is recognised in the statement of changes in equity* **not** *the statement of profit or loss).*

40.17 C

	$
30,000 2% $1 Irredeemable preference shares	30,000
100,000 $0.50 Equity shares	50,000
	80,000

Tutorial note: *Irredeemable preference shares do not have to be repaid and are therefore treated as equity. Redeemable preference shares have to be repaid and so are regarded as debt (i.e. a liability on the statement of financial position).*

40.18 D The steps to answering this question are as follows:

(1) Calculate the nominal value of the bonus issue:

1 for 5 bonus issue ($100,000 ÷ 5) $20,000

This is a credit to the share capital a/c.

(2) Use the share premium to the extent possible:

Debit share premium a/c $15,000.

(3) Balance of $5,000 is therefore debited to retained earnings.

Retained earnings balance is now $455,000 ($460,000 – $5,000).

Tutorial note: *A bonus issue is where new shares are issued to existing shareholders in proportion to their existing shareholding. The company receives no cash. Usually the share premium a/c and/or retained earnings are used to record the debit side of the transaction.*

Answer 41 RESERVES AND ISSUES

(a) Reserves

(i) Meaning

Reserves are balances in a company's statement of financial position forming part of the equity interest and representing surpluses or gains, whether realised or not.

(ii) Examples

- Share premium account: The surplus arising when shares are issued at a price in excess of their par value.
- Revaluation surplus: The unrealised gain when the amount at which non-current assets are carried is increased above cost.

Tutorial note: *Other examples would be given credit on their merits.*

(b) Issues

A "bonus issue" is the conversion of reserves into share capital, with shares being issued to existing members in proportion to their shareholdings, without any consideration being given by the shareholders.

A "rights issue" is again an issue of shares to existing members in proportion to their shareholdings, but with payment being made by the shareholders for the shares allotted to them.

The fundamental difference between them is that the rights issue raises funds for the company whereas the bonus issue does not.

Answer 42 ARMANI

(a) Bonus issue

	Marks
■ A bonus issue is a capitalisation of reserves. There is no consideration (cash) so it would not raise any capital for the company.	1 1
■ To raise capital a rights issue (or an issue at full market price) would be necessary.	1
■ For either a bonus issue or a rights issue to be possible, the authorised capital would have to be increased.	1
■ There are insufficient reserves to make a bonus issue of $750,000 worth of shares. The maximum amount available, assuming no dividends are paid from retained earnings, is $525,000.	1 1
	max 4

(b) $0.05 dividend per share

	Marks
3,000,000 × $0.05 = $150,000. This is twice the retained earnings available for distribution. Retained earnings are insufficient to pay a dividend of more than $0.025 per share.	½ + ½ + 1
	max 1

(c) Increasing revaluation surplus

	Marks
■ Although purchased goodwill may be written down subsequently (for impairment) it can never be revalued (upwards).	1

(d) Combining reserves

	Marks
■ Reserves cannot be combined into a single figure as suggested without any additional disclosure.	1
■ IAS 1 *Presentation of Financial Statements* requires that contributed equity and reserves are disaggregated into various classes (e.g. paid-in capital, share premium and reserves), either in the statement of financial position or in the notes.	1 1
	max 2
	8

Answer 43 MCQs IAS 2

Item	*Answer*	*Justification*
43.1	A	(2) is a distribution cost and (4) an administration cost; neither are manufacturing costs
43.2	C	(1) is a cost of materials purchase and (3) and (4) are production overheads.
43.3	B	When prices are rising (which is usual) profit would be understated if overheads are excluded altogether. Factory management costs are a production overhead to be included.
43.4	C	Inventory is only carried at net realisable value where it is less than cost.
43.5	A	Selecting the lower of cost and NRV applied to each item: 100 + 170 + 150 + 120 + 170 = $710.

43.6 A

Inventory is valued at lower of cost and net realisable value. Net realisable value is expected sale proceeds (17,500) less selling costs (3,000).

43.7 C

FIFO means that the 430 kg inventory includes:

	$
All of the delivery on 28 Nov 300 kg at $60	18,000
Part of the delivery on 19 Nov 130 kg at $52	6,760
Inventory value	24,760

43.8 D

Inventory should be valued at the lower of cost or net realisable value. This means that the painting should be valued at $1,200 (selling price is lower than cost), the necklace at $900 (cost) and the ear-rings at $800 (cost).

43.9 B

	Necklace	*Bracelet*	*Pendant*
	$	$	$
Purchase cost	12,000	31,000	45,000
Restoration costs to date	6,000	5,000	2,000
Cost at 31 May 20X7	18,000	36,000	47,000
Expected selling price	25,000	38,000	53,000
Further costs before sale	2,000	3,000	1,000
Net realisable value 31 May 20X7	23,000	35,000	52,000
Lower of cost and NRV	18,000	35,000	47,000

Total inventory value = $100,000

43.10 D

Inventory is included in the statement of financial position at the lower of cost and net realisable value (NRV). Comparison must be made on an item-by-item; not on the total inventory value.

The NRV of a unit of product A is $17 selling price less $5 modifications costs i.e. $12.

	$
Product A 2,000 units × $12 (NRV) =	24,000
Product B 5,000 units × $16 (Cost) =	80,000
Total inventory	104,000

Answer 44 SAMPI

Inventory valuation

Continuous weighted average cost

	Number of units	*Weighted average cost*	*Total value of closing inventory*
		$	$
Opening inventory	4,000	13.00	
8 March	3,800	15.00	
Balance	7,800	13.97	
12 March	(5,000)		
	2,800	13.97	
18 March	(2,000)		
	800	13.97	
22 March	6,000	18.00	
	6,800	17.53	
24 March	(3,000)		
	3,800	17.53	
28 March	(2,000)		
	1,800	17.53	31,554

Tutorial note: *Or 31,558 without rounding differences.*

Answer 45 P, Q & R

(a) Value of closing inventory

Model P

Cost	100 + 20 + 15 =	135[1]
Net realisable value	150 – 22 =	128[2]
Lower of cost and net realisable value		$128

Model Q

Cost	(200 + 30 + 18)	248[1]
Net realisable value	(300 – 40)	260[2]
Lower of cost and net realisable value		$248

[1] purchase cost + delivery costs from supplier + packaging costs
[2] selling price – delivery costs to customers

(b) FIFO values

Year 1	*Purchases*	*Cost of sales*	*Inventory*	*Sales*
Buy 10 at 300	3,000		3,000	
Buy 12 at 250	3,000		6,000	
Sell 8 at 400		2,400[3]	3,600	3,200
Buy 6 at 200	1,200		4,800	
Sell 12 at 400		3,100[4]	1,700	4,800
	7,200	5,500	1,700	8,000
Year 2				
Opening inventory (8)			1,700	
Buy 10 at 200	2,000		3,700	
Sell 5 at 400		1,100[5]	2,600	2,000
Buy 12 at 150	1,800		4,400	
Sell 25 at 400		4,400[6]	0	10,000
	3,800	5,500	0	12,000

[3] 8 at 300
[4] 2 at 300 + 10 at 250
[5] 2 at 250 + 3 at 240
[6] 3 at 200 + 10 at 200 + 12 at 150

		FIFO
	$	$
Year 1		
Sales revenue		8,000
Opening inventory	0	
Purchases	7,200	
	7,200	
Closing inventory	1,700	
Cost of sales		5,500
Gross profit		2,500
Year 2		
Sales revenue		12,000
Opening inventory	1,700	
Purchases	3,800	
	5,500	
Closing inventory	0	
Cost of sales		5,500
Gross profit		6,500

Answer 46 MCQs Revenue

Item	*Answer*	*Justification*
46.1	A	The accruals basis concerns the timing of recording of transactions. A transaction (e.g. a sale) is recognised when it occurs (i.e. recorded in the period to which it relates) and not when cash is received. So (1) and (3) are correct. (2) is incorrect as the accruals basis applies to both income and expenses. The "matching concept" concerns the measurement of profit. When revenue is recorded (under the accruals basis) a cost must be matched with it (even if this is only an estimate). However, revenue cannot be anticipated on costs having been incurred. So (4) is incorrect.
46.2	B	A contract for the sale of goods is a performance obligation that will be satisfied at the point in time when the customer obtains control of the goods. Payment for goods is not an indicator of the transfer of control. **Tutorial note:** *That the customer has an obligation to pay (e.g. because they have accepted the goods)* **is** *an indicator. If the customer pays in advance of the seller dispatching the goods the performance obligation is not yet satisfied.*
46.3	C	\$500 revenue per month for 6 months = \$3,000
46.4	B	Only revenue for three months should be recognised; the advance payment for the second three months is presented in current liabilities.
46.5	D	The criteria for revenue recognition have not yet been met so the advanced payment should be recognised as a current liability.

Answer 47 MCQs IAS 16

Item	*Answer*	*Justification*
47.1	C	48,000 + 400 + 2,200 = \$50,600
47.2	B	Depreciation: $^1/_{40} \times 1{,}000{,}000$ = \$25,000 Revaluation: 1,000,000 – (800,000 – 2% × 10 × 800,000) = \$360,000
47.3	D	Assets with indefinite lives (e.g. land) are not depreciated. Goodwill cannot be revalued.
47.4	D	A, B & C are examples of revenue expenditure. Only capital expenditure can be recognised as an asset under IAS 16 (i.e. to acquire physical assets).
47.5	C	Total cost of machine is \$15,000 + \$1,500 + \$750 = \$17,250 10% deprecation for the year \$1,725 Carrying amount at the end of year = \$15,525 **Tutorial note:** *Repairs of \$400 is an expense and not capitalised (IAS 16).*
47.6	C	Purchase cost (124,760) + delivery (1,250) + installation (3,750) = \$129,760. **Tutorial note:** *Maintenance costs are a revenue expense which will be charged to profit or loss on a time-apportioned basis (e.g. if the reporting date is 31 December \$1,600 (2,500 × $^8/_{12}$) will be expensed in the current year and the remainder in the following year).*

47.7 C

The carrying amount of the factory is $100,000 less than its market value. $40,000 of this loss must be recognised against the previously recognised revaluation surplus of $40,000 (i.e. the amount relating to the factory). The balance of $60,000 must be expensed to profit or loss.

The correct balance on the revaluation surplus (in the statement of changes in equity) will be:

$000	*Head office*	*Warehouse*	*Factory*	*Total*
Balance b/f	186	68	40	294
Increase in year	40	5	–	45
Loss recognised			(40)	(40)
Balance c/f	226	73	–	299

47.8 A

The profit on the sale is a realised gain recognised in the statement of profit or loss. The revaluation surplus is an unrealised gain that is recognised in other comprehensive income.

47.9 D

The fall in value of the factory cannot be offset against the surplus for the head office; therefore the value of the revaluation surplus is $1,339,000 (1,257 + 82).

47.10 D

The loss of $45,000 on the second property must be expensed entirely to profit or loss; it cannot be offset against the surplus on another asset.

47.11 D

The increase is recognised in other comprehensive income (the gain in the period) and the statement of financial position (in the carrying amount of the asset and revaluation surplus). The statement of changes in equity shows the movement on the surplus in the reporting period.

47.12 D

When a property has been revalued, the charge for depreciation should be based on the revalued amount and the remaining useful life of the asset. The increase of the new depreciation charge over the old depreciation charge may be transferred from the revaluation surplus to retained earnings:

Dr Revaluation surplus	$20,000	
Cr Retained earnings		$20,000

Therefore: Retained earnings = $895,000 (875,000 + 20,000)
Revaluation surplus = $180,000 (200,000 – 20,000)

47.13 B

The consequence of the revaluation to $432,000 is a higher annual depreciation expense. The difference between the new expense based on the revalued carrying amount and the old expense based on £400,000 original cost is "excess depreciation". IAS 16 permits a transfer of the amount of the excess depreciation from the revaluation surplus to retained earnings within equity.

Old depreciation ($400,000 ÷ 40 years)	$10,000
New depreciation ($432,000 ÷ 36 years)	$12,000

An amount of $2,000 can therefore be transferred each year from the revaluation surplus to retained earnings. The correct accounting entries would be:

Dr Revaluation surplus	$2,000	
Cr Retained earnings		$2,000

Answer 48 NON-CURRENT ASSETS

(a) Accounting terms

(i) Asset

An asset is a resource controlled by the entity as a result of past events and from which future economic benefits are expected to flow to the entity.

(ii) Current asset

A current asset is defined in IAS 1 *Presentation of Financial Statements* as one which is:

- expected to be realised in, or is held for sale or consumption in, the normal course of the entity's trading cycle; or
- held primarily for trading purposes or for the short-term and expected to be realised within 12 months after the reporting period; or
- cash or a cash equivalent asset which is not restricted in its use.

(iii) Non-current asset

A non-current asset is defined in IAS 1 as any asset not within the definition of current asset in (ii) above. A non-current asset is thus an asset held for the long term to be used in carrying on the activities of the entity and not held for resale.

(iv) Depreciation

Depreciation is defined in IAS 16 *Property, Plant and Equipment* as the systematic allocation of the depreciable amount of an asset over its useful life. The depreciable amount is the cost of an asset, or other amount substituted for cost in the financial statements, less its residual value.

(b) Assets

(i) A screwdriver

This is strictly within the definition of a non-current asset, however, on application of the concept of materiality such items would usually be written off to profit or loss as an expense.

(ii) A machine hired by the business

As the asset has not been acquired and is not controlled by the business on a permanent basis the machine cannot be regarded as an asset. If the hire were on a long-term basis then there could be an argument that in fact the machine was controlled by the business and therefore the right to use the machine is an asset.

(iii) The good reputation of the business with its customers

This is usually one component of the asset of goodwill. However as goodwill is usually created and not purchased, it is common for goodwill not to be valued as an asset in the accounts (as it is difficult to meet the recognition criteria of an asset).

(c) Meaning of $4.5

The non-current assets have a value of $4.5 million, made up of $3 million of land, $1 million of buildings and $0.5 million of plant and equipment. The land is stated at valuation, which means that it is stated at a value such as market value rather than original cost.

The buildings are stated at their original cost, which may have been incurred some time ago and which may be out of line with the current value of the building.

The plant and equipment figure is made up of the original cost of the plant after deduction of an amount of $1.5 million for depreciation to come to the carrying amount of $0.5 million.

The depreciation is an attempt to spread the cost of the plant, as an expense to profit or loss, over its useful economic life. Thus the $0.5 million is the remaining cost yet to be expensed to profit or loss in future years.

The total of $4.5 million therefore consists of three figures calculated on entirely different bases. It is therefore questionable whether this figure gives any meaningful information to the shareholders.

Answer 49 MCQs IAS 38

Item *Ans9er* *Justification*

49.1 D IAS 38 does not specify a maximum period for amortisation, therefore not (1). If the conditions exist, asset recognition is not an option, therefore not (2). Amortisation is an expense in profit or loss, therefore not (4).

49.2 C Goodwill can never be revalued upwards. Internally-generated goodwill cannot be capitalised. Purchased goodwill is not amortised (but tested annually for impairment).

49.3 A Development expenditure *must* be capitalised if certain conditions are met.

49.4 C Research expenditure can never be capitalised.

49.5 C Expenditure on both Projects 175 and 393 is research expenditure which must be expensed as incurred.

Expenditure on Project 254 is development expenditure that must be capitalised. Amortisation commences with production, not sale. Therefore the amount to be amortised is $1.6m ÷ 4 years × $^{3}/_{12}$ = $100,000.

Therefore expensed to profit or loss is:

Project 175	$2.5m	
Project 254	$0.1m	
Project 393	$4.8m	Total $7.4m

49.6 A

(1) Is incorrect as many internally-generated intangibles are not recognised (e.g. development costs that do not meet all the asset recognition criteria).

(2) Is incorrect as some internally-generated assets (e.g. development costs that meet the asset recognition criteria) may be recognised.

(3) Is incorrect. Goodwill (like any other asset) must be carried at an amount that is less than cost if its realisable amount is less than cost.

49.7 D All research expenditure must be expensed to profit or loss as incurred. If relevant criteria are met development expenditure must be capitalised.

49.8 C Only the $600,000 qualifies for capitalisation as it is development expenditure. (The $300,000 is research expenditure and must be written off as incurred.) Thus the expense for the current year is amortisation: $600,000 ÷ 8 = $75,000.

Answer 50 LION

(a) Research and development

	Carrying amount at 1 April 20X6	*New expenditure*	*Profit or loss Amortisation*	*Profit or loss Research*	*Carrying amount at 31 March 20X7*
	$000	$000	$000	$000	$000
Project Q	1,000				
	(200)		(100)		700
R	400	250			650
S				(140)	
	1,200	250	(100)	(140)	1,350

Equipment

	Carrying amount at 1 April 20X6	*New expenditure*	*Depreciation*	*Carrying amount at 31 March 20X7*
	$000	$000	$000	$000
Cost	500	180		680
Depreciation	(200)		(136)	(336)
Carrying amount	300	180	(136)	344

Headings

The amortisation of deferred development expenditure ($100,000) and the research expenditure ($140,000) and the depreciation of the research equipment ($136,000) will be included in the statement of profit or loss as part of cost of sales.

The total deferred development expenditure ($1,350,000) will be shown in the statement of financial position under intangible non-current assets.

(b) Disclosure notes

Statement of profit or loss

The aggregate amount of research and development expenditure recognised as an expense during the period was $376,000, all charged in cost of sales.

Statement of financial position

Movements on deferred development expenditure during the year were:

	Cost	*Amortisation*	*Carrying amount*
	$000	$000	$000
Balance at 1 April 20X6	1,400	(200)	1,200
Year ended 31 March 20X7			
Amortisation		(100)	(100)
New expenditure	250		250
	1,650	(300)	1,350

Answer 51 AIRCRAFT

(a) Statement of profit or loss

Project	$000
A17 ($^1/_8$ × $16 million)	2,000
A20	3,000
	5,000

Statement of financial position

	Cost	Amortisation	Carrying amount	
	$000	$000	$000	
A17	16,000	4,000	12,000	1
J9	5,500		5,500	1
	21,500	4,000	17,500	4

(b) Accounting concepts applicable to development expenditure

The main applicable accounting concepts are accruals, prudence and going concern. ½ each

The accruals concept favours capitalisation of development expenditure. The cost is then matched by charging annual amortisation against the future income generated. 1 1

The prudence concept however argues for the exercise of a degree of caution, having regard to the lack of certainty about the successful outcome of the development project. Prudence therefore suggests that development expenditure should be expensed when incurred. However, the exercise of prudence does not allow the deliberate overstatement of expenses (understatement of assets) where an asset should be recognised (as meeting the asset recognition criteria). 1 1 1

The going concern concept is relevant if it is in doubt. If the asset recognition criteria are no longer met development expenditure, including that which has been previously capitalised, must be expensed. max 2

max 6

Answer 52 MCQs IAS 37

Item	*Answer*	*Justification*
52.1	D	No provision can be made for future operating losses. Non-adjusting events are disclosed. Contingents assets are not recognised until virtually certain.
52.2	A	
52.3	C	A contingent asset cannot be recognised as an asset when it is merely probable, so not (1). Adjusting events do not all need to be detailed as they have been adjusted, so not (3).
52.4	A	(1) A provision must be made for the best estimate of the liability (in the light of past experience). A provision cannot be made for (2) because it is not probable; nor can it be ignored (because it is not remote), therefore disclose.
52.5	C	IAS 37 requires a provision to be recognised if, at the reporting date, an event has taken place which means that it is probable that a transfer of economic benefits will be required, and the amount of the transfer can be reliably measured.

In this case, as the company has accepted liability, it is clear that compensation is highly likely to be paid at some point in the future. Although the customer has claimed $250,000 and the company has offered $100,000, the best estimate is the amount estimated by the legal representatives ($150,000).

52.6 B The legal claim gives rise to a possible liability; the offer of a relatively small settlement is not an admission of liability. A provision is not required as liability is not probable (based on legal advice).

Tutorial note: *A provision of $5,000 would be appropriate if the customer had accepted the offer but this amount had not been paid at the reporting date.*

52.7 D Legal advice indicates that a liability of the full amount, $85,000, should be recognised. As the case will not be going to court until July 20X7, more than one year after the reporting date, the liability should be classified as non-current.

52.8 A Liabilities and provisions are recognised in the statement of financial position, contingent liabilities may be disclosed (e.g. if only possible).

Answer 53 RESERVES

(a) Reserves; cash in hand

Reserves are the ownership interest in the business other than the share capital itself which for limited companies must always be shown separately as such. Reserves represent claims by the owners on business resources. Reserves include Share premium account, Revaluation surplus and Retained earnings. The bigger the reserves then, other things equal, the bigger the resources in the business attributable to the owners. Cash in hand, on the other hand, means the amount of actual money - coin or note - which is owned by a business at the relevant date. Cash in hand is an asset, indeed the most liquid asset of all. Reserves are one of the claims on the assets. Reserves are not cash.

(b) Ownership interest; capital employed

Ownership interest is the total of share capital and reserves. It is the total ownership claim on a business. It indicates the total resources held in a business at a point of time which "belong" to the owners, both put in by the owners and gained by successful business activity, according to the measurement bases used in the accounts.

Capital employed is the total of ownership interest plus long-term (i.e. non-current) liabilities. It represents the "permanent" sources of finance being used by the business. Capital employed therefore considers funds put into the business by the shareholders (owners) and those that have merely loaned money to the business.

(c) Liability; expense

A liability is an existing obligation of a business, arising from past events, the settlement of which is expected to involve the outflow of future economic benefits. Liabilities are claims on the business assets other than claims from the owners.

An expense arises through the use or consumption of an asset or resource. When a resource has been used for its beneficial purpose then the recorded figure for the resource becomes an expense and the resource is no longer regarded as an asset. If the expense is recognised before the resource is acquired then a liability will also arise. In this situation the expense and the liability form the two parts of the double entry for the transaction.

(d) Contingent liability; provision

A contingent liability is a possible or potential liability which may or may not actually occur. It relates to a past event but there may very well be no crystallisation of a liability, and therefore there may be no outflow of economic resources. An example would be a court case where no actual liability exists unless or until the judgement goes against the business.

A provision is an estimated liability. The existence of the liability is known (unlike with a contingent liability), but the precise amount of the liability or the timing is not.

Answer 54 MCQs IAS 10

Item	*Answer*	*Justification*
54.1	A	(2) and (3) are non-adjusting events (as conditions did not exist at the end of the reporting period).
54.2	A	Non-adjusting events (3) and (4) will be disclosed.
54.3	D	The "conditions" of (1) and (3) do not exist at the end of the reporting period.
54.4	D	
54.5	B	
54.6	B	As the fire occurred after the reporting date, it concerns conditions which did not exist at the reporting date. As 30% of inventory would be considered material (but not affect the going concern basis of preparation of the financial statements) this is a non-adjusting event. The uninsured portion of the loss ($90,000) should be disclosed in a note. It cannot be recognised in profit or loss.
54.7	D	Both events occurred after the reporting date and are therefore classified as non-adjusting. The reported profit for 20X7 will therefore not be affected by the two events.
54.8	C	The accident occurred before the reporting date. The correct treatment would have included expensing the uninsured loss ($30,000). The letter provides further evidence relating to a condition that existed at the reporting date. It informs the accountant that there is an additional loss ($245,000) that must be recognised.
54.9	D	Information received from the insurance company relates to conditions at the reporting date, the information is therefore an adjusting event. As only $12,500 is now receivable there is an expense of $112,500 to be recognised in profit or loss and a receivable of $12,500.

Answer 55 ALUKI

(a) Closing inventory

Inventory should be measured at the lower of cost and net realisable value (IAS 2 *Inventories*). The 3,000 skirts should therefore be included at cost $40,000 as this is less than $62,000 net realisable value.

The jackets should be measured at net realisable value:

	$
$25,000 less $1,800	23,200
$20,000 less $2,000	18,000
	41,200

(b) Employee dismissal

IAS 37 *Provisions, Contingent Liabilities and Contingent Assets* requires contingent liabilities of this kind and degree of probability be disclosed in a note, detailing the nature of the contingent liability and an estimate of the financial effect.

The $100,000 should therefore be reversed and the note disclosure given. However, provision should be made for legal expenses to be incurred.

(c) Warehouse fire

According to IAS 10 *Events after the Reporting Period* the fire is a non-adjusting event. Disclosure in a note is required, giving details of the event and its financial effect (a loss of $180,000 plus $228,000 = $408,000) as the matter is material enough to influence a user of the financial statements.

Answer 56 QUAPAW

(a) One-year warranty

The correct treatment is to provide for the best estimate of the costs likely to be incurred under the warranty, as required by IAS 37 *Provisions, contingent liabilities and contingent assets*. A best estimate might be calculated as the expected percentage of product returns multiplied by the average cost of rectifying a defect (which should not exceed the cost of replacing the product returned).

(b) Damaged goods

The inventories should be valued at the lower of cost and net realisable value (IAS 2 *Inventories*). Cost is $80,000, net realisable value is $85,000 less 10% (i.e. $76,500). The net realisable value of $76,500 should therefore be the carrying amount of these inventories at the end of the reporting period.

Answer 57 UMBRIA

(1) Fire at factory

- The factory was in working condition at 30 June 20X7 and the fire does not provide evidence of a condition existing at that date. Therefore the fire is a non-adjusting event according to IAS 10 *Events after the Reporting Period.*
- The fact of the fire occurring should be disclosed in a note to the financial statements together with an estimate of the loss suffered showing separately the estimated cost of the fire and the estimated insurance recovery.

Tutorial note: *It would be insufficient information for users of financial statements to disclose only a net loss. Any reimbursement of costs through insurance is a completely separate transaction/event.*

(2) Overdraft guarantee

- According to IAS 37 *Provisions, Contingent Liabilities and Contingent Assets*, such contingent liabilities must be provided for as soon as it becomes probable that a liability will arise.
- A provision should therefore be made for the best estimate of the cost that will arise in respect of the guarantee.

Tutorial note: *An estimate can always be made for such a provision. For example, the cost would not be expected to exceed the balance on the overdraft or the amount guaranteed (whichever is the lower).*

(3) Director's dismissal

- The assessment of a future aware of damages as "probable" makes it a contingent asset under IAS 37.
- This pending litigation should be disclosed in a note to the financial statements, explaining its nature and, if possible, an estimate of the financial effect.

Tutorial note: *The action by the company is not an event after the reporting period as it would appear to have commenced before 30 June 20X7. The event under consideration here is the probable subsequent award of damages.*

(4) Revaluation gain

- It is incorrect to include it in the statement or profit or loss, because the gain is unrealised. It should be included separately in other comprehensive income.
- It will then be included in a revaluation surplus in the statement of changes in equity and shown in the statement of financial position as a reserve. (IAS 16 *Property, Plant and Equipment* and IAS 1 *Presentation of Financial Statements*).

Answer 58 MCQs IAS 7

Item	*Answer*	*Justification*
58.1	B	
58.2	D	Proposing dividends and issuing bonus shares are not cash flow transactions.
58.3	D	
58.4	B	Acquisitions and disposals of non-current assets are investing activities. A profit on disposal is not a cash flow and therefore deducted.
58.5	A	Additions = $15,000 cash outflow Cash inflow from disposal = $3,000 (gain) + $2,000 (carrying amount) = $5,000 Net cash out flow = $15,000 - $5,000 = $10,000
58.6	B	Increase in inventory = $20,000 outflow Increase in receivables = $35,000 outflow Increase in payables = $40,000 inflow Net effect = $15,000 outflow

58.7 A

	$000
Cash flows from financing:	
Issue of share capital (120 + 60) – (80 + 40)	60
Repayment of bank loan (100 – 150)	(50)
Net cash inflow from financing	10

Tutorial note: *Movement in retained earnings is not a cash flow.*

Item	*Answer*	*Justification*
58.8	D	An increase in trade receivables means that some of the sales in the year were not realised as cash during the year. The other three changes would have caused the opposite effect.
58.9	B	The full cost of purchase of non-current assets is $687,000 (regardless of how it is financed) and proceeds from the sale of non-current assets is $60,000 (75 – 15).

58.10 C

Sold	Carrying amount	$273,790	Purchases	$568,900 outflow
	Loss	$15,850		
Cash received		$257,940 inflow	Net cash outflow	$310,960

Item	*Answer*	*Justification*
58.11	B	Increase in assets and decrease in liabilities both affect cash flows in the same manner. Both will be cash outflows.
58.12	B	2,110 – (1,945 – 270) = $435. Movements in equity and non-current loans are financing activities.

Answer 59 CRASH

(a) Statement of cash flows for the year ended 31 March 20X7

	$000	$000
Profit	405	
Adjustments for:		
Depreciation	1,500	
Profit on sale of non-current asset	(75)	
Interest expense	150	
	1,980	
Operating profit before working capital changes		
Increase in inventories	(135)	
Decrease in receivables	60	
Increase in payables	90	
	1,995	
Cash generated from operations		
Interest paid	(150)	
Net cash from operating activities		1,845
Cash flows from investing activities		
Purchase of property, plant and equipment (W1)	(2,700)	
Proceeds from sale of non-current asset	375	
Net cash used in investing activities		(2,325)
Cash flows from financing activities		
Proceeds from issuance of share capital	1,200	
Repayment of loan notes	(750)	450
Decrease in cash		(30)
Overdraft at beginning of period		(135)
Overdraft at end of period		(165)

WORKING

(1) Movement in non-current assets

Non-current assets – cost

	$000		$000
Opening balance	9,000	Transfer disposal	1,500
Revaluation	750		
Net assets purchased	2,700		
		Closing balance	10,950
	12,450		12,450

(b) Ratios

		20X7	20X6
(i)	*Gearing*		
	Debt ÷ (Debt + Equity):		
	$750 ÷ $8,745	8.6%	
	$1,500 ÷ $7,140		21%
	Or		
	Debt ÷ Equity:		
	$750 ÷ $7,995	9.4%	
	$1,500 ÷ $5,640		26.6%
(ii)	*Current ratio*		
	$2,745 ÷ $1,350	2:1	
	$2,625÷ $1,185		2.2:1

Non-current assets – depreciation

	$000		$000
Transfer disposal	1,200	Opening balance	3,300
Closing balance	3,600	Profit or loss	1,500
	4,800		4,800

Non-current assets – disposal

	$000		$000
Transfer cost	1,500	Transfer depreciation	1,200
Profit or loss	75	Proceeds of sale	375
	1,575		1,575

Answer 60 MARMOT

(a) Net cash flow from operating activities – direct method

	$000	$000
Cash receipts from customers		12,800
Cash paid to suppliers	4,940	
Cash paid to employees	2,820	
Cash paid for expenses	2,270	
		10,030
Net cash flow from operating activities		2,770

(b) Net cash flow from operating activities – indirect method

Profit before taxation	2,370
Adjustment for: Depreciation	880
Operating profit before working capital changes	3,250
Increase in inventories	(370)
Decrease in receivables	280
Decrease in payables	(390)
Net cash from operating activities	2,770

Answer 61 RENADA

(a) Statement of cash flows for the year ended 31 October 20X6

Cash flows from operating activities	$000	$000
Profit before taxation	200	
Adjustments for:		
Depreciation	120	
Loss on sale of office equipment	50	
Operating profit before working capital changes	370	
Increase in inventory	(1,000)	
Increase in receivables	(530)	
Increase in payables	1,050	
Cash used in operations	(110)	
Income taxes paid	(120)	
Net cash used in operating activities		(230)
Cash flows from investing activities		
Purchase of non-current assets (W)	(700)	
Proceeds from sale of non-current assets	30	
Net cash used in investing activities		(670)
Cash flows from financing activities		
Proceeds from issuance of share capital	500	
Net cash from financing activities		500
Net decrease in cash and cash equivalents		(400)
Cash and cash equivalents at 31 October 20X5		140
Cash and cash equivalents at 31 October 20X6		(260)

WORKING

Non-current assets – carrying amount

	$000		$000
Balance	1,000	Transfer disposal	80
Revaluation surplus	300	Depreciation	120
Assets purchased (balancing figure)	700	Balance	1,800
	2,000		2,000

(b) Ratios

		20X6	20X5
(i)	*ROCE*		
	$200 ÷ $2,800	7.1%	
	$600 ÷ $1,840		32.6%
(ii)	*Quick ratio*		
	$1,800 ÷ $2,400	0.75:1	
	$1,410 ÷ $1,170		1.2:1

Answer 62 SIOUX

(a) Statement of cash flows for the year ended 31 December 20X6

	$000	$000
Cash flows from operating activities		
Profit before taxation	2,350	
Adjustments for:		
Depreciation (W2)	1,250	
Profit on sale of plant (W3)	(150)	
Interest expense	300	
Operating profit before working capital changes	3,750	
Decrease in inventories	400	
Increase in receivables	(900)	
Increase in payables	500	
Cash generated from operations	3,750	
Interest paid	(300)	
Income taxes paid	(600)	
		2,850
Cash flows from investing activities		
Purchase of non-current assets (W1)	(3,300)	
Proceeds of sale of non-current assets	500	
Net cash used in investing activities		(2,800)
Cash flows from financing activities		
Proceeds of issue of loan notes	1,000	
Dividends paid	(750)	
Net cash from financing activities		250
Net increase in cash		300
Cash at 1 January 20X6		100
Cash at 31 December 20X6		400

WORKINGS

(1) **Non-current assets – cost**

	$000		$000
Opening balance	8,000	Disposal	800
Revaluation surplus	500		
Cash (balancing figure)	**3,300**		
		Closing balance	11,000
	11,800		11,800

(2) **Non-current assets – accumulated depreciation**

	$000		$000
Disposal (800 – 350)	450	Opening balance	4,800
Closing balance	5,600	Profit or loss	**1,250**
	6,050		6,050

(3) **Non-current assets – disposal**

	$000		$000
Cost	800	Accumulated depreciation	450
Profit on sale	**150**	Cash	500
	950		950

(b) **Ratios**

Tutorial notes:

(i) *The receipt of cash from customers does not change total of current assets.*
(ii) *An increase in loan notes will increase non-current liabilities and cash.*
(iii) *A payment to suppliers will decrease current assets and current liabilities.*

(i) *Current ratio*

6,600 ÷ 2,400 2.75:1

(ii) *Quick ratio*

3,200 ÷ 2,400 1.33:1

(iii) *ROCE*

4,000 ÷ 9,600 41.7%

Or

4,000 ÷ 5,600 71.4%

Answer 63 JOYCE

Statement of cash flows for the year ended 30 June 20X7

	$000	$000	
Cash flows from operating activities			
Profit before taxation (W1)	22,200		2½†
Adjustments for			
Depreciation	13,000		½
Interest expense (8% × ½ (8,000 + 10.000))	720		1
	35,920		
Increase in inventories	(4,900)		½
Increase in receivables	(8,900)		½
Decrease in payables	(2,100)		½
Cash generated from operations	20,020		
Interest paid	(720)		½*
Income taxes paid	(6,200)		½
Net cash from operating activities		13,100	½
Cash flows from investing activities			
Purchase of property plant and equipment (W3)	(19,000)		2½†
Net cash used in investing activities		(19,000)	
Cash flows from financing activities			
Proceeds of issue of share capital	2,000		½
Proceeds of issue of loan notes	2,000		½
Dividends paid	(4,000)		½
Net cash from financing activities		–	
Net decrease in cash and cash equivalents		(5,900)	½
Cash and cash equivalents at 1 July 20X6		4,600	
Cash and cash equivalents at 30 June 20X7		(1,300)	½
			12

* Award for the same amount as is included in the adjustment.
† Includes 2 for amount (W) and ½ for inclusion in statement.

WORKINGS

(1) Calculation of profit for year

	$000		$000
Dividends	4,000	Opening balance	18,000
Tax expense (W2)	8,200	Profit for year	
Closing balance	28,000	(balancing figure)	22,200
	40,200		40,200

(2)

Income taxes

	$000		$000
Cash	6,200	Opening balance	6,000
Closing balance	8,000	Expense (balancing figure)	8,200
	14,200		14,200

(3)

Non-current assets

	$000		$000
Opening balance	130,000	Depreciation	13,000
Revaluation gain	12,000		
Purchases (balancing figure)	19,000	Closing balance	148,000
	161,000		161,000

Answer 64 MCQs CONSOLIDATED FINANCIAL STATEMENTS

Tutorial note: *Consolidation will not be examined using objective test questions in the F3 examination. These questions are provided for revision only.*

Item *Answer* *Justification*

64.1 C

	$000
Cost of investment (assumed fair value)	1,400
Fair value of net assets acquired ((600 × 0.5) + 50 + 20))	(370)
Goodwill on acquisition	1,030

64.2 D

	$000
Fair value of non-controlling interest on acquisition (200,000 × 20% × $3.10)	124
Post-acquisition profits (50,000 × 20%)	10
	134

64.3 B (1) is incorrect –The only exception to consolidation of a subsidiary is if control is known to be temporary at the date of acquisition (IFRS 3). (2) is correct (IAS 1).

64.4 D

	$000	%
Sales value	1,044	100
Cost of sales	783	75
Profit	261	25

Tutorial note: *Margin is "on sales" therefore sales value is 100%. If margin is 25%, cost is 75%.*

Unrealised profit in inventory is $261,000 × 60% = $156,600

Alternatively: (60% × $1,044,000) × $^{25}/_{100}$ = $156,600

64.5 D (576,000 + 140,000) – (180,000 + 108,000) = 428,000

64.6 C 140,000 + (20% × 144,000) = 168,800

64.7 B

	$
Parent as per question	1,224,000
Post-acquisition share of Malta (80% × ((680,000 – 3,000) – 476,000))	160,800
	1,384,800

Unrealised profit is 20% on cost price, $18,000 is selling price so profit element is $^{20}/_{120}$ = 3,000

64.8 B 60% × ($^{25}/_{125}$ × $200,000) = $24,000

64.9 C An investment in an associate is only carried at cost initially. (Thereafter the carrying amount is increased or decreased to recognise the investor's share in profit or loss post-acquisition.)

64.10 D More than half of the voting power constitutes control. Significant influence is a power that does not amount to control.

64.11 B Since an investment in an associate is shown as a single line item in the consolidated statement of financial position under the equity method the carrying amount includes any goodwill (i.e. excess of the cost of the investment over the net fair value of the investor's share of the associate's identifiable assets and liabilities).

64.12 B There is no requirement to value assets at fair value.

64.13 C Under the equity method an investment in an associate is calculated as original cost plus the parent's share of post-acquisition profits.

	$
Cost of investment	960,000
Share of post-acquisition profits (25% × (1,710 – 1,080))	157,500
	1,117,500

64.14 A Bram's payables 244,000 + Stoker's payables 40,000 – owed to Bram 6,000 = 278,000
Bram's receivables 360,000 + Stoker's receivables 150,000 – owed by Bram 6,000 = 504,000

64.15 D Only the "full goodwill" (also called "fair value") method of valuing non-controlling interest is examinable. So all that is required is to complete the proforma calculation:

	$
Fair value of consideration:	
Cash paid (75% × 100,000 × $2)	150,000
Shares issued (75% × 100,000 × $1.75)	131,250
Fair value of non-controlling interest	82,000
	363,250
Less: **Fair value** of net assets at acquisition	(215,500)
Goodwill at acquisition	147,750

Tutorial note: *The examiner reported that only 20% of candidates answered this question correctly with the most popular incorrect answer being C (i.e. failing to include shares issued at fair value rather than nominal value).*

64.16 D

	$000
At acquisition	450
% Post-acquisition (4,000 – 3,200) × 10%	80
	530

64.17 C

$9{,}000 + (9{,}000 \times 3\%) + (12{,}000 \times {}^{7}/_{12}) + 6{,}000 = 22{,}270$

Tutorial note: *Any "elimination" of inter-group transactions is irrelevant because the question concerns the separate financial statements of the parent.*

64.18 C

Jamee has 1 million ($500,000 × $0.50) shares in issue.
Harvert holds 400,000 shares or 40% of the share capital.
With a holding of 40% and one nominated director, it is virtually certain that Harvert can exercise significant influence over the operating and financial policies of Jamee, but cannot exercise control.

64.19 B

The group recognises 100% of every asset (and liability) of any subsidiary in the consolidated statement of financial position. Only the share capital of the parent is included in the consolidated statement of financial position.

64.20 D

As Orius has not acquired sufficient shares to control the voting at any meeting of members, but has a representative on the board of directors, it is in a position to exercise significant influence over, but not to control, Eerus. This means that Eerus is an associate of Orius.

The correct accounting treatment of an associate is equity accounting (acquisition accounting is applied to subsidiaries).

64.21 D

$\$100{,}000 + ({}^{4}/_{12} \times \$62{,}000) - \$6{,}000 = \$114{,}667$

When answering questions on the preparation of consolidated financial statements, there are two important facts to establish quickly:

(1) What is the size of the holding acquired?
(2) What is the date of acquisition?

Panther acquired 80% of Seal's equity shares and therefore has a controlling interest (> 50%). Thus Seal will be consolidated as a subsidiary, on a 100% line-by-line basis to reflect control.

However, as the interest was acquired on 31 August, Seal was only a subsidiary for 4 months of the year. Therefore, only the post-acquisition results of the subsidiary are consolidated.

As intra-group sales were all made in October, in the post-acquisition period, they must be eliminated in full.

64.22 D Goodwill is calculated as:

	$
Consideration transferred (W1)	1,500
Fair value of non-controlling interest	300
	1,800
Less Fair value of net assets acquired (W2)	(1,585)
Goodwill	215

When calculating goodwill on acquisition, it is important to determine:

(i) The date of the acquisition (i.e. when control was gained). This was 1 April, not the year end date of 30September;

(ii) Consideration transferred to gain control;

(iii) The fair value of the non-controlling interest (given as $300);

(iv) The fair value of the net assets on acquisition (1 April).

WORKINGS

(1) Consideration transferred: (75% × 1,000 shares) × $2 a share = $1,500

(2) Fair value of net assets acquired:

	$
Equity share capital	1,000
Retained earnings ($710 – ($^{6}/_{12}$ × $250))	585
	1,585

Tutorial note: *The tricky part is determining the fair value of Bee's net assets at acquisition. Although there are no fair value adjustments, the financial statement extracts are as at the year-end date (30 September). Therefore, net assets at 1 April must be calculated by deducting the amount of retained earnings earned in the six months after the acquisition.*

Answer 65 HAYDN & STRAUSS

(a) Consolidated statement of financial position as at 31 December 20X6

	$
Non-current assets	
Goodwill (W2)	41,000
Tangible (131,500 + 144,000)	275,500
	316,500
Current assets (57,000 + 110,400 – 3,000)	164,400
	480,900
Share capital	50,000
Revaluation surplus (W4)	59,000
Retained earnings (W5)	222,000
	331,000
Non-controlling interest (W3)	58,500
Total equity	389,500
Current liabilities (32,000 + 62,400 – 3,000)	91,400
	480,900

WORKINGS

(1) S net assets

	Reporting date	*Acquisition*	*Post-acquisition*
	$	$	$
Share capital	36,000	36,000	–
Share premium	24,000	24,000	–
Revaluation surplus	12,000	–	12,000
Retained earnings	120,000	24,000	96,000
	192,000	84,000	108,000

(2) Goodwill

	$
Fair value of consideration	93,500
Non-controlling interest on acquisition (25% × 36,000 × $3.50)	31,500
Less: Net assets acquired (100%)	(84,000)
	41,000

(3) Non-controlling interest

Fair value (W2)	31,500
Share of Strauss post-acquisition (25% × 108,000)	27,000
	58,500

(4) Revaluation surplus

	$
Haydn as per question	50,000
Share of Strauss post-acquisition (75% × 12,000)	9,000
	59,000

(5) Retained earnings

	$
Haydn as per question	150,000
Share of Strauss post-acquisition (75% × 96,000)	72,000
	222,000

(b) C All of the subsidiary's revenue is included in consolidated revenue and all intra-group sales are cancelled on consolidation.

(c) C (1) and (4) are both indicators of control and in these instances Bach would be a subsidiary. (2) and (3) are possible indicators of significant influence (IAS 28 *Investments in Associates and Joint Ventures).*

Answer 66 DUBLIN & BELFAST

Consolidated statement of financial position as at 31 December 20X6

		$
Non-current assets		
Goodwill (W2)		6,250
Tangible (157,000 + 82,000)		239,000
Other investments		12,000
		257,250
Current assets		
Inventory (73,200 + 35,200 – 3,000(W5))	105,400	
Trade receivables (96,800 + 46,900 – 28,000)	115,700	
Cash and bank (8,000 + 25,150)	33,150	
		254,250
		511,500
Share capital		250,000
Revaluation surplus (W4)		12,000
Retained earnings (W5)		53,000
		315,000
Non-controlling interest (W3)		23,500
Total equity		338,500
Non-current liabilities: 6% Loan		20,000
Current liabilities (123,000 + 58,000 – 28,000)		153,000
		511,500

WORKINGS

(1) Belfast net assets

	Reporting date	*Acquisition*	*Post-acquisition*
	$	$	$
Share capital	50,000	50,000	–
Share premium	6,250	6,250	–
Revaluation surplus	15,000	–	15,000
Retained earnings	40,000	10,000	30,000
	111,250	66,250	45,000

(2) Goodwill

	$
Fair value of consideration	58,000
Non-controlling interest on acquisition	14,500
Less: Net assets acquired (100% × 66,250)	(66,250)
	6,250

(3) Non-controlling interest

	$
Fair value on acquisition	14,500
Share of Belfast post-acquisition (20% × 45,000)	9,000
	23,500

(4) Revaluation surplus

	$
Share of Belfast post-acquisition (80% × 15,000)	12,000

(5) Retained earnings

	$
Dublin as per question	32,000
Share of Belfast post-acquisition (80% × 30,000)	24,000
Unrealised profit on inventory (25% × $12,000)	(3,000)
	53,000

Answer 67 HELIOS & LUNA

(a) Consolidated statement of financial position as at 30 June 20X7

	$000
Non-current assets	
Goodwill (W2)	199
Tangible assets (280 + 490 + 20)	790
	989
Net current assets	390
	1,379
Share capital	600
Share premium account	350
Retained earnings (W4)	232
	1,182
Non-controlling interest (W3)	197
	1,379

(b) Parent-subsidiary factors

A, B, F and H are all indicators of a parent-subsidiary relationship; the other factors are indicators of significant influence and would lead to a parent-associate relationship.

WORKINGS

(1) **Luna's net assets**

	Reporting date	*Acquisition*	*Post-acquisition*
	$000	$000	$000
Share capital	400	400	–
Share premium	200	200	–
Fair value adjustment (land)	20	20	–
Retained earnings	150	60	90
	770	680	90

(2) Goodwill

	$000
Fair value of consideration	700
Non-controlling interest on acquisition	179
Less: Net assets acquired (100% × 680)	(680)
	199

(3) Non-controlling interest

	$000
Fair value on acquisition (W2)	179
Share of Luna's post-acquisition (20% × 90)	18
	197

(4) Retained earnings

	$000
Helios as per question	160
Share of Luna's post-acquisition (80% × 90)	72
	232

Answer 68 BRADSHAW & MARTIN

(a) Goodwill on acquisition of Martin

	$000	$000
Fair value of consideration		34,000
Fair value of non-controlling interest		7,408
Less: Net assets at acquisition		
Share capital	23,150	
Retained earnings	5,338	(28,488)
		12,920

(b) Financial statements

Consolidated statement of profit or loss for the year ended 31 October 20X6

	$000
Revenue (125,000 + 77,900 – 15,000)	187,900
Cost of sales (65,000 + 38,500 – 15,000 + 2,500 unrealised profit)	(91,000)
Gross profit	96,900
Distribution costs (6,750 + 8,050)	(14,800)
Administrative expenses (17,500 + 9,780)	(27,280)
Finance costs (20 – 15)	(5)
Profit before tax	54,815
Income tax expense (19,250 + 10,850)	(30,100)
Profit for the year	24,715
Profit attributable to:	
Owners of the parent	22,575
Non-controlling interest (20% (W) × 10,700)	2,140
	24,715

WORKING

Group share is 80%, therefore non-controlling interest is 20%.

(c) Parent-associate factors

C, D, E and G are all indicators of a parent-associate relationship; the other factors are indicators of control and would lead to a parent-subsidiary relationship.

Answer 69 MCQs INTERPRETATION OF FINANCIAL STATEMENTS

Item	*Answer*	*Justification*
69.1	B	Future trends cannot be predicted accurately.
69.2	A	A company may not have a known share price. All the other matters will affect the company's ability to pay interest (and capital) and therefore be of concern.
69.3	A	Trend analysis concerns the pattern of results over time.

69.4 B These are the key accounting ratios for the assessment of short-term liquidity.

69.5 D Cost of sales has been overstated by $48,000 ($24,000 of opening inventory valuation was not an expense + carry forward of $24,000 expense in closing inventory valuation). If inventory days is calculated using average inventory there is no error in average inventory but cost of sales in the denominator is overstated so turnover days are lower than they should be. (If closing inventory was used turnover days will have been even lower.) Current assets in the current ratio were understated so this was also lower.

69.6 D Cost of sales will be increased (as higher cost purchases will be expensed first) so gross profit will be lower. Current ratio will also be lower as inventory valued at average cost will be lower than FIFO basis when prices are increasing.

69.7 C

69.8 A Increase in inventory ⇒ increase in working capital
Decrease in bank ⇒ decrease in working capital
Increase in payables ⇒ decrease in working capital
$500 – $600 – $1400 = total decrease of $1,500

69.9 A Current assets (124,800) less current liabilities (64,290).

69.10 A FIFO uses the most recent prices to value inventory.
As prices are falling, this will lead to a lower inventory value.
A lower inventory value will lead to a shorter inventory turnover period (i.e. fewer days).

69.11 B The reduction in inventory means that the net assets will be reduced, leading to a reduction in the current ratio. The new loan will increase the level of debt, leading to an increase in the gearing ratio.

69.12 C ROCE = Net profit margin × Asset turnover = 14.7% × 2.3 = 33.81%

69.13 B As both companies have the same profit before interest and tax it is obvious that Light's interest cover is higher that Murky's because Light pays less interest:

	Light	*Murky*
5% × $375,000 (W)	$18,750	
5% × $525,000 (W)		$26,250

WORKING

$\text{Gearing} = \dfrac{\text{Long-term debt}}{\text{Equity}} = \dfrac{\text{Long-term debt}}{\$1{,}500{,}000}$	25%	35%
Therefore, long-term debt	$375,000	$525,000

Tutorial note: *This question calls for an understanding of two key ratios: gearing and interest cover. Gearing is the ratio of external debt (e.g. outstanding loans) to equity. This can be used to calculate the long-term debt of each company. The following calculations of interest cover are shown for completeness:*

	Light	*Murky*
$\text{Interest cover} = \dfrac{\text{PBIT}}{\text{Interest payable}}$	$\dfrac{\$100{,}000}{\$18{,}750} = 5.3$	$\dfrac{\$100{,}000}{\$26{,}250} = 3.8$

Answer 70 BETA

(a) Ratios

(i) Profitability		*Zeta*	*Omega*
Gross profit as % of revenue	1,000 ÷ 4,000	25%	
	1,200 ÷ 6,000		20%
Net profit as % of revenue	500 ÷ 4,000	12.5%	
	(400 + 400) ÷ 6,000		13.3%
Return on capital employed (ROCE)	500 ÷ 1,950	25.6%	
	800 ÷ 6,890		11.6%
Return on equity (ROE)	500 ÷ 1,950	25.6%	
	400 ÷ 2,890		13.8%

Tutorial note: ***Only two measures were required.***

(ii) Liquidity			
Current assets/current liabilities	1,350 ÷ 1,200	1.13:1	
	1,880 ÷ 990		1.90:1
Quick assets/current liabilities	950 ÷ 1,200	0.79:1	
	1,080 ÷ 990		1.09:1

(iii) Efficiency			
No. of days' cost of sales in inventory	400 ÷ 3,000 × 365	49 days	
	800 ÷ 4,800 × 365		61 days
No. of days' revenue in receivables	800 ÷ 4,000 × 365	73 days	
	900 ÷ 6,000 × 365		55 days
No. of days' purchases in payables	800 ÷ 3,200 × 365	91 days	
	800 ÷ 4,800 × 365		61 days

(b) Comparison of companies

(i) Profitability

Zeta's gross profit percentage is higher than that of Omega, possibly indicating different pricing policy, with Omega offering lower prices to raise market share and therefore revenue.

Zeta's ROCE and ROE are both much higher than those of Omega. This may be partly due to the fact that Zeta's buildings do not appear to have been revalued as Omega's have. A revaluation would increase the carrying amount of Zeta's assets and hence reduce its ROCE.

This difference in accounting policy is a problem when trying to compare accounts of two companies.

(ii) Liquidity

Omega's liquidity ratios are comfortable, while Zeta's are much lower, almost dangerously so. However, Zeta should be continuing to make profits in the current year, and the cash generated from those profits should increase both liquidity ratios within a few months. If Zeta has been managing with these levels for a number of years then there may not be a major problem.

(iii) Efficiency

Zeta succeeds in controlling inventory levels better than Omega, but is less successful in keeping receivables down.

Zeta's shortage of working capital as evidenced by the low liquidity ratios has led to slowness in settling accounts payable. A delay of 91 days is enough for the company to start losing the goodwill of suppliers. If receivables collection could be improved to Omega's level, receivables would be reduced to about \$600,000 (55 ÷ 73 × \$800,000), liberating about \$200,000 to improve the payables' payment position or indeed to eliminate the overdraft. As indicated under (ii) above, future cash flows should enable Zeta to reduce the time taken to settle payables in any case.

(c) Implication of gearing

High gearing implies a high financial risk. As long as Omega has a ROCE in excess of the 10% interest payable on the loan, all is well. A downturn in trade could, however mean that Omega's ROCE drops from 11.6% to below 10%, leading to a negative return on the loan capital with adverse effects for shareholders. Zeta, with negligible loan capital, could survive a greater downturn without moving into a loss.

An upturn in profitability would benefit Omega more than Zeta, because the loan interest would continue at 10% while the profit earned from the employment of the loan capital rose.

Answer 71 WEDEN

(a) Ratios

		Year ended 31 March *20X7*	*20X6*
(i)	*Return on capital employed (ROCE)*		
	550 ÷ 3,900	14.1%	
	500 ÷ 2,550		19.6%
(ii)	*Return on equity (ROE)*		
	350 ÷ 1,900	18.4%	
	400 ÷ 1,550		25.8%
(iii)	*Current ratio*		
	1,380 ÷ 1,480	0.93:1	
	1,010 ÷ 430		2.35:1
(iv)	*Inventory turnover*		
	3,000 ÷ 500	6.0 times	
	2,300 ÷ 300		7.67 times
	(full credit given for correct answer in days	61 days	48 days)
(v)	*Payables' days*		
	1,400 ÷ 3,200 × 365	160 days	
	380 ÷ 1,800 × 365		77 days

(b) Comment

All ratios show a marked deterioration in 20X7 compared with 20X6.

ROCE and ROE are at reasonable levels in 20X7, but considerably below the levels in 20X6. A possible cause is the decline in the gross profit percentage caused by reducing prices to increase sales.

ROE shows a return in excess of ROCE in both years, and well in excess of the interest payable on the loan, showing that the shareholders are continuing to benefit from the gearing effect of the loan.

The current ratio is seriously reduced to a potentially dangerous level. The consequence is the slowness in paying suppliers, which must be eroding suppliers' goodwill, evidenced by the increase in payable days from 77 days to 160. In effect, suppliers' money is being used to finance the very heavy purchasing of non-current assets.

The inventory turnover ratio has declined, indicating a possible slowing of activity. The decline could be caused simply by a large purchase of goods just before the end of the reporting period.

Answer 72 APILLON

(a) Year ended 31 March

			20X7	*20X6*
(i)	*Current ratio*			
		1,420 ÷ 860	1·65:1	
		990 ÷ 430		2.3:1
(ii)	*Quick ratio*			
		700 ÷ 860	0·8:1	
		450 ÷ 430		1·05:1
(iii)	*Inventory turnover*			
		720 ÷ 2,400 × 365	109 days	
		540 ÷ 1,900 × 365		104 days
(iv)	*Average period of credit allowed to customers*			
		700 ÷ 3,700 × 365	69 days	
		450 ÷ 2,800 × 365		59 days
(v)	*Average period of credit allowed by suppliers*			
		690 ÷ 2,580 × 365	98 days	
		410 ÷ 2,080 × 365		72 days

Tutorial note: *All amounts are $000.*

(b) Comments

- The current ratio and quick ratio are both down by over 20%.
  The drop in the quick ratio to below 1:1 could indicate liquidity problems.
- The increase in sales, and hence in receivables, purchases and payables, is placing strain on the working capital, evidenced by the increase in the receivables and payables payment periods.
- The business is one requiring large holdings of inventory, but inventory control appears to have deteriorated slightly between the two years.
- Cash sales have decreased considerably in 20X7. Making more sales for cash could contribute to an improvement in the current and quick ratios because this would reduce the overdraft.

Tutorial note: *Other comments would be considered on their merits.*

SPECIMEN EXAM ANSWERS

Section A

Item	*Answer*	*Justification*	
1	A	Opening net assets (capital) + Profit for the period – Drawings + Capital introduced = closing net assets. Therefore Profit = Closing net assets + Drawings – Capital introduced – Opening net assets.	
2	B	An imprest system has a pre-determined "float" of petty cash. Expenditure reimbursements out of the float are replaced with a voucher stating the amount and nature of the expense. The float is replenished periodically by replacing vouchers with cash.	
3	C	In a limited liability company the shareholders' exposure is limited (to the extent of any unpaid share capital) but the company's liabilities are not limited.	
4	C		$
		Payables:	
		Balance b/f	60,000
		Cash paid to suppliers	(302,800)
		Discounts received	(2,960)
		Contra	(2,000)
		Purchases (balancing figure)	331,760
		Balance c/f	84,000
5	D	If a cheque from a customer was credited to cash (incorrectly) and credited to receivables (correctly) the trial balance will have more credits than debits. Rent received is an income account in the general ledger and therefore should be extracted to the trial balance as a credit; if extracted as a debit the totals on the trial balance will not agree.	
6	B		$
		Loan asset	12,000
		Interest (12,000 × 12%)	240
		Prepayment ($^{8}/_{12}$ × 9,000)	6,000
		Accrued rent	4,000
		Current assets	22,240
7	C		$
		Draft profit	83,600
		Purchase of van	18,000
		Depreciation 18,000 × 25%	(4,500)
		Adjusted profit	97,100
8	C	Liquidity has deteriorated as evidenced by (i) falling current ratio; and (ii) lengthening of the cash conversion cycle from 50 – 45 + 35 = 40 days to 75 – 30 + 42 = 87 days	

9 D The direct and indirect methods give the *same* figure for net cash from operating activities. Cash raised from a rights issue is a financing activity. A revaluation surplus does not involve any cash. Cash received from a non-current asset disposal is an investing activity; any profit on disposal is an adjustment in deriving cash from operating activities.

10 D

	$
Balance b/f (advance)	28,700
Balance b/f (arrears)	(21,200)
Cash received	481,200
Balance c/f (advance)	(31,200)
Balance c/f (arrears)	18,400
Rental income	475,900

11 B A sole trader's financial statements may be required by third parties such as banks (providing loans) and the tax authorities.

12 C Ratio analysis is particularly valuable to identify trends and benchmark against industry average (sector) data.

13 A The balance c/f at the end of the current period will be b/f as the opening balance at the start of the following period. As the balance represents the cost of an asset it will be a debit balance.

14 A As per the disclosure requirements of IAS 38 *Intangible Assets.*

15 A IAS 38 *Intangible Assets* does not specify a maximum permitted amortisation period. Research expenditure must be written off as an expense but, if certain criteria are met, development expenditure must be recognised as an intangible non-current asset,

16 A

	$
Balance b/f	550
Expense incurred (cash)	5,400
Accrual c/f	650
Electricity expense for the year	6,600

17 C

	$	$
Debts written off		37,000
Movement in allowance (517 – 37) × 5%	24,000	
Less opening allowance	39,000	
		(15,000)
Receivables expense		22,000

18 D

	$
Balance per ledger	438,900
Less contra	(980)
Posting error	(90)
Corrected balance	437,830

19 B Inventory valuation must include all costs incurred to bring the inventory to its current location and condition (IAS 2 *Inventories*). Therefore carriage inwards (delivery costs charged by suppliers) should be included but carriage outwards (cost of delivering goods to customers) should be excluded (as, by definition, inventory has not yet been sold),

Production overheads (e.g. depreciation of factory plant) should be included but non-production overheads (e.g. administration costs) excluded.

20 B Cost of sales = 6,700 + 84,000 – 5,400 = 85,300. Revenue = 85,300 + 20% = 102,360. Gross profit = 102,360 – 85,300 = $17,060

21 B

	Share capital	*Share premium*
	$	$
Balance b/f	125,000	100,000
Rights issue	62,500	187,500
Bonus issue	37,500	(37,500)
Balance c/f	225,000	250,000

22 C Per IAS 1 *Presentation of Financial Statements.*

23 D

	$
Jan–Mar: 240,000 × 20% × $^{3}/_{12}$	12,000
Apr–Jun: (240,000 – 60,000) × 20% × $^{3}/_{12}$	9,000
Jul–Dec: (180,000 + 160,000) × 20% × $^{6}/_{12}$	34,000
Depreciation charge for the year	55,000

24 C Return on capital employed = Profit before interest and tax ÷ (Equity + Non-current liabilities) = 10,200 ÷ 42,500 = 24%

25 A Sales tax is collected by the seller and suffered by the consumer. It is income for the government, not the seller who records revenue net of sales tax.

26 B Any error that causes an imbalance between debits and credits will require an entry to the suspense account to correct it.

Tutorial note: *(1) has $3.000 excess debit. (2) has excess $2,800 credit; entry in asset a/c should have been debit. (3) is omission of a debit balance. (4) a transposition error.*

27 C If there is only a 20% chance of defeating the claim then there is an 80% chance that the claim will be successful – therefore it is "probable" that Cannon will have to pay compensation and a provision must be made (for the full amount).

28 D 1,040 – 25 = $1,015.

Tutorial note: *Maintenance costs must be expensed, not capitalised. The purchase is recorded net of sales tax which will be reclaimed (offset against sales tax payable).*

29 B

	$
Overdraft per bank statement	(3,860)
Less: Unpresented cheques	(9,160)
Add: Outstanding lodgements	16,690
Cash at bank	3,670

30 B Per the *Conceptual Framework for Financial Reporting* faithful representation requires neutrality, accuracy and completeness.

31 D

Receivables ledger control account

	$		$
Opening balance	308,600	Cash	147,200
Credit sales	154,200	Discounts allowed	1,400
Interest charged on overdue accounts	2,400	Contras	4,600
		Irrecoverable debts	4,900
		Closing balance	307,100
	465,200		465,200

32 B Adjustment is required if the event provides evidence of conditions which existed as at the reporting date.

33 A

	$
50 × $190	9,500
500 × $220	110,000
300 × $230	69,000
Closing inventory	188,500

34 A

	$
Opening assets	569,400
Opening liabilities	(412,840)
Capital introduced	65,000
Drawings (800 × 12)	(9,600)
	211,960
Profit (balancing figure)	32,400
Closing net assets (614,130 – 369,770)	244,360

35 C Discounts received represent a reduction in cost and should be extracted as a credit balance (like income).

Answer 1 KESWICK

(a) Consolidated statement of profit or loss for the year ended 31 May 20X6

	$000
Revenue (W1)	10,100
Cost of sales (W1)	(4,950)
Gross profit	5,150
Operating expenses (W1)	(3,160)
Profit before tax	1,990
Tax (W1)	(740)
Profit for the year	1,250

(b) A

(c) Non-controlling interest = $80,000 ($400,000 (W1) × 20%)

(d) The factors that illustrate the existence of a parent–subsidiary relationship are B, C, D, E.

WORKINGS

(1)

	Keswick Co	*Derwent Co*	*Adjustments*	*Consolidated*
	$000	$000	$000	$000
Revenue	8,400	3,200	(1,500)	10,100
Cost of sales	(4,600)	(1,700)	1,500	(4,950)
Unrealised profit	(150)			
Operating expenses	(2,200)	(960)		(3,160)
Tax	(600)	(140)		(740)
	850	400		

Answer 2 MALRIGHT

Statement of profit or loss for the year ended 31 October 20X7

	$000
Revenue	1,800
Cost of sales (W1)	(1,284)
Gross profit	516
Administrative expenses (325 + 10 (W4) + (16 (W3) – 10))	(341)
Profit for the year	175

Statement of financial position as at 31 October 20X7

	$000	$000
Assets		
Non-current assets (W2)		731
Current assets		
Inventories	75	
Trade receivables (W3)	304	
Cash	20	
		399
Total assets		1,130
Equity and liabilities		
Equity		
Share capital	415	
Retained earnings (130 + 175)	305	
Share premium	80	
		800
Current liabilities		
Trade and other payables (250 + 10 (W4))	260	
Bank overdraft	70	
		330
Total equity and liabilities		1,130

WORKINGS

(1)

	$000
Cost of sales	
Opening inventory	160
Purchases	1,140
Closing inventory	(75)
	1,225
Depreciation (W2)	59
	1,284

(2)

	Property	*Plant*	*Total*
	$000	$000	$000
Cost	740	220	960
Depreciation b/f	(60)	(110)	(170)
Depreciation for year			
740 × 5% (37)			
(220 – 110) × 20%		(22)	(59)
Net book value 31 October 20X7	643	88	731

(3) Trade receivables

Allowance = 320,000 × 5% = $16,000
320,000 – 16,000 = $304,000

(4) Energy cost accrual

15,000 × $^2/_3$ = $10,000

ABOUT BECKER PROFESSIONAL EDUCATION

Becker Professional Education provides a single solution for students and professionals looking to advance their careers and achieve success in:

- Accounting
- International Financial Reporting
- Project Management
- Continuing Professional Education
- Healthcare

For more information on how Becker Professional Education can support you in your career, visit www.becker.com/acca.

Becker Professional Education
is an ACCA approved content provider